1

IT IS the principle concern of the banker to keep our money safe, and there is nowhere safer than behind locked doors. To this end, banks severely restrict their branch opening hours to just a few hours a day, closing completely at weekends. During the short periods when they are open, the banks once again protect our money by drastically restricting the number of cashiers on duty.

2

THE days when your local bank manager knew each of his customers by name are gone. But in today's high tech banking world, there is still room for the personal touch, and today's manager still likes to call his customers in for a regular chat. It is his duty to spend a couple of minutes making sure that his bank is providing the tailored financial service we require. After that he will launch into a two-hour sales pitch inviting us to upgrade our account, take out loans we didn't know we needed and purchase costly, non-functional insurance schemes that will automatically debit money from our accounts for decades to come. It's all part of the service.

BANKERS' salaries often hit the headlines, courting criticism from left wing moaning minnies, especially since their recipients had to be bailed out to prevent their institutions failing as a result of a global recession that they themselves directly caused. But what is often forgotten amongst all the talk about huge wage packets and even huger bonuses is that bankers pay much more tax than the rest of us, and that money goes directly into the economy. After they have channelled their money through a complex series of Jersey-based tax efficiency maximisation schemes, many bankers pay out up to 1% of their income in tax. On their vast salaries, this figure typically amounts to much more than the 25-40% of his wages paid by the ordinary man in the street.

NEITHER a borrower or a lender be, so goes the old saying. But you'll not hear a bank manager say it, because one of the most important parts of his job is to lend money so that businesses can grow, providing jobs, revenue and tax income that benefits the whole economy.

THE LISTENING BANK

5

6

PLEASE DO NOT ASK FOR CREDIT AS A REFUSAL OFTEN OFFENDS

Here, a plumber finds that he has so much work coming in that he has taken on two new employees, and now needs to buy a second van so that his business can grow. He approaches his friendly local bank manager for a short term loan of £2000. However, the plumber has failed to understand the extreme complexity of banking, which means that the manager is unable to advance him the cash he requires. Neither a borrower or a lender be, so the old saying goes, and it is a saying that this small businessman would do well to heed.

IT IS often said that money makes the world go round, and in today's global marketplace that statement is truer than ever. Without bankers to look after all the money, the modern world would grind to a halt and [...] is [...] to [...] of co[...] be[...] ec[...] that [...] ankers that the world is not teetering on the brink of such an economic abyss.

9

D1080259

Next month:

Heroes of Our World~
Somalian Pirates

Duck and Cover. It's

Viz

THE
DUTCH OVEN

A heady brew of the choicest releases from issues 212~221

Windy Millers
Graham Dury and Simon Thorp

Dutch Afterburners
Mark Bates, Tim Briffa, Alex Collier, Gareth Dunn, Simon Ecob, Tom Ellen, Barney Farmer, Lee Healey, Andy Hepworth, Carl Hollingsworth, Davey Jones, Alex Morris, Graham Murdoch, Paul Palmer, Ian Stacey, Lew Stringer, Tim Sull, Cat Sullivan and Nick Tolson.

Dutch Caps
Russell Blackman and Stephen Catherall

Published by Dennis Publishing Ltd
30 Cleveland Street, London W1T 4JD

ISBN 9781781063705
First Printing Autumn 2014

© Fulchester Industries/Dennis Publishing Ltd. All rights reserved.
No part of this book may be copied, reproduced or forced under the duvet whilst somebody farts without the written permission of Fulchester Industries and/or Dennis Publishing.

Subscribe online at www.viz.co.uk

ROGER MELLIE
THE MAN ON THE TELLY

1975... WELL, THAT'S IT FOR THIS SERIES OF "ROG'LL SORT IT"... BUT WE'LL BE BACK IN THE SPRING WHEN I'LL BE MAKING MORE DREAMS COME TRUE...

UNTIL THEN, IT'S BYSIE-WYSIE, NOWSIE-WOWSIE!

ROG'LL SORT IT!

ROG'LL SORT IT!

EEURGH! EEURGH! EEURGH!

CUT!

HOW'S THAT, TOM?

GREAT, ROGER... BUT WE'LL JUST HAVE TO RE-SHOOT THE CLOSING REMARKS

OH!?..

...HAIR IN THE GATE WAS IT, TOM?.. OR WAS ONE OF THE KIDS PICKIN' THEIR NOSE?

OY! WHICH ONE OF YOU CUNTS WAS PICKIN' THEIR NOSE, EH?.. YOU DIRTY BASTARDS!

HOW MANY FUCKIN' TIMES?

NO...

THIS VIDEO TAPE COSTS A GRAND A FUCKIN' MINUTE! NOW FUCKIN' BEHAVE YOUR-SELVES... F' FUCK'S SAKE!

RIGHT! I'VE SORTED THE LITTLE FUCKERS OUT... LET'S GO AGAIN AN' THEN HIT THE BAR, EH, TOM?

NO... IT'S NOT THE KIDS...

IT'S WHAT YOU SAID ABOUT BEING BACK IN THE SPRING... THE SHOW'S BEEN AXED

AXED!?! SAYS WHO?

THE HEAD OF PROGRAMMING I'M AFRAID... IT'S A DIKTAT THAT CAME FROM THE DG'S OFFICE

WELL WE'LL FUCKIN' SEE ABOUT THAT!

SHORTLY...

HEY! WHAT'S THIS I HEAR ABOUT YOU CANNING ROG'LL SORT IT?

AH, ROGER

LET ME EXPLAIN...

YOU SEE... ROG'LL SORT IT WAS A GREAT CONCEPT.. MAKING KIDDIES' DREAMS COME TRUE... BUT.. RECENTLY IT SEEMS TO HAVE DRIFTED FROM ITS ORIGINAL FORMAT

EH?

I MEAN... JUST LOOK AT THE LAST SHOW, ROGER...

"DEAR ROGER, PLEASE COULD YOU SORT IT FOR ME AND MY FELLOW STUDENT NURSES TO ACCOMPANY YOU ON AN ALL EXPENSES PAID TRIP TO LAS VEGAS. THANK YOU."

BLESS 'EM... THEY WORK HARD, NURSES... THEY DESERVED THAT BREAK

OR THIS ONE... "DEAR ROGER, I'M A 19-YEAR OLD LINGERIE MODEL AND I'D LOVE TO POSE FOR A GLAMOROUS CALENDAR...

..PLEASE COULD YOU SORT IT FOR ME AND YOU TO GO TO BALI FOR A PHOTO SHOOT

...TELLY GOLD, IT WAS

YOU SHOULD HAVE SEEN HER FACE LIGHT UP...

"DEAR ROGER. MY MATE FROM THE RUGBY CLUB IS GETTING MARRIED NEXT SUMMER...

CAN YOU SORT IT FOR TEN OF US TO SPEND A STAG WEEKEND IN A STRIP CLUB IN AMSTERDAM...

P.S. YOU CAN COME TOO IF YOU LIKE"... ROGER, THIS IS A SATURDAY TEA-TIME SHOW AIMED AT CHILDREN

IT WAS TASTEFULLY FILMED. AND IT WAS ONLY A TITTY BAR... IT WASN'T FANNY OUT

NO, I'M SORRY, ROGER... IT'S SIMPLY NOT THE SHOW WE ORIGINALLY COMMISSIONED

YOU'RE MAKING A BIG MISTAKE, YOU MARK MY WORDS... IT COULD RUN FOR ANOTHER 20 YEARS!

...IT'S A SHIT HOT FORMAT, I TELL YOU

I AGREE... IT'S NOT THE FORMAT WE'RE GETTING RID OF... IT'S THE PRESENTER

WHAT!?

WE HAVE TO THINK OF OUR REPUTATION

THE BBC SIMPLY CANNOT AFFORD TO HAVE A CONTRO-VERSIAL FIGURE LIKE YOURSELF HOSTING A CHILDREN'S SHOW.

I'M AFRAID WE'LL HAVE TO REPLACE YOU WITH A SAFER PAIR OF HANDS, ROGER... SOMEONE WE CAN TRUST

2012... BACKED THE WRONG FUCKIN' HORSE THERE, DIDN'T THEY, EH, TOM?

CERTAINLY DID, ROGER

FUCKIN' BIG TIME

PAEDO SHAME OF NGEBIE SAVILE

IT WAS late in the afternoon on Christmas Eve as shepherd Andrew Selkirk and his faithful border binliner Black Bag set out across the newly fallen snow which coated the glens and valleys of Peebles up to and in excess of a depth of two feet. Andrew was carrying his trusty axe as he had a very special job to do. "Come on, Baggie," he smiled. "Let's go tae the woods and cut doon a wee Christmas tree tae decorate oor crofter's cottage tae celebrate yon festive season."

"OCH, this one will look michty braw sitting in the corner of oor hoose festooned wi' baubies, tinsel an' fairy lichts," said Andrew, looking at a fine young spruce. The brawny shepherd lifted his axe and swung it against the trunk with all his might. The sharp blade and the crofter's strong muscles made short work of the wood and after a few strokes it was ready to come down. "Och the noo!" shouted Andrew as he stood back. "Timber!"

BUT just as the tree began to fall, a sudden gust of wind caused it to twist violently. The shepherd wasn't quick enough to get out of the way, and the trunk crashed down on top of his leg, pinning him to the snow. "Help, m'boab!" he cried. "I'm trapped! I cannae move! The weight of yon tree is pressin' doon tae hard awa' ma leggie. Fetch help, laddie." Bag knew how quickly the nights drew in and darkness would soon be falling, so as fast as the breeze could take him, he set off to raise the alarm.

DUSK was already beginning to gather as Black Bag made his way over the hillside. The snow was deep, and he was cold, wet and exhausted, but the faithful polythene binliner knew his master was relying on him, and he pressed on. Just when he thought he could go no further, he spotted the headlights of a car that was snaking its way along the Auchtermuchty Pass. He knew his only hope was to somehow stop the car and alert the driver to his master's plight.

BAG stood by the side of the road, flapping frantically to attract the motorist's attention. But amongst the wintry gloom, the driver hadn't seen him, and Bag looked on in despair as he failed to slow down. Then, as luck would have it, just as the car sped by a sudden breeze picked the exhausted border binliner off the snow and flung him against the windscreen. "Jings and crivvens!" cried the driver. "Whit the fuck...!?" Unable to see, he swerved off the icy road and the car crashed into the burn.

THE driver got out of his car to survey the damage. It was Doctor Buchan, and he was none too pleased with Bag. "Look whit ye've done, ye little shitehoose," he cried. But then in the distance he saw Andrew the shepherd, still lying trapped under the tree. "Och, Baggie, I see noo. Yir master's in trouble!" he said. "Let's get awa' there the noo and come tae his aid." With Bag leading the way, the two of them raced over to the stricken crofter.

DR BUCHAN took stock of the situation. "It's nae looking tae guid, Andrew," he said. "This is a michty braw tree. And I cannae shift the bugger by ma sel'." He shook his head sadly. "I'm afraid it's muckle bad news. Yon leg will have tae come off awa' the knee, the noo." The doctor opened his bag and began preparing to carry out an emergency operation to save the stricken shepherd's life. "I'm afraid I dinnae hae nae anaesthetics, Andrew, so this might sting a wee bit," he said.

NEXT day, the events of Christmas Eve were soon forgotten, and amidst the excitement of the festivities, Andrew Selkirk barely gave his anaesthetic-free amputation another thought. "Thank you, Baggie. If it hadnae been for your quick thinkin', I'd be deed, the noo," he said. He pointed at the tree that had caused all the trouble, which now stood by the window, decorated with shiny tinsel and twinkling fairy lights. "And on twelfth nicht, I'm goin' tae whittle thae bastard doon into a wooden leg!" he laughed.

Letterbocks

LETTERBOCKS
VIZ COMIC
PO BOX 841
WHITLEY BAY
NE26 9EQ

ST★R LETTER

★ **I'M NO** economist, but if the Greeks stopped smashing all their plates after every meal, maybe their economy wouldn't be up shit creek.

Terry Corrigan, e-mail

I HAD £10 on Sachin Tendulkar to get his one hundredth century against the West Indies in the recent test match, and was annoyed to find that he was out for 94. Now if a man of his supposed ability can't score 6 runs then he's hardly one of the best batsmen in the world as all these so-called experts like to mention. I regularly get more than 6 runs for Blubberhouses 2nd team and I'm shit.

Al Hogg, Ilkley

DID you know that a group of roe deer is

called a bevy? I mention this to avoid any misunderstandings should any of your readers be invited to go for a drink in Newcastle.

Alan Heath, e-mail

I'VE just found seven pips in a satsuma, including three in a single segment. I don't want to know if any *Viz* readers can beat it, I just thought they'd like to know.

Sebastian, e-mail

B&Q now stock 'No Nonsense' branded PVA Glue. Does anyone know what is so nonsensical about the alternative PVA glue which they also still sell?

David Milner, Durham

A PARAGLIDER recently explained to me that his experience and know-how enables him to land on a sixpence. Surely if he was that knowledgeable, he would know that we went decimal in 1971.

Grant B Warner, NZ

I DO hope Jimmy Savile made his trademark "Ur-ugh ur-ugh ur-ugh' yodelling sound as he

expired. You can add this to the pile with all the others.

Steve Duffield, e-mail

∗ *ACTUALLY, Mr Duffield, there was no pile to add it to. Your letter, seeing fit to poke fun at the death of a man who raised countless millions for charity, and who only ever*

brought joy and happiness to the world, sat alone, a testament to its author's spite. Shame on you, Mr Duffield.

SO Jimmy Savile was buried at 45° in order that he could have a view of the sea. It seems to me that unless he was actually buried under the sea, his view going to be somewhat hampered by basic geometry. Surely it would have been better if he had been buried vertically with his head poking out above the ground.

Stuie Taybun, e-mail

∗ *OH, actually, there was this one as well. Sorry, Mr Duffield.*

VEGETARIANS wear shoes made from plastic rather than leather. But everyone knows that plastic comes from petroleum which is made of dead dinosaurs over millions of years. This is surely less ethical because dinosaurs are extinct, whereas cows are plentiful. I think the shoe is well and truly on the other foot for these so-called animal lovers.

Angel Victorio, e-mail

T★P TIPS

KLINGONS. Save money on expensive cloaking devices by painting all your ships black.

Greg, e-mail

TEACHERS. Take a tip from local shops and dramatically reduce your workload by putting one of those signs on your classroom door which says 'No more than 2 schoolchildren at a time.'

Darren Conway, e-mail

MAKE candles out of carrots. That way you can see better in the dark without having to eat the disgusting things.

Dave Bosh, e-mail

POP lyricists. Stuck for a rhyme? It's a little known fact that 'fire' rhymes with 'desire'. And if you are feeling daring, try 'ocean' and 'emotion'.

Smaug, e-mail

SAVE a fortune on your wife's hair by simply getting a wife with the right colour hair to start with.

John Tipex, e-mail

OLYMPIC athletes. Disguise the fact that you've taken anabolic steroids by running a bit slower.

Max E Padd, e-mail

DOG owners. Solve problems of muck, hair shedding and smell by simply applying a generous coat of varnish to your pet. Done in sideways stripes creates an armadillo look and enables movement once dried.

James Lewis, e-mail

AN old toilet seat can be used as a tasteful frame for a large photograph of a beloved, deceased relative.

Richard Astridge, e-mail

It's every monarch's dream to be able to live a normal life. So we asked the lady Crowned Heads of Europe what they would do if they were...

Not Queen For a Day

ELIZABETH II OF THE COMMONWEALTH

BEING Queen, I have staff to perform even the most simple tasks for me, and I sometimes think it would be wonderful to do some of the things that common people take for granted. If I weren't Queen for a day, I think I'd cook my own breakfast, put the toothpaste on my toothbrush myself and wipe my own arse after a shit.

QUEEN BEATRIX OF THE NETHERLANDS

THE Netherlands is a wealthy country, but like all countries, it has a terrible homelessness problem. If I weren't Queen for a day, I think I would go around the poorest areas of Amsterdam and look at the poverty that some people live in. This would make me really appreciate the fabulous, carefree oppulence in which I spend my life.

MARGRETHE II OF DENMARK

IF I were not Queen for a day, I would go into a cafe or pub and have a drink

with normal people, something I cannot do as their Queen. For one day I would chat to them as an equal and find out what they really thought about their royal family. Then the next day I would have anyone who criticised us arrested on trumped-up charges.

QUEEN SILVIA OF SWEDEN

IT'S A hard life being queen and I often wish I could switch off completely. If I were an ordinary person for the day, I would just flop on the settee, eating Pot Noodles and drinking White Lightning whislt watching the Swedish equivalent of Jeremy Kyle. Then the next day it would be back to the grind of sitting around on a big velvet-cushioned throne most of the day, eating caviar and drinking Moët et Chandon.

QUEEN SOPHIA OF SPAIN

I REALLY like being a queen, so if I found myself not being queen for a day, I would fly to America and go on the show *Queen for a Day* and hope that I won.

IF I could travel back in time I'd go back to Germany in the 1930s, and tell Hitler to shave that little moustache off. He looked absolutely ridiculous with it.

Craig Scott, e-mail

HOW about a picture of the Rt Hon Jack Straw MP eating some mice?

J Monkbottle, Carlisle

*NO problem, Mr, Mrs, or indeed to avoid any accusations of sexism, Ms Monkbottle.

WHY DO people moan so much about Ryanair being so shit and uncomfortable? My grandad was a rear tail gunner in WW2 and he never grumbled, and he didn't have the luxury of having a gay Irishman climbing into his gun turret and asking him to put his seat forward.

Terry Corrigan, e-mail

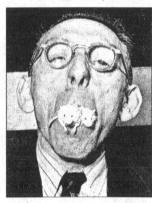

THEY say that man was created in God's image, but I'm 20-stone and have terrible piles. Surely any omnipotent deity worth his salt could have set a slightly better example.

MK Kirk, Knottingley

WHILE channel flicking recently I came

TOP

SAVE money on expensive 3D televisions by watching your normal TV with your eyes crossed.

Leopold Stough, e-mail

BUTCHERS. Increase sales by punching your customers, giving them a black eye. They will then buy an additional piece of steak to take down the swelling.

M Bonde, e-mail

MAKE your penis appear bigger in pictures by holding a fun size Mars bar or one of those tiny cans of coke next to it.

Darren Cassell, e-mail

WETHERSPOON'S staff. Confused over which customer to serve next? Simply look to see whose beard has grown the most since their arrival.

Steve Jefferson, e-mail

UNABLE to afford an exotic Parrot? Simply use old Airfix model paint to spruce up a retired racing Pigeon.

Phil Mc, Cumbria

CAN'T find your wallet/purse/car keys when you wake up in the morning?

Pop them in the fridge last thing at night and you will find them when you have your breakfast.

Russ Young, e-mail

WHEN driving on wet or muddy roads, cover the whole of your car in clingfilm. It can be removed afterwards and the car will be clean.

Colin Bell, e-mail

MODEL railway enthusiasts. Create an authentic winter backdrop for your electric trains by placing the layout outdoors for 3 weeks in January.

Craig Campbell, e-mail

MOTORISTS. Don't waste money buying oil for your car. Simply invest in a longer dipstick.

Henry Walton, e-mail

IF you find yourself face to face with an angry ostrich, put your hat on top of a stick and raise it slowly above your head. The ostrich will think you are much bigger than itself and will back off.

Mma Ramotswe, Botswana

TIPS

toptips@viz.co.uk

upon *Songs of Praise* and was greatly impressed to see the congregation performing an - albeit sanitized - version of *'Who's the bastard in the black?'* Well done the C of E. Reworking popular football chants as hymns will undoubtedly show that the church has got the common touch and it might even encourage more people to attend.

Dr W Basinger, Pimlico

THE man behind me in the queue at Sainsbury's is refusing to put anything on the conveyor belt without a divider. I'm not sure what he's worried about. The worst case scenario is that I might pay for his shopping.

Christina Martin, e-mail

EARLIER today I farted and experienced what is commonly known as following through. I always thought this was an old wives' tale or something. Well, I guess every day's a school day.

Hugh Dong, e-mail

HAS anyone seen a more crestfallen looking model than the one I saw on Littlewoods' website today? I don't know about you but he makes me want to buy that hat because I feel so sorry for him.

Stephen Usher, e-mail

COMMON DENOMINATOR

=SLURP!=

2/3

DON'T LOOK NOW, BUT HE'S EATING HIS SOUP WITH A DESSERT SPOON.

Dear AB of C!

with Dr ROWAN WILLIAMS, the Archbishop of Canterbury

Dear AB of C.

MY WIFE and I recently visited the Basilique du Saint-Sang in Bruges, where they keep a tiny piece of cloth bathed in Christ's blood. Visitors are allowed to touch this most holy relic, which is kept in a glass vial, and are asked to make a donation towards the upkeep of the church in return. I put a 2 Euro coin in the box before my wife and I touched the sacred artefact. However, I am now worried that God might not realise that my payment was intended to be 1 Euro each for both of us, and He may now be under the impression that my wife hasn't paid. I'd hate Him to think she had dodged the charge, and am worried that He might decide to punish her with a plague of boils or a mighty flood or some such, because He does have a bit of form in that department.

Cedric Riddle, Otley

The AB of C says...

● FIRST of all, God is omniscient. I would imagine that He probably knows that your payment of 2 Euros was intended to cover both you and your wife's touching of the cloth. But even if He doesn't, don't worry, for The Lord saves His wrath for real sinners, such as fornicators, blasphemers and their wives and children even unto the seventh generation. I doubt He could be bothered to summon up one of His trademark biblical plagues simply because He thought your wife had turked Him out of a Euro, which is only about 87p! At worst, He'd probably just smite her with piles, which can be cleared up with an over-the-counter cream from your chemist.

Dear AB of C.

MY GRANDFATHER died last week at the ripe old age of 91. He had lived a sin-free life, and as a result I am sure he has gone to spend the hereafter up in Heaven, sitting at God's right hand. However, all his life he was allergic to feathers. He couldn't go near birds, and he had to have a special pillow stuffed with artificial fibres . Now I'm worried that he'll have itchy eyes, a runny nose and constant sneezing fits for all eternity, on account of all the feathers off the angels' wings.

Yootha James, Hull

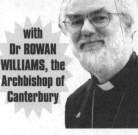

The AB of C says...

● THE FEATHERS on an angel's wing are not made of the same substance as earthly bird feathers. They are fashioned from the purest gossamer gold and so it is unlikely they will provoke an allergic reaction in your late grandfather. However, if he does find himself coughing and sneezing due to dander when he's near the heavenly host, he should simply go and get Jesus to cure him. After all, He raised the dead, turned water into wine and made the lame walk. I'm sure He could fix a simple feather allergy with His eyes shut!

Dear AB of C.

MY HUSBAND recently passed on following a long illness. He was buried at the local churchyard, but after the service we realised we had forgotten to put his glasses in the coffin with him. The vicar said it shouldn't matter, because in Heaven everyone is restored to their prime age, which he thought was probably about 25. The trouble is, my husband had needed glasses ever since the age of 3, when he caught eye worms off a dog dirt, so even in his prime he couldn't manage without them. What can I do?

Audrey Gazpacho, Uttoxeter

The AB of C says...

● I AM sure your late husband should be able to borrow a pair of glasses off someone who was buried with theirs but no longer needs them due to having been restored to their prime in Paradise. Either that, or you could bury his glasses so they go up to Heaven and become angel glasses. However, you would have to inter them in consecrated ground, so it may be worth approaching your local vicar and checking that he doesn't mind you using a trowel to dig a small grave in his churchyard for your hubby's specs.

9

10

SPOILT BASTARD

How to SPOT TRAINS

TRAINSPOTTING is one of the most exciting hobbies you can take up, but many people are put off trying it because they think it's too complicated. But whilst it may seem daunting at first, it's actually quite straightforward.

Here, NIGEL SEXCASE, chairman, treasurer and founder member of the Gateshead & District Association of Railway Enthusiasts, answers YOUR questions and explains everything you need to know in order to take up this wonderful, thrilling and rewarding pastime.

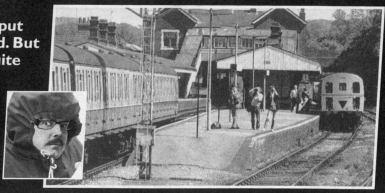

Q1: Is trainspotting easy?

*A veteran of over 5000 spots makes it look easy at Crewe Central.

A: NO. DON'T think you you can just wander onto the nearest railway platform and spot the next train that comes by. If it was that easy, everybody would be doing it. Lots of beginners make the mistake of underestimating this demanding discipline, and they pay the price big style because spotting trains is much more difficult than it looks. The trainspotters you see huddled at the end of the station platform make it look easy, but you have to remember they're seasoned experts. You need years of experience, specialist knowledge and quite a bit of fancy kit before you can go out and spot a train with any measure of success.

Q2: What equipment will I need?

*Trainspotter's arsenal. Kagoule, notebook, pencil, sandwich, flavoured crisps.

A: AT THE BAREST minimum, you're going to need a kagoule. And not just any kagoule will do. It's going to need a pocket on the front big enough for your notepad, a pencil, *flavoured* crisps and a Dairylea cheese sandwich on white bread. And make sure your mum wraps that bad boy *tightly* in clingfilm - the last thing any spotter wants is getting cheese sandwich sweat on his numbers. And like trawlermen, trainspotters are a hardy bunch who pursue their hobby in all weathers, even quite heavy showers, so your kagoule should have a string round the hood that can be pulled up tight to keep the rain out, leaving a small circle to peer out at trains through.

Q3: Will I need anything else?

A: UNLESS YOU'VE got superhuman vision, you're going to need a pair of binos - preferably at least 10x35 if you're at all serious about taking up the hobby. The more warning you have that a train's approaching, the better prepared you'll be, both mentally and physically, to spot it as it comes past. And unless you can remember nearly 10,000 numbers off the top of your head, kit yourself out with a notebook and pencil. Take a tip from a pro - make it a 2H. Anything softer and you'll find yourself missing numbers while you sharpen it. Any harder and you might end up tearing the paper in the excitement of the moment.

Q4: What sort of notebook is best?

*The correct notebook could make the difference between getting that number down...and NOT

A: MAKE SURE it's not too big. Like a wild west gunslinger, you've got to be able to whip that baby out of your kagoule at a second's notice. A Silvine ready-ruled 72-page memo book is the trainspotter's best friend.

Q5: Do I need a flask?

A: A FLASK goes with the territory. On one of my first trainspotting trips, I missed a Class 57 Deltic because I'd nipped to the station cafe for a can of pop. Believe you me, I didn't make that mistake again.

Q6: Could I bring a carton of juice instead?

A: TO THE experienced trainspotter, nothing screams "Amateur hour" more than a carton of juice. It's a flask or nothing. Frankly, if you're not going to take the hobby seriously, then stay at home.

Q7: Where do I go to spot trains?

A: MOST PEOPLE know that the railway station is the best place to go if you're going to spot trains properly. But railway stations are big places, and believe it or not, they are usually packed with bozos who aren't interested in spotting trains. Novices often make the mistake of trying to spot trains from the middle of the platform, but there's nothing more annoying than getting your view of the number obscured by a load of ruddy passengers trying to get on or off.

＊King's Cross station. At peak times, over 10,000 people per hour get in the ruddy way.

Q8: So where should I stand to best spot the trains?

A: POSITION IS everything. On my first spotting venture many moons ago, I went up on a footbridge thinking I'd get the best view of the train. How I laughed at my fellow spotters on the platform below... untill the train came past! I got a great view of the top of the train, but the number was on the *side!* The laugh was well and truly on me. Again, it's a mistake I made only the once. So stick to the platform, and go to the very end away from all the pain-in-the-backside commuters.

HERE ✔

HERE ✔ NOT HERE ✘

Q9: Okay, I'm standing on the platform and there's a train coming. What now?

A: GET INTO THE habit of running through a mental checklist. Kagoule? *Check.* 2H pencil? *Check.* Notebook? *Check.* Small erection? *Check.* It's at this point that a lot of novice trainspotters come unstuck. They get excited, their glasses steam up and before they know what's happening the train's come right past and they've forgotten to spot the number. So keep calm and concentrate on the 4 or 5 big digits painted on the side of the locomotive. Don't allow yourself to be distracted by any other numbers you might see written on the train. These might refer to axle weights or something; they're meaningless and it would be utterly pointless and a complete waste of time to try to spot them.

＊The Money Shot. This is the number the spotters are after.

＊A series of utterly pointless and meaningless figures.

wt 15,000 kgs

Q10: What do I do with the numbers I've written down?

A: AT THE END of the day your 'spots' have to be transferred from your notepad into your main spotting log using a ballpoint pen. A pencil isn't a permanent record, and there's no telling when you might need to refer back to a train you spotted years ago. It's never happened to me yet, but it might do, and if it does I want all my numbers there at my fingertips. In ballpoint. Once you have done that, they can be cross-referenced and marked off in your official records, using a recognised tabulated system. Remember - the digits on the side of a train are a code, not a number. The individual figures do not represent place values, so you must line them up on the left rather than the right.

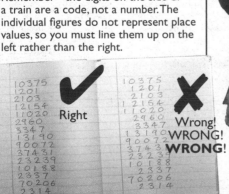

Right ✔   Wrong! WRONG! **WRONG**! ✘

Q11: Will I make lots of new friends?

A: LIKE BRAIN SURGEONS, air traffic controllers and concert pianists, trainspotters have to concentrate 100% at all times. For this reason, although you will be surrounded by fellow train spotters for hours every day, they will not talk to you, and you must never talk to them. A split second's distraction, such as a question about the power of a fellow spotter's binos or the hardness of his pencil, and the train could be past, and its number lost for ever. No, a good train spotter is a lone wolf, ploughing a solitary furrow through life. A completely friendless existence may seem a high price to pay for pursuing your hobby, but when you look at your Silvine A6 books full of neatly-tabulated four- and five-digit numbers, you'll know it has been worth it.

Q12: Is it a good way to meet girls?

A: NO. But but it's a great way to meet lots of middle-aged men on the Sex Offenders' Register.

Next week: How to Do It - *Bus Spotting*

BOXING CLEVER

IN THE PAST, TV documentaries were invariably presented by elderly, bespectacled academics. After spending decades studying their subjects in dusty university libraries, earnest eggheads like Lord Clark and Jacob Bronowski brought a sense of gravitas, seriousness and authority to our televisions. However these days, such old-fashioned fuddy-duddy male presenters are increasingly being pushed off our screens by a voluptuous new generation of female academics. As broadcasters compete to recruit the hottest documentary hosts, sexy telly experts like **BETTANY HUGHES, LUCY WORSLEY** and **CHARLOTTE UHLENBROEK** are setting Britain's couch potatoes's pulses racing... and viewing figures are going through the roof as a result.

Ian Turdbridge, Head of Factual Programming at Channel 4 says that time is finally running out for ageing male presenters like wrinkly naturalist David Attenborough, slap-egg-headed chemist Jim Al-Khalili and hairy-arsed historian Mick Aston off Time Team. He told us: "It's such a simple idea. I don't know why nobody thought of it before."

illuminations

"That recent BBC4 series about medieval illuminations is a case in point. You're off to a bad start because the subject's so crushingly dull in the first place. If you filmed it with a whiskery old Cambridge professor peer-ing through half-moon glasses into the camera, it'd be a recipe for disaster. The host might know his stuff, but you'd be lucky to pull in 10,000 viewers tops, and most of them would be struggling to stay awake," he continued.

"But get the same script read out by some busty PhD in high heels, spice it up with a few low-level shots of her tripping up the steps of the British Library, and your audience numbers will go through the roof."

"There's no point sending a film crew half way round the world to make a documentary about broken pots on Skiathos unless you're sure people are going to tune in. And the only way to get bums on seats is to put tits on screen," said Turdbridge.

tower

"That's not sexism. It's just commercial pragmatism. Get your presenter delivering a piece to camera in a flimsy frock with the sun behind her and you're on a guaranteed ratings winner. It's as simple as that," he added.

But the new trend for attractive female presenters has met with an angry response from women's libbers. "Whilst it's high time more women were seen on screen, these academic bimbos are mere eye candy pandering to the disgusting sexual desires of male viewers," said Andrea Lesbos, chairperson of feminist pressure group Clit Power.

"What we need is more boot-faced women on the television who wear men's suits, smoke pipes and have buzz haircuts and whiskers on their chins," Ms Lesbos added.

SEX OF THE BEST

THESE days, when we're bombarded with a veritable bevy of bootylicious brainboxes every time we turn on the television to watch a documentary, it's often difficult to know which one is on the screen. So here's a handy cut out & keep round-up of the Top 5 scholarly saucepots on the box.

PRESENTER
CHARLOTTE UHLENBROEK

ACADEMIC FIELD
BIOLOGY

AS presenter of BBC nature shows like *Chimpanzee Diary*, *Congo's Secret Chimps* and *Going Ape*, Dr Uhlenbroek has brought her unrivalled knowledge of primate behaviour to a wide television audience.

She may have spent 5 years studying zoology at Bristol University, but her own Bristols are a much more fascinating area of her study for her legions of male viewers, who go bananas every time she monkeys around on screen!

SEXPERT RATING
Ooh! Ooh! Aah! Aah! We wouldn't mind "gibbon" her a seeing-to!
8/10

PRESENTER
LUCY MOORE

ACADEMIC FIELD
HISTORY

LUCY has presented many history programmes on TV, including a biography of Lord Nelson for the BBC's recent *Great Britons* series.

But after watching the gorgeous Edinburgh-educated brunette strolling around the Bay of Naples in a skimpy red dress, the one-eyed hero of the Battle of Trafalgar wasn't the only viewer who ended up with an enormous column and his hand pushed firmly inside his clothes!

SEXPERT RATING
We love Lucy and we can't wait to see "Moore" of her!
8/10

PRESENTER
LUCY WORSLEY

ACADEMIC FIELD
SOCIAL HISTORY

WORSLEY boasts a First Class degree from Oxford University, and when she's not making telly programmes such as top-rated BBC4 series *If Walls Could Talk*, this first class bird is chief curator of the Tower of London, scene of many executions.

Well, we're sure there's a good few viewers who get their own choppers out and lose their heads every time this posh blonde bombshell pops up on screen!

SEXPERT RATING
Oi Lucy, we've got a bit of beef here for you to eat!
8/10

PRESENTER
BETTANY HUGHES

ACADEMIC FIELD
ANCIENT CIVILISATIONS

OXFORD graduate Bettany boasts a degree in Classical Civilisations, and she's a classy piece of crumpet to boot. She's taught at Bristol, Manchester, Oxford, Cambridge and London Universities, and is a familiar face presenting landmark documentary series about the Pharaohs of Ancient Egypt.

But it's Dr Hughes's own pair of Nefertitis that all her randy viewers really want to know about!

SEXPERT RATING
Oh Mummy! Get your pyramids out for the lads, Bettany!
8/10

PRESENTER
ALICE ROBERTS

ACADEMIC FIELD
PALAEOPATHOLOGY

SCIENTIFIC anthropologist Alice Roberts is well known to viewers of programmes like *Coast*, *Extreme Archaeology* and *Digging for Britain*. She's got three degrees from the University of Wales as well as a PhD. from the University of Bristol, and is an expert in osteoarchaelogy... the study of dirty old bones.

We'd be willing to bet there's a few viewers with dirty old bones of their own that they wouldn't mind getting this saucy young boffin to take a look at!

SEXPERT RATING
Hey, doctor. We'd happily take you three times a day after meals!
8/10

Let's take a whistle stop tour of the perfect documentary presenter to see what gives her

THE SEX FACTOR

THE ANATOMY OF ATTRACTION

LIPS
Pout saucily when pronouncing words such as "Prebyzantine", "Schrodinger's Cat", "Constantinople" or "Nitrogen fixation".

HAIR
Tossed seductively or played with coquettishly when interviewing someone, looking at a model of a DNA or leafing through an old book.

DRESS
Figure-hugging to show off curves, and semi-translucent when the sun is behind a presenter standing next to a glacier, a pyramid or a Parthenon

RACK
Kept in shot at all times to keep viewers awake during boring accounts of physics experiments, royal marriages and allegiances between medieval dukes etc.

ARSE
Wiggles from side to side whilst walking away from the camera towards henges, radio telescopes and Iron Age burial mounds.

PINS
Filmed from a low angle whilst presenter is walking about looking thoughtful. Can also be provocatively crossed and uncrossed to create a frisson of sexual tension whilst interviewing a curator of Mayan Pottery at the British Museum, an architectural historian or a particle physicist at CERN.

HANDS
Good for close-ups when pointing at manuscripts or test-tubes; can also be used to suggestively grasp the cylindrical wooden banister on the stairs at the British Library.

The Spice of Life on Earth

How would YOU sex up Attenborough's boring documentaries?

THERE is no doubt that **SIR DAVID ATTENBOROUGH** is a national treasure. But after sixty long years on our screens, is his appeal beginning to tarnish? Put up against the new breed of raunchy female documentary presenters, how does the white-haired octogenarian presenter of such landmark series as *Life on Earth*, *Life in the Freezer* and *The Blue Planet* measure up? We went out on the streets to see what the Great British Public thought.

● "I'D take substance over style every time. What Attenborough lacks when it comes to va-va-voom, ohh-la-la and the phwooarr factor, he more than makes up for with the in-depth knowledge and infectious enthusiasm he has for his subject."

Frank Balthazar, plumber

● "THERE'S already quite enough sex in Attenborough's programmes, if you ask me. You can't turn one of his shows on without being subjected to explicit footage of courtship rituals, animals mating or chimpanzees having a wank."

Audrey Kaspar, housewife

● "ATTENBOROUGH'S had his day. It's time to give Joe Public what he wants. I think the BBC should do a proper, in-depth programme about the mechanisms of Darwinian Natural Selection, fronted by a big-titted stunner in a skimpy wipe-clean zoo keeper's uniform, like they sell at the Ann Summers shop."

Joe Public, teacher

● "THEY should re-make *Life on Earth*, but instead of Attenborough they should get a bra-less Biology graduate in a white T-shirt and pith helmet to present it. Then, when they did the episode about elephants, she could get sprayed with water so you could see her tits."

Sid Melchior, teacher

● "WHY can't we have the best of both worlds? Attenborough could continue to present his programmes, bringing his gravitas to the subject and maintaining the BBC's commitment to educate and inform, whilst a go-go dancer stands next to him rubbing her tits, thus fulfilling the entertainment part of the corporation's remit, and ensuring good ratings."

Garth Herod, janitor

● "I'M fascinated by polar bears. A series about these endangered predators would be a great way to inform the public about their fragile habitat and the threat posed to it by man-made climate change. However, I'd only watch such a series if it was hosted by a sexy bird who occasionally took off her anorak and rubbed some snow onto her nipples to make them go hard."

Dave Nebuchadnezzar, postman

● "ALL this talk of nature programmes being presented by sexy young pieces makes me laugh. I'm Britain's oldest woman and recently celebrated my 112th birthday, so to me 86-year-old David Attenborough is a sexy young piece. Phwooarr!"

Ada Clitworth, retired munitions worker

● "IT'S time for Attenborough to wake up and smell the coffee. A film of a caterpillar crawling over an 86-year-old man's hand is never going to pull in as many viewers as a film of a caterpillar crawling over a sexy young female zoologist's hand, preferably with a good view of her cleavage in the shot at the same time. Actually, you could do away with the caterpillar too, as they're not particulary interesting."

Ian Beelzebub, fast food worker

● "I DON'T want my nature programmes hosted by some air-headed blonde bimbo fresh out of college. I'd prefer them to be presented by a middle-aged woman, preferably wearing glasses and with her hair in a bun. And I'd like her to deliver the information in a stern way, perhaps with a slight German accent, whilst she slaps a riding crop against the side of her thigh-high leather boots."

Norman Ezekiel, optician

Continued over...

BIG VERN

...AND THIS IS MY WORKSHOP, VERN.

ERM...NO...

LIKE IT, ERNIE. THESE ARE THE PLANS FOR YOUR NEXT TICKLE..? BIG JOB, IS IT? BULLION HEIST UP WEST... SUNNINK LIKE THAT?

I GETCHA, ERNIE, SAY NO MOWAH. NO NAMES, NO PROVERBIAL, EH? DON'T WORRY, YOU CAN TRUST YER OLD PAL VERN TO KEEP SCHTUMM.

WHAT'S ALL THIS GEAR FOR..? SAWIN' THE END OFF YA SHOOTA? MELTIN' DAHN A LOAD OF HOOKY TOM?

NO, VERN - THAT'S MY LATHE. I'M MAKING MYSELF A CHESS SET, YOU SEE.

YESTERDAY I TURNED ALL THE PAWNS, ROOKS, BISHOPS AND KINGS... SO THIS AFTERNOON I'LL BE TURNING QUEENS.

DO WHAT!? TURNIN' FACKIN' QUEENS!? YOU BARSTAD, ERNIE! I ALWAYS KNEW YOU WAS A FACKIN' SQUEALAH! WELL YOU AIN'T GUNNA GET THE CHANCE TO GRASS ME UP THIS TIME...!

NO! VERN!

BLAM!

...AND I'M NOT LETTIN' THE FACKIN' FILF FIT ME UP FOR THIS ONE NEITHAH!

BLAM!

FESTIVE HATSTAND FUN with **ROGER IRRELEVANT**

ROGER IS GOING INTO TOWN

YARR! GIT ALONG THAR!

KEEP IT ROLLIN', YER ORNERY CRITTERS!

FULCHESTER TOWN CENTRE

WE GOTTER REACH MICHAEL SHARVELL-MARTIN'S KITCHEN UTENSIL RANCH BY SUNDOWN, Y'HEAR?

SHORTLY WATERWORKS BOOKS

NOW, WE'LL START WITH 'ONCE IN ROYAL DAVID'S CITY'. IS EVERYONE READY?

SALLY BASH BAND

'APPEN T'CALF'S PRESENTIN' IN BREECH POSITION, VET'NARY. WE'LL 'AVE TER PERFORM CAESAREAN!

HOY! GET OFF MY EUPHONIUM!

I SAID GET OFF IT!

BUT FRANCESCA, I DID IT ALL FOR YOU! I THOUGHT THAT STEALING COLIN MONTGOMERIE'S CHEEKS WOULD BRING US CLOSER TOGETHER!

RWORKS BOOKS

WAH!

YOU'VE MADE ME DROP IT, YOU FOOL!

F'ZNARK

CLANG RKS BOOKS

OOF!

GOOD GRACIOUS!

THE AUTHOR WILL SELF HAS BEEN KNOCKED UNCONSCIOUS BY A EUPHONIUM WHILST ON HIS WAY TO GIVE A READING AT OUR BOOKSHOP!

OH DEAR. OUR CUSTOMERS WILL BE DISAPPOINTED NOT TO HEAR MR SELF READING PASSAGES FROM HIS NEW EXPERIMENTAL NOVEL, "UMBRELLA".

IF ONLY WE HAD SOMEONE TO REPLACE HIM...

...HMMM...

AND SO

SNIBBIT FORBES CATTLEGRID FONDUE SET

BLIP BIBBLE

LET ME VARNISH YOUR CLAVICLE, MRS DISREALI

ETC.

MM, YES, A TOUR DE FORCE OF JOYCEAN STREAM OF CONSCIOUSNESS

TRULY A MODERNIST CLASSIC FOR OUR AGE.

The 12 WA-HEYS of SEXM

Celebrity Tips to Spice-Up your YULETIDE LOVE LIFE

CHRISTMAS is the busiest time of the year. After we've worn ourselves out trailing round the shops, decorating the tree and wrapping endless presents, it's a sad fact that we're often too exhausted to think about anything more exciting than slumping on the sofa with a large egg-nog and a mince pie. Amidst all the frantic excitement of the festive season, our sex lives can all too easily get put on the back-burner.

It's a frightening made-up statistic that fewer than 2% of us manage to find the time for a bit of yuletide slap and tickle amongst the Christmas turkey and tinsel. But it needn't be like that. With just a little bit of forethought and planning, it's easy to put the XXX back into Xmas! We've asked twelve celebrity sexperts to reveal their secret red hot tips to ensure that the festive season goes with a bang. And a couple of blowjobs.

Dr Pamela Stephenson
Jan Leeming impersonator, 63
Sexpert qualification: *Pamela abandoned comedy to become a fully-qualified sexual physio cycle-therapist.*

IT CAN be quite difficult to find time for love-making during a busy Christmas schedule, but as a fully-qualified clinical psycho-sexual physiotherapist I would argue that it is important to make time during the festive season to at least talk about sexual matters in a frank and mature manner. My husband Billy Connolly and I discuss my erogenous zones whilst peeling the sprouts, have a frank exchange of views about ways of delaying his climax whilst writing our Christmas cards, and analyse Billy's transvestite tendencies whilst fishing for the giblet bag up the turkey.

The Krankies
Unsettling novelty act, 80
Sexpert qualification: *The comedy double act shocked the nation last year when it was announced that they were swingers.*

ME AND my wife Wee Jimmy spend Christmas Eve wrapping up presents, and we always like to finish off the night with our favourite saucy sex-game. She strips off her blazer, cap and shorts and climbs into a shoe-box, which I gift-wrap and pop under the tree with all the other presents. In the morning, I excitedly open my "surprise parcel" to reveal just what I always wanted - a naked Jeanette Krankie. We then make mad, passionate love under the Christmas tree. Fanny-dabidozi!

Ben Dover
Veteran cocksmith, 56
Sexpert qualification: *Ben (real name Linseed Honeybunch) has written, directed and starred in over 10,000 erotic movies.*

A SPOT OF role-playing is a great way to spice up a jaded sex life. Every Christmas Eve, I dress up in a Santa costume, complete with red tunic, heavy boots and a false beard, whilst my wife waits for me in the front room in a see-through negligee. Then I get my ladder out the shed, climb up on the roof and make my way down the chimney for a saucy romp. The flue's quite narrow and it takes about two hours to get down, and I'm all covered in soot and sweating by the time I emerge out the fireplace to give her one on the hearth-rug and empty my sack. Over the years, it's proved a great way to put a bit of Christmas spice into our marriage. The only problem is that I always end up spending Christmas day on the roof, re-pointing the chimney, fixing loose slates I've dislodged and re-attaching the TV aerial so my mum can watch the Queen's Speech.

Jordan
Proper Author, 34
Sexpert qualification: *Jordan (real name Katie Boyle) has posed for hundreds of high class lads', jazz and bongo mags.*

I ONLY ever date very shallow men, such as premiership footballers, third-rate pop singers and cage-fighters. To get them in the mood for a bit of festive slap and tickle, I like to take myself off on December 24th for a relaxing Christmas makeover at my local cosmetic surgery clinic. I have tinsel surgically grafted onto my knockers, baubles attached to my nipples, and I get my fanny vajazzled with flashing fairy lights. It never fails to put whichever muscly no-mark I happen to be banging at the time in the mood for a bit of the other. I book myself back into the clinic on January 6th to have all my decorations taken down, as it is bad luck to leave them up after Twelfth Night.

Robin Askwith
Seventies Confessions actor, 73
Sexpert qualification: *In the 1970s Robin starred in several of the most unerotic screen sex romps ever committed to film.*

I LOVE the scene in *Nine and a Half Weeks* where Mickey Rourke smears Kim Basinger in food from the fridge and then licks it off her naked body. After Christmas dinner, I like to cover my wife Ada in any left over brandy butter on the table, rubbing it sensuously into her breasts, thighs and buttocks. However, I don't like the taste, so she usually ends up going off and having a bath to wash all the greasy butter off her skin before it goes rancid and starts to stink.

Pamela Anderson
Baywatch panto actress, 45
Sexpert qualification: *Former Playboy bunny girl who appeared as a naked waitress at Hugh Hefner's 100th birthday party.*

CHRISTMAS is always an extremely hectic time in the Anderson/Lee out of Mötley Crüe household, but we always find time for a bit of how's-your-father on Christmas Day. As soon as I've put the sprouts on, me and Tommy out of Mötley Crüe catch a private jet to the Caribbean, where we get on our yacht and I suck him off. Once he's shot his bolt, we fly home so I can turn the sprouts down before they go too mushy.

Ron Jeremy
Pornographic film legend, 59
Sexpert qualification: *During his 30-year career in hardcore movies, Ron is reputed to have done it with more than 8.3 million women.*

FINDING time for a bit of you-know-what over the holiday season isn't a problem for me as, after years of practice, I'm really quick at it - they don't call me "one-take Ron" for nothing! Just like in all my films, I simply sit on a sofa next to a lady - in this case my wife, Ada. Ten seconds later I'm copping a feel of her whatsits, and then half a minute after that I've got my finger up her doodah and she's sucking my unmentionable. It's a short step from there to actually having thingie with her, and I'm all finished inside a couple of minutes - only about the same time it takes to put the fairy on the top of the tree. So we don't have a fairy on the top of the tree in our house. **"**

Ken Barlow
Coronation Street stalwart, 72
Sexpert qualification: *In a recent interview with Piers Morgan, Ken claimed to have bedded 1,000 women.*

IT'S A well known fact that I'm a druid, but what you might not realise is that us druids don't celebrate Christmas. As a result, during the time when most people are wrapping presents, stuffing the turkey and cutting them little crosses in the bottom of their sprouts, me and the missus have plenty of spare time to enjoy a bit of the other. We generally do it outdoors at a henge to coincide with the winter solstice when we celebrate the ancient druid festival of Saturnalia. Saturnalia is a very important time for us druids. We give each other presents and enjoy a big meal of turkey with all the trimmings, including sprouts with little pagan crosses cut in them. **"**

Mick Hucknall
Ruby-toothed minstrel of soul, 52
Sexpert qualification: *During his 1980s musical career, the Manchester-born carrot-top's soulful ballads left millions of ladies weak at the knees.*

OVER THE years I've found that sweet music is the way to a woman's heart. On Christmas Eve, my wife Gabriella and I make sure that we get our jobs done early so we can chill out and enjoy some time together. I turn the lights down low, put another log on the fire and pour her a glass of mulled wine as she relaxes on the sofa. Then, to get her in a romantic yuletide mood, I sing her a medley of seasonal songs in my inimitable soulful style. I do all the standards; everything from *White Christmas* and *Let it Snow* to the *Bells of St Mary* and *Kissin' by the Mistletoe*. By the time I get round to *Wombling Merry Christmas*, she's frothing like bottled Bass and I'm in. **"**

Paris Hilton
Hotel 'It' girl heiress, 31
Sexpert qualification: *Paris's 2003 video, in which she did ESD, Belgian biscuit and sticky belly flapcock with an ex-boyfriend, went viral on the internet.*

I'M ONLY too aware of how busy this time of year can be for the ordinary person in the street, and it can be even busier for someone like me who has got lots of houses which all need to be got ready for Christmas. That's why I simply hire lackies to do all my jobs for me; everything from decorating the tree, buying, wrapping and opening presents to preparing and eating my Christmas dinner. This leaves me with the whole holiday season free to fart about with a little dog in a handbag, do whatever it is I do and make grainy sextapes. **"**

Hugh Grant
Unversatile actor, 52
Sexpert qualification: *Hugh was found engaging the services of a call girl called Pancake in Hollywood.*

GOSH, well, me and my wife Liz Hurley always seem to end up hosting a mass gathering of the clans at Christmas, actually. The house is full of endless cousins, half-cousins, uncles, grandparents and maiden aunts, and we never seem to get a moment to ourselves. However, during dinner, when everyone's sat down at the table and tucking into turkey with all the trimmings, we do manage to find time for a sneaky spot of festive naughtiness. At a given signal, Liz gets up and announces that she's going outside to fetch some logs for the fire. Ever the gentlemen, I offer to help to help her and we both leave the room. Then, while she fetches the logs in, I nip to the upstairs toilet and have a wank. **"**

Hugh Hefner
Playboy boss, 100
Sexpert qualification: *Despite advanced yerars, Hugh still manages to date young women in multiples of three.*

CHRISTMAS at the Playboy mansion is my favourite time of year, but there's so much to be done to get the place ready for the festive season that it often feels like there aren't enough hours in the day to have sex with my three pneumatic blonde girlfriends. But over the years it's become a tradition that we always make time on Christmas Day for a sexy romp. After lunch, the giggling girls dress in sexy Santa outfits - complete with stockings, suspenders and balconette bras - and make their way upstairs. I don my Father Christmas costume and follow them on my stairlift. Once in the bedroom, they frolic on my giant circular waterbed, rubbing each other with oil whilst I sit in my chair and have a nap. After about an hour, the girls fetch out a selection of sex toys, with which they take turns bringing each other to orgasm, each one more shattering than the last, whilst my nurse brings me my afternoon indigestion pills, laxatives and statins. Eventually, the girls collapse on the bed, exhausted and spent, whilst I have a another little nap. **"**

Next Issue: HAPPY SCREW YEAR!
Celebrities Give their Top Tips for Successful Sex over the busy Hogmanay Season

ELDERLY gentlemen. Make your frequent trips to the toilet due to a weak bladder look like a cool cocaine habbit by dabbing some flour on your nose.

Richard Eckley, e-mail

PETER Andre. Save money when ordering tailored shirts by not ordering the first 5 buttons, (or first 4 buttons for winter shirts).

Dan Waite, e-mail

GOOSEBERRIES. Make people like you more by not having as many seeds and not tasting like fucking battery acid.

Tam Dale, e-mail

WHEN you catch a mouse in a trap, make its head into a trophy by mounting it on a Blue Peter badge painted brown, and then sticking it above your fireplace.

Fredward Thompson, Edinburgh

DOG owners. Avoid having to pick up your dog's poo by sliding a bowler hat underneath it as it squats.

Nisbet Crawford, e-mail

ALLIGATORS make excellent replacement crocodiles for people who haven't got any crocodiles.

Derek Klaus, e-mail

CONVINCE your neighbours that you are doing an episode of Come Dine With Me by arranging to have a fat black woman, an overtly-gay man, a lonely looking geek and a middle-aged tart to call at your house at 5-minute intervals one evening.

Terry Corrigan, e-mail

RESTLESS sleepers. Fry two eggs close enough together so that they form an albumen bridge in the middle. Hey presto! You have an eye mask that you can eat the next morning.

Skodaboy, e-mail

toptips@viz.co.uk

Letterbocks

...Viz Comic, PO Box 841, Whitley Bay, NE26 9EQ ...e-mail letters@viz.co.uk

STAR LETTER

MY BROTHER Eric is 52, yet he's the dead spit of Farrah Fawcett-Majors when she was in her twenties. He regularly gets *Charlie's Angels* fans coming up to him and asking for his autograph.

Stan Nemesis, Ilkeley

APPARENTLY the recently-deceased dictator of North Korea Kim Jong-il was not only the World's greatest sportsman and warrior, but also the greatest lover ever known to mankind. That's pretty incredible for a bloke that looked just like my mother-in-law. Actually, I reckon the North Koreans should have kept quiet about his death and hired my mother-in-law to secretly take his place. This would have benefited everyone as they could have kept up the legend of the great leader and she'd be 8000 miles away from me.

Richard Evans, Colwyn Bay

I LIKE to put the insides out of yesterday's newspaper inside the cover of today's paper, and leave it on the seat of the bus. Then I sit back and wait for the fun to start!

Ron Bongo, Kenilworth

I BOUGHT a pair of shoes from TK Maxx the other day. They were reduced from £159 to just £19.99. I didn't like them very much and they weren't my size. And I haven't got any legs after I had a road accident last year. But I just can't resist a bargain.

D Bistro, Penge

I RECENTLY placed a large bet on a horse and it didn't win. But when I went to the betting shop to get my money back, the manager didn't want to know and sent me out with a flea in my ear. In any other shop, if you paid for something and it didn't work they'd give you your money back. No wonder bookies drive round in such big cars.

N Bukkake-San, Yeovil

ASK THE Viz LAWYER

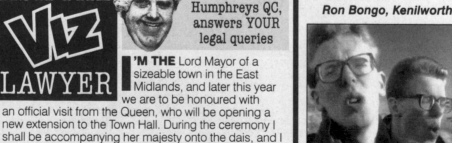

Mr Michaelmas Humphreys QC, answers YOUR legal queries

I'M THE Lord Mayor of a sizeable town in the East Midlands, and later this year we are to be honoured with an official visit from the Queen, who will be opening a new extension to the Town Hall. During the ceremony I shall be accompanying her majesty onto the dais, and I was wondering what would happen if I were to take the opportunity to kick her up the arse. Many years ago, I kicked an old lady up the arse in a shop. It was just a little tap with the side of my foot, and she wasn't badly injured or anything. On that occasion I was done for Common Assault and fined £100. Would the penalty for punting the monarch up the mudflaps be comparable, do you think? If so, I reckon I'll probably have a go.

LA (address withheld)

WELL, it's a bit of a legal grey area, I'm afraid. It depends on so many factors that I can't really offer you a hard and fast answer. That'll be 650 guineas, please.

I WISH Johnny Rotten would make his mind up. When he was on *I'm a Celebrity*, he famously called the British public "fucking cunts", but now when he wants us to buy his butter, he comes on all chummy and nice. Come on, Johnny, make your ruddy mind up!

Mrs Doreen Hubris, Joskyn St. Mary

MY local greengrocer displays his produce on the street. I like to put a few Golden Delicious apples in with the Granny Smiths and vice versa. Then I retire to the café over the road and wait for the fun to start!

Ron Bongo, Kenilworth

THE Proclaimers said that they'd walk '500 Miles' and then '500 more', if necessary, to knock at 'their baby's door', which means that they could be walking up to 1000 miles. As Britain is only 600 miles long, I assume they must have walked into the sea and drowned. A tragic loss.

Ron Wibble, Cleck Heaton

MY mum always used to say that if you don't have something nice to say about somebody, then you shouldn't say anything at all. Well, I think Adolf Hitler was always very nicely turned out, Peter Sutcliffe always kept his beard nice and tidy and Pol Pot was very nice to his mum.

Audrey deVere, Roehampton

WHY is it that sunbathers in hot countries don't get any smaller as they lay on the beach? Yet when I put a rasher of bacon in the pan it shrinks to 60% its size in seconds. It seems like bacon suppliers have got a nice little racket going on, making us buy 40% more bacon than we need.

Ronald Purple, e-mail

MY mum informed me that my Dad gave a chocolate from the Christmas tree to his godson, despite me having been told since I was a kid that we were not allowed them till Christmas Eve. Personally I think this takes the piss. He's supposed to be a role model, not some sort of anarchic, Anti-Christ, who goes against years of tradition at the drop of a hat.

Catherine James, e-mail

WHAT a waste of time these road signs are. I don't even drive a car and I really resent my local council spending money on them.

Edna Potatoes, Cheadle

I HAVE just joined the Jewish RAC. They offer comprehensive roadside breakdown assistance 24/6.

Rabbi Alan Heath, e-mail

I LIKE to pull up at the garage and fill my petrol car with diesel. Once I've paid, I get back into the driver's seat and wait for the fun to start!

Ron Bongo, Kenilworth

I RAN into a bus queue whilst drink driving last year killing several young people. I was heavily criticised for my action, but any one of those young people might have grown up into somebody like Hitler. So my actions have possibly saved millions of lives. This thought is a great comfort to me.

Len Plywood, Stoke

I PAUSED an advert with Steffi Graf using my Sky+ to take a good look at her tits. Then I remembered I had an iPad and could view endless images of a much younger, fitter Steffi on that. What a wondrous age of technology we live in!

Jamie Wood, e-mail

THIS summer I read a poster informing me that dogs die in hot cars. Without seeming pedantic, I would like to point out to the author of this poster that dogs will die in cars of any temperature, if left for long enough.

Dave Garley, e-mail

I LIKE to put a bucket of my own urine inside the door behind my letterbox just before the postman arrives with my morning mail. Then I sit back on the stairs and wait for the fun to start!

Ron Bongo, Kenilworth

WHEN Roy Wood wrote 'I Wish It Could Be Christmas Every Day', I bet the bearded cunt wasn't driving around Tesco's car park for half an hour on Christmas Eve, trying to find a fucking space.

PB, e-mail

BABY CHANGING

BABY CHANGING

Lucky Harry Horseshoe's
LUCKY LETTERS

LUCKY HARRY HORSESHOE is Britain's leading expert on luckology - the scientific study of luck, happenstance and serendipity. Send him your lucky letters and he'll put them in his column... *if you're lucky!*

I BOUGHT a black cat for luck, and for the first few weeks it worked a treat. I won the lottery, had it off with a Page 3 girl and everything. Then my wife noticed that it wasn't lucky at all as it had a few white hairs on its chest. Sure enough, a week later I got piles and my wife died.

Charlie Hall, Birmingham

THEY SAY that rabbit's paws are lucky, but my neighbour's rabbit's got four of them and he's not particularly lucky. In fact, I just reversed the car over him and he's in a right old state. I might have to go and finish him off with a spade.

James Finlayson, via text

LIKE Mr Hall (above) I bought a black cat for luck. However, as I walked about the house it kept crossing my path, which is bad luck. These two lucks cancelled each other out and I found my life carrying on much as it had before, being neither particularly lucky nor particularly unlucky either.

Mrs Fartwell, Colchester

THEY say horseshoes are lucky, but I'm not convinced. My neighbour's horse has got four of them and he's not particularly lucky. In fact, I just drove round a corner on the wrong side of the road whilst texting and ran into him, and he's in a right old state. I might have to go and finish him off with a spade.

James Finlayson, via text

THEY say chimney sweeps are lucky, but I'm not convinced. My neighbour's a chimney sweep and he doesn't seem to be particularly lucky. At the moment he's lying unconscious in the middle of the road after being knocked off his horse. I might have to go and finish him off with a spade.

James Finlayson, via text

McFlys like a Bird

TEEN pop sensations McFLY yesterday revealed that they're throwing their weight behind a particular species of British bird.

"We really are all in favour of this specific type of avian," the boys told a packed press conference. "And we're absolutely 110% behind it," they added.

A spokesman for the Royal Society for the Prevention of Birds said he was delighted to hear that the band were giving their support to a particular variety of winged egg-layer.

He told us: "We're over the moon that McFly are giving their backing to this type of feathered friend." ~ Reuters

SELFISH PRICK
I CAN'T BELIEVE YOU MADE YOURSELF A COFFEE AND DIDN'T OFFER ME ONE!
I'M SORRY. I WASN'T THINKING. DO YOU WANT ME TO MAKE YOU ONE ESPECIALLY?
NO! DON'T BOTHER! I'LL DO IT MYSELF!!
STOMP!

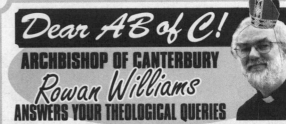
Dear AB of C!
ARCHBISHOP OF CANTERBURY
Rowan Williams
ANSWERS YOUR THEOLOGICAL QUERIES

Dear AB of C,
I'VE RECENTLY been hearing voices in my head telling me to take my firstborn son up onto a hill and there sacrifice him unto the glory of God, and I'm not sure what to do for the best. I know that I'm either going mad or the Lord is demanding a demonstration of my love for Him. If it is God speaking to me, I obviously don't want to displease Him and provoke His mighty wrath, but equally I don't want to end up cutting my son's throat for no good reason if I'm going a bit mental. What should I do?

Dr. Hazelnut Monkbottle, Tring

The AB of C says...
IN THE Book of Genesis, God commands Abraham to sacrifice his son Isaac as a test of faith. As Abraham raises his sword, The Lord stops his hand and provides a goat for him to sacrifice instead. If God is indeed the source of the voices in your head, I am confident that He is probably just testing your faith in a similar way. If you do take your firstborn infant up onto a hill and prepare to cut his throat in honour of Him, I'm 99% sure God will step up in the nick of time and provide some sort of an alternative for you to sacrifice, such as a lamb or a cat. However, just to be on the safe side, it may be wise to take a joke-shop dagger with a spring-loaded blade up onto the hillside and stab your son in the neck harmlessly using that. That way, if it does turn out that you're undergoing some sort of catastrophic mental breakdown, then there's no harm done. The third possibility is that it is actally the voice of God you are hearing, and He does actually want you to sacrifice your son unto His glory. Having read the Bible a couple of times for work, I wouldn't put anything past Him, I can tell you.

Dear AB of C,
MY BROTHER passed away yesterday after a long illness. The trouble is, he owed me £200 at the time and I'm a bit short at the moment. I know that Jesus can raise the dead, as He did it with Lazarus in the Bible, so I was wondering if He could bring my brother back to life long enough for him to pop down the bank and get my money. If I pray really hard, do you think it would be possible? Only He'll have to be quick as we're cremating him on Thursday.

Terry Damocles, Cardiff

The AB of C says...
IN ALL MY years as an Archbishop, I've never known Jesus bring anybody back, and certainly not for a sum as small as £200. If it was over a grand, then you might stand a chance of Him interceding and raising your late brother for a trip to the cashpoint, but I certainly wouldn't get your hopes up on this occasion.

Dear AB of C,
IS THE Communion wafer literally the body of Christ, as it says in the New Testament? Only I'm a strict vegetarian and I wouldn't like to think I was eating meat.

Glenda Drab, Eccles

The AB of C says...
AH, THE old chestnut of the transubstantiation of the Host. Well, I've had a look at the packet, Mrs Eccles, and the main ingredients are corn starch, corn syrup, guar gum and xanthin. There's no mention of any meat products, so you can munch away to your heart's content!

BIFFA BACON

WOT'S THAT YUZ'RE DEEIN' SON? HURMWORK IS IT?

AYE!..FUCKIN **HISTORY** MUTHA

AN' IT'S AS FUCKIN' BORIN' AS FUCKIN' FUCK AN'AALL

BORIN'? NAH, BIFFA...YUZ'RE JUST GANNIN' ABOOT LORNIN' IT IN THE WRANG FUCKIN' WAY, MAN. WORRA YUZ READIN' ABOOT?

THE FUCKIN' CIVIL WAR

AYE?.. WELL YUZ'LL NEVAH LORN ABOOT THAT FROM READIN' A FUCKIN' **BOOK**!

WIVVEN'T AH?

NAH, SON...THE FUCKERS WOT WRITE THESE FUCKIN' BOOKS DIVVEN'T KNAA SHITE MAN

THE BEST WAY T'LORN HISTORY IS T'EXPERIENCE IT **FORST HAND**, SON.

YUZ'VE GORRA BRING THE PAST T'LIFE, BIFFA...

EH? HOO D'YUZ MEAN?

YER REET THERE, MUTHA. WUZ'LL RE-ENACT A BATTLE FROM THE CIVIL WAR T'SEE WOT IT W'REALLY LIKE

YEE CAN BE THE CAVA-LEE-YAZ BIFFA...ME AN'YER MUTHA'LL BE THE ROONDHEEDS.

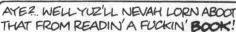
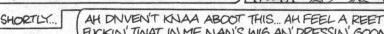

SHORTLY...

AH DIVVEN'T KNAA ABOOT THIS... AH FEEL A REET FUCKIN' TWAT IN ME NAN'S WIG AN' DRESSIN' GOON

AH, STOP YER FUCKIN' MITHERIN' BIFFA... Y'WANT T'DEE WELL IN YUZ EXAMS, DIVVEN'T YUZ, SON?

REET!..WHICH BATTLE ARE WUZ GANNA DEE, FATHA?

WORRABOOT THIS'UN. ...THE BATTLE OF ADWALTAN MOO-AH? THORTIETH O'JUNE, SIXTEEN FAWATY THREE

AHEM..."THE TWO ARMIES MET ON A BATTLEFIELD ENCLURSED BY HEDGERURS WHICH PUT THE ROYALIST CAVALRY...

THAT'S **YEE**, BIFFA

... AT AN ADVANTAGE, EVEN THUR THEY WAS HEAVILY COTNUMBAD..."

HOO!.. HAD ON, MUTHA... IT SEZ THE ROONDHEEDS WAS AWA-OPTIMISTIC AN'ENDED UP GEDDIN' FUCKIN' CHINNED

EH?... WELL WUZ CANNAT RE-ENACT THAT 'UN, FATHA...IT'LL BE UNREPRESENTATIVE O' THE WAR AS A HURL

URKAY...THE BATTLE O'ROONDAWA DOON... AHEM... "THE ROYALISTS WAS IN A BAD WAY AFTAH A PREVIOUS BATTLE, AN' PARLIA-MENTARIAN GENERALS..." THAT'S ME AN'MUTHA..."PUSHED THEM BACK, FORCING A CONFRONTATION AT ROONDAWA DOON...

GEDDIN!

CRACK!

NAH, HAD ON AGAIN, MUTHA...THE ROYALISTS ENLISTED THE HELP O'HEPTON, AN'THE ROONDHEEDS GOT SANDWICHED BETWEEN TWO CAVA-LEE-YAH ARMIES AN' 'AD T'FLEE THE BATTLEFIELD

FUCKIN' **EH?**

HEH!

GIZ THAT FUCKIN' BOOK, FATHA MAN... I'S'LL FIND A BATTLE WHERE THE CAVA-LEE-YAZ GET THEIR FUCKIN' HEEDS KICKED IN...

SNATCH!

LET'S 'AVE A LOOK...HMM... EDGEHILL...NEWBURY... MARSTON MOO-AH...

...HOO...'ERE WE GAN... THE BATTLE O'NASEBY

25

RAFFLES

The Gentleman Thug

THE LONDON OLYMPIC GAMES 1908...

CONGRATULATIONS, MONSIEUR BOULON! YOU HAVE WON THE GOLD MEDAL IN THE THREE FURLONG EXPEDITIOUS DASH!

VOCALISE WHAT?

YOU WERE SECOND, LORD RAFFLES. A MOST CREDITABLE PERFORMANCE, IF I MAY SAY SO.

TESTICLES.

ARE YOU FUCKING DEVOID OF OPHTHALMOLOGICAL ACUITY? I PREVAILED AT THE FINISHING LINE WITH CASUAL ADROITNESS. I URINATED THAT RACE.

WELL FOR MY PART, YOUR GRACE, I AVER THAT THE FRENCHMAN FINISHED STRONGLY AND CAME FROM BEHIND..!

THAT, SIR, IF YOU DON'T MIND ME SAYING SO, IS THE IDIOMATIC LOCUTION VOUCHSAFED BY YOUR OWN MATERFAMILIAS.

AM I TO TAKE IT, SIR, THAT YOU ARE IMPUGNING THE HONOUR OF MY MOTHER?

TAKE IT ANY WAY YOU LIKE... MUCH IN THE MANNER I AM GIVEN TO UNDERSTAND THAT SHE DOES...

FURTHERMORE, MIGHT I POLITELY ENQUIRE WHAT FUCKING ACTION YOU PROPOSE TO UNDERTAKE WITH REGARD TO THE MATTER..?

I SHALL ENGAGE YOU IN FISTICUFFS, LORD RAFFLES. NO MAN QUESTIONS THE VIRTUOUS PROBITY OF MY MATRIARCH.

COME ON. PUT UP YOUR DUKES LIKE A GENTLEMAN, YOUR GRACE.

VERY WELL. I'LL BE WITH YOU IN A SECOND...

EXCUSE ME... MIGHT I MOMENTARILY APPROPRIATE YOUR HAMMER, MY GOOD MAN..?

?

SPANG!

26

Take a Shit

WINNER
MAGAZINE OF THE YEAR
~Take a Shit Magazine of the Year Awards

A Fling of the Past

FLINGS ain't what they used to be...and that's official. According to a new government report, over the last decade the number of British women having holiday romances with local Spaniards has fallen to an all-time low. As the tourist season gets underway, UK girls traditionally look forward to a fortnight of sun, sea and Spanish sex. But whilst the first two are guaranteed, the supply of the latter has all but dried up, leaving many Brits facing the prospect of returning home without having had a bit of the other.

At their peak in the mid-seventies, 98% of British women enjoyed a loveless fling with a waiter, hotel worker or pool cleaner whilst on holiday. But after decades of decline, that figure today stands at a mere 40%. And now the government has expressed concern at the dwindling rate.

"A combination of factors is responsible for this worrying position," said Minister for Foreign Sexual Affairs Tarquin Quim MP. "Ironically it is the popularity of foreign travel that has caused the problem. Thanks to the availability of cheap flights, favourable

Brit Girls Return Home Without Tasting Spanish Nookie

exchange rates and the fragile Spanish economy, the numbers of Brits holidaying in Spain has soared."

"As a consequence, the local waiters and barmen are becoming choosy about where they put it," he continued. "In the 70s a woman only had to have a pair of knockers and a pulse and Spanish men would be buzzing round her like flies round shit. These days, with so many girls stepping off every aeroplane, the bar has been raised."

"It's a sad fact that the majority of lady holidaymakers now return home without having had any sort of dalliance with a swarthy Don Juan," Mr Quim added.

Spanish Prime Minister Mariano Rajoy also expressed his concern at the situation. He told the Spanish Parliament: "Most British girls come to our country to experience the caress of a Latin lover. If they do not find this shallow, transient affection in our country, next year they may decide to look for it elsewhere. Perhaps in the arms of an Italian table wiper in Sorrento or a Greek who hires out pedalo boats on a beach in Corfu."

LADIES! A FREE FLING with a Spanish Waiter for EVERY reader!
See page 29

"I have loved and lost... *18 times!*"

The Real Fling

Globetrotter Janice Lifts the Lid on her Life of Holiday Romance Heartbreak...

Photographs and memories ~ All that remain of the loves Janice has lost.

As told to **Vaginia Discharge**

WE'VE all had a holiday romance. Once we set foot on foreign soil, there's something about the heady combination of cold sangria, hot sun, and even hotter locals that all too often leads to us losing our inhibitions and embarking on a whirlwind fortnight of passionate abandon. And to most of us, that's all it is. Two weeks of meaningless fun and some nice memories to cherish - or perhaps blush over - as we get back on the plane and return to our mundane lives.

Rarely does anyone meet their soulmate whilst on holiday, and very few casual poolside affairs ever blossom into the sort of true love that lasts a lifetime. But amazingly, one Derbyshire woman has found the love of her life on holiday not once... but EIGHTEEN times in the past eighteen years.

JANICE BUNIONS may be a serial holiday romancer, but the 38-year-old DHS filing clerk prides herself on never having had a casual holiday fling. "Every single one of my eighteen holiday romances has been the *real thing*," she says.

Speaking exclusively to *Take-a-Shit* magazine, Janice tells how she has loved and lost repeatedly on her yearly fortnight break abroad.

"I sometimes think fate is conspiring against me, because every time I meet the man with whom I'm destined to spend the rest of my life, something happens to tear us apart," she told us.

Janice was nineteen when she went on her first foreign holiday - a package to Magaluf. She went with three or four girls from the office

Continued over...

where she worked, and romance was the last thing on her mind. But as soon as they arrived, she discovered it was the first thing on her friends' minds.

"Before we had even unpacked our bags, they were off to the pool to try to 'cop off' with a party of lads they had been eyeing up on the coach.

I wasn't interested in that kind of behaviour. I had come abroad to widen my horizons and experience other cultures and ways of life. I went to the hotel restaurant and ordered egg and chips.

Carefree Janice with friends ~ Just an hour later, her life was a partnership.

Pablo ~ Swept Janice off her feet.

I had only been sitting at my table for a couple of minutes when the waiter brought my meal over. I remember to this day the first words he spoke to me. His rich, deep voice and exotic Spanish accent immediately swept me off my feet. "You English?" he asked. I said I was. Then he came straight out with it and told me from the heart: "You are very beautiful lady. You are most beautiful lady I ever see." And that was it.

Until that moment I had never believed in love at first sight. But then I knew it was real. Because we fell head over heels in love with each other, there and then.

Over the course of my egg and chips we got to know each other better. The waiter's name was Pablo, and he was a medical student at Magaluf University, paying his way through college by

working in the hotel. As he brought me the tomato sauce and a clean knife, I knew I had met my soul mate. Later, as he took my plate away, he opened his heart once more.

In faltering English, he asked me to come back to his room and make love. I told him that although I knew he was the one, I wanted to take things easy. I explained that I wasn't like the girls I had come away with who were just after a cheap fling in the sun, and I asked him to be patient with me. But then Pablo dropped his bombshell.

He was terminally ill. He didn't have the English to tell me what was wrong, but he said that he had just a few days to live. As the terrible news sank in, a sobering realisation dawned on me. I knew that if we didn't cement our love immediately, we might never have the chance. So I said yes.

He told me to meet him behind the kitchens at 2.30 when the lunch shift finished. I went to my room, showered and put on my best dress. We meant so much to each other, and I wanted this to be a very special moment. When I got to the back of the kitchens, Pablo was sitting on a dustbin, having a cigarette. Looking at him, with his olive skin, jet black hair and deep brown eyes, he seemed the picture of health. It was hard to believe that his life was soon to be cut cruelly short by some un-named disease that was ravaging him.

When he saw me, Pablo stood up and started undoing his trousers. Gently, but very quickly, he took my arm, leading me through a door and down some stairs into the hotel basement. We eventually came to a mattress behind the boiler. Before I knew what was happening, he had taken me in his arms, tenderly pulled my dress up and pushed me down on the mattress. He seemed conscious of the fact that he could die at any second, and he didn't want to waste a single second of the precious time we had left together. So he didn't do any foreplay.

It was very beautiful and tender. And when it was over he jumped straight up, lit a cigarette and ran off, leaving me lying next to the boiler in the afterglow with my dress up around my neck.

We made love on that mattress every afternoon for the whole fortnight, and our love grew ever stronger with each stolen minute of passion. As my holiday drew to an end, I was heartbroken at the prospect of leaving Pablo behind. He said he couldn't come to the airport to wave me off as he was putting in an extra shift, but he promised that he would follow me to England and marry me. I left him my address and he promised to write to me every day until we could be together again.

But the fairytale was to have no happy ending. Pablo must have died that very day, because I never received a letter from him."

After the tragic loss of Pablo, Janice thought she would never love again. And she felt she could never return to Magaluf, as the memories were simply too painful. So the following year she booked a fortnight in Port Andratx, three miles down the coast.

"Once again, romance was the last thing on my mind; my memories of Pablo were still too raw. This time I went with my friend Susan who worked in accounts. Back home, she was shy and retiring, but as soon as we were abroad she showed her true colours. On our first day there she copped off with the first bloke who showed an interest in her. I was appalled, and I went to the beach alone to read my book.

I hadn't been there five minutes when I suddenly heard a man's voice.

"You English?" he asked in a husky, Majorcan accent.

He was tall and handsome, with jet black hair, olive skin and brown eyes. He sat down beside me, and we got talking. I felt flattered that of all the girls on the beach, he had been attracted to me.

He told me his name was Roberto, and that he lived locally. He seemed fascinated by my hair and glasses, and he told me I was the most beautiful girl he had ever seen. It's the sort of line that a lot of Spanish boys use on holiday-making girls who they see as easy prey. But when I looked into Roberto's loving eyes, I could tell that he meant every word.

After the heartache of Pablo's death I had thought I could never know true happiness again. But now, as I sat chatting to Roberto, I could feel myself falling in love once more. In his halting English, he explained that he had a scooter, and he asked me if I'd like to come back to his house as his mum and dad were out. My doomed romance with Pablo had taught me to seize every moment, and so I said yes.

As I clung to his sweaty vest, I knew that I never wanted to let him go. I was in love again

Janice with friend Susan, just before finding her soulmate Roberto

After all, I was sure I had found the man with whom I was going to spend the rest of my life.

Five minutes later I was hurtling along a dirt road on the back of Roberto's scooter. I was intoxicated by the heady musk of his aftershave combined with the fumes from his cigarette and the tiny 2-stroke engine. And as I clung to his sweaty vest, I knew that I never wanted to let him go. I was in love again.

Eventually, we turned into the drive of his house. When we got off the moped, he seemed rather agitated. He explained that his parents had arrived back unexpectedly.

Janice with a hat ~ a parting gift from her ice-cream vendor fiancé José. He promised to come to England to retrieve it and marry her. That was 12 years ago.

"He bent me over a sit-on lawn mower and expressed his love for me in the only way he knew how"

I was quite excited at the prospect of meeting my future in-laws, but Roberto didn't seem in any hurry to introduce me as he pushed me towards a detached garage at the side of the house.

Once inside he kicked off his flip-flops and told me to get out of my dress. I told him that although I loved him, I wanted to save myself for our wedding night. Roberto frowned. And then he dropped his bombshell.

He told me that like all Spanish eighteen-year-olds, he had to do twelve months of military service. His conscription papers had come through that very morning and he was to enlist in two weeks' time. The room began spinning as I felt the bottom fall out of my world once more. It seemed that cruel fate had again conspired to scupper my chance of happiness. Time was not on our side, and as Roberto held me close, I knew he wanted to compress our courtship into these two fleeting weeks. He tenderly pulled down my knickers and bent me over a sit-on lawn mower before expressing his true love for me in the only way he knew how.

After he had finished, I remained bent double, holding the steering wheel in the afterglow while Roberto pulled up his cut-off jeans and lit another cigarette. He explained that he couldn't take me back to the hotel for one reason or another, but I didn't mind. It was a pleasant forty-minute walk down a dusty road In the midday sun, and it gave me time to reflect on our love for each other and to plan our future together after he completed his spell in the forces.

During the rest of my holiday, we spent many a passionate few minutes in that garage, cementing our love. And when it finally came time for me to return home, I was heartbroken. But worse was to come, for Roberto told me that he would be unable to write to me, as he would probably be going into the Spanish Submarine Service, where he would be under the sea for the entire year.

Those twelve months I waited for Roberto were the longest of my life. Being apart from my true soulmate was almost more than I could bear. It was only the thought of hearing from him once again after his national service that kept me going.

But I was never to hear from him again.

I can only imagine that Roberto must have been killed in action, as I never received a letter or phone call from him after his twelve months were up. They say it is better to have loved and lost than never to have loved at all. But I'm not so sure. The pain of knowing that his body is lying somewhere at the bottom of the sea in a crashed submarine tortures me to this day."

Most women would count themselves extremely unlucky to have two romances cut so cruelly short. But Janice's ill-fortune seemed to know no bounds. Over the next seven summers she was swept off her feet by a series of Spanish men who in turn fell deeply in love with her. Today, thumbing through fading holiday snaps as she sits in her Belper home, she recalls the other loves who were not to be, including...

• FERNADO, a table-wiper from a fish & chip cafe in Port de Pollenca, who she believes was eaten by a shark shortly after the end of her holiday.
• PEDRO, a taxi driver from Las Maravillas who she believes must have perished after his brakes failed on a winding mountain pass.
• JUAN, a barman in a Saint Agusti Karaoke pub, who she fears must have lost his memory and now remembers nothing of the fourteen days they spent planning their future together in 2001.

In 2003, Janice once again packed a case and headed off for two weeks in the sun-soaked resort of Cala Vinyes. Every year, thousands of English girls fall prey to Spanish men who are only interested in one thing. But Janice was a street-wise, seasoned traveller and after years of holidaying, she wasn't going to fall for their glib patter and superficial flattery.

"I'd never been to Cala Vinyes before," she said. "It is completely unspoilt by tourism; a labyrinth of winding narrow streets, fascinating traditional amusement arcades and little Irish bars.

On my first evening there I decided to take a stroll along the harbour front where local artisans pitch their wares in a little market. It was fascinating to wander between the stalls looking at all the traditional goods for sale - belts, handbags, sombreros, straw donkeys and football shirts with Fabregas written on the back. It really was like taking a step back in time to a simpler age. One stall that caught my eye was selling paintings. They were beautifully done, and the artist clearly had a wide repertoire, including tigers, hula dancers, crying clowns and Al Pacino holding a gun. He saw me admiring his work and came over to chat.

"You English?" he asked in a rich, Spanish brogue. I replied that I was, and he told me that I was a very beautiful woman, and that he would love to paint me. Of course I was flattered, who wouldn't be? But there was another feeling beginning to stir inside me ... a burgeoning excitement deep in my heart that I hadn't felt for about a year.

He told me his name was Sergio and that he had studied painting at the finest art schools in the world. He had wild, Bohemian eyes that seemed to hold a spark of genius, and as he spoke I could see he sensed in me a kindred free spirit. He told me he had to paint me, that night. He said I was his muse and he

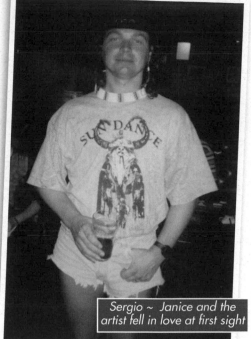

Sergio ~ Janice and the artist fell in love at first sight

had never before felt such desire to paint someone.

I was dizzy with excitement and love. Sergio was the one.

He called over to his friend who was selling fudge and asked him to look after his stall whilst we went his studio. The friend grinned and made a traditional Majorcan arm gesture as we got into Sergio's van. During the five-minute journey to his studio, neither of us spoke. We didn't have to. The muse was upon Sergio and both of us understood that words were superfluous.

Continued over...

LADIES! There's a FREE FLING with a SPANISH WAITER for EVERY reader!

WITH VISITOR NUMBERS soaring thanks to cheap flights and Spanish waiters becoming more choosy, British ladies are finding it harder than ever to have a fling while they're abroad.

Gone are the days when a female holidaymaker could find herself in bed underneath a waiter while her suitcase was still going round on the baggage carousel. These days, valuable vacation time is all too easily wasted in pursuit of a swarthy man called Pedro or Mario, and it's a sad fact that following a frantic fortnight of fruitless flirting, many

British girls end up boarding the plane home without having copped off at all. That's why we're stepping in to make sure you don't have to Wait for your Waiter. And we've teamed up with the Spanish Tourist Board to give a FREE FLING with a Spanish waiter to every lady Take a Shit reader!

Just clip out the coupon, take it with you on holiday and present it to any waiter in your hotel. The voucher is valid in any resort on mainland Spain and the Balaeric Islands and entitles you to one hurried, loveless scuttle per day with the olive-skinned lothario of your choice for up to a fortnight.

Free Holiday Fling with a Spanish Waiter

Resort...........................Hotel............................. No. of days (número de días) 7 ☐ 14 ☐

Arrival (llegada) ..../....../...... Departure (salida) ..../....../......

Por favor, dele al poseedor de este vale 1 (uno) encuentro sexual superficial y triste por día por toda la duración mostrada. Al fin de la estancia, no está obligado ni a despedirle al poseedor de este vale al aeropuerto, ni a contactar con él, ni siquiera a pensar en él.

To be filled in by the waiter

Aseguro que, que yo sepa, hasta esta fecha, no tengo ni ladillas ☐   ni gonorrea ☐
ni sífilis ☐   ni clamidia ☐   ni herpes ☐   ni verrugas genitales ☐   Fecha ....../....../.....

Terms and conditions: Take a Shit, its employees and representatives are not responsible for any pregnancies, sexually transmitted diseases, broken hearts and fights that result from the use of this voucher.

Sergio's caravan studio in the hills above Calla Vinyes

When we got to his caravan studio we went inside. Sergio then said that he had forgotten his brushes, but he didn't need them anyway. I asked him what he meant. He explained that my body was his canvas and that his love for me was his brush. Our night together would be the greatest masterpiece the world had ever known, he told me as he began taking his trousers off. His passion for me was so intense that that piece of art took him less than five minutes to complete.

As I lay back in the afterglow on the pull-down bed of the caravan, he dressed quickly and said he had to get back to his stall as Saturday nights were very busy, and he didn't really trust the fudge seller that much. We got in his van and drove back to the market. Again we didn't speak. We didn't have to. Mere words could not describe the beauty of what we had just created together.

He asked if I would come back the next evening so he could paint me again, and of course I said I would. Sergio was my love. He was my life.

I returned to the market the following night, but I found that the fudge seller was minding the art stall again. I asked him where Sergio was, but he didn't speak any English, and he just chuckled and made the same traditional Majorcan

arm gesture I had seen him do the previous night. I felt lost without my Sergio, but then my heart leapt as I saw his van approach. He got out with a woman, and I waved to him. He didn't seem to recognise me, probably because it was quite dark, and it was only when I went up and spoke to him that the penny dropped. He was thrilled to see me.

The woman in his van was his sister, who spoke perfect English with a strange Majorcan accent that made her sound like someone from Birmingham. I reminded him of his promise to paint me again. Sergio looked pained and told me that he had already done a painting that night, and he couldn't do another one so soon after. He could see I was disappointed.

But then he told me that he was thinking of doing a sculpture of me, and asked if he could take some photographs for reference. I was delighted and honoured, and the fudge seller was soon minding Sergio's stall again as we went back to the caravan.

It was to be a highly detailed statue, he told me. And it was to be a study of the nude. I would not normally pose naked for anyone, but the bond of trust between Sergio and myself was so strong that I instantly agreed.

For nearly an hour he snapped away with his mobile phone, taking the most intimate of shots as I struck a series of artistic poses for him. And every night for the next fortnight I returned to his caravan where he photographed me, or used me to create his art.

Sergio and I decided to live together. He was to come to Derby with me, where he would do paintings of the Peak District and sell them on a stall at the Eagle Centre Market. On the final night of my holiday I went to see him at the harbour front to finalise our plans. But I was met with the worst news I could imagine.

Sergio was dead. His identical twin brother Ramos was running the stall, and he explained how Sergio had killed himself in a fit of artistic rage after being unable to get the stripes right on a tiger. I felt like the bottom had fallen out of my world once again. I had had happiness within my grasp, only for it to be snatched away like a candle in the wind."

After such a run of ill fortune, no one would have blamed Janice for giving up on love and seeking solace in a series of shallow physical holiday flings. But she is a romantic and believes that true love is worth waiting for, no matter how long it takes. And

He explained that my body was his canvas and that his love for me was his brush

Janice on the harbour front in Cala Vinyes, snapped by her love Sergio ~ one of the few respectable shots the artist took

I would never sleep with anyone on a first date unless I was sure I would spend the rest of my life with them, and with Raoul, I was sure

in 2009 when she packed her suitcase and once more jetted off to foreign climes, she found not one love of her life... but two!

"I'd booked to go to Costa de la Calma with my friend Coleen who worked in the next office. At the airport we got on the coach that was to transfer us to our hotel. The driver was a young man who introduced himself as Raoul, and he made sure that Coleen and I sat on the front two seats. He was handsome, with jet black hair, brown eyes and olive skin. All the way to the resort he was chatting to us and looking at my legs in his mirror. I felt a spark of something stirring deep within me, a spark that I had felt many times before.

When we arrived at the hotel he helped us get our cases out of the bus and asked if he and his friend could take us for a drink later, and straight away I said yes. I wasn't in love with him at that point, but I could feel there was something between Raoul and I.

Raoul turned up later that evening with his friend Carlos, who I thought was rather coarse. He had greasy black hair, brown eyes and a dark complexion, although Coleen seemed to like him. We spent the night in a local taverna, and half way through the evening Coleen went back to our hotel room with Carlos. I must admit I was disappointed with the way she had cheapened herself, jumping into bed with the first Spaniard who came her way.

The love between me and Raoul deepened as the night went on. He told me that I was the most beautiful woman he had ever seen, and he wanted to make love to me, and to me only, for the rest of his life. Now I would never sleep with anyone on a first date unless I was sure I would spend the rest of my life with them, and with Raoul, I was sure. We were a match made in heaven. We left the taverna and went over to a dark, secluded patch of ground where there was some building work going on, and we made love.

As I lay there on some bags of cement in the afterglow, Raoul dressed quickly. He explained he had to go as he had to look after his elderly mother. That was typical of the caring Raoul that I had come to know and love. He asked if he could meet me again the following evening, and I said of course. "You bring your friend, too, eh?" he said. I was so touched at his kindness. He clearly didn't want Coleen to feel left out.

Three's company ~ Janice and her boyfriend Raoul, 5 mins before he copped off with Coleen (behind)

But the next night, a change seemed to have come over him. The four of us went to the same taverna as before, but Raoul was a little distant, and he seemed to be paying more attention to Coleen than me. In fact he was openly flirting with her, and she was lapping it up. I was so upset with myself for being taken in by Raoul, who I now clearly saw as a womaniser. Half way through the evening, he and Coleen went off to the hotel room together, and quite frankly I thought good riddance to both of them. But I was still upset. I had loved Raoul deeply and it was going to take time to get over him.

Carlos could see that I was upset and came over and sat at my side. He put his arm around me and told me that I looked beautiful when I cried. He picked up a napkin from the table and wiped my tears away. He was handsome, with shiny, black hair, deep brown eyes and a dark complexion, and I was so cross with myself for having misjudged him.

For the rest of the evening I poured my heart out to Carlos, telling him how Raoul had hurt me. He was very understanding. He kept kissing my ear, telling me everything would be alright and cupping my breasts. He was very tender and by the end of the evening we loved each other more than life itself."

The finger that so very nearly wore a wedding ring 18 times

Next week...

How Janice was cruelly betrayed by Carlos the following day, but found true love with his friend Esteban on the Wednesday.

1 PALAEONTOLOGISTS believe the first holiday romance happened more than 25,000 years ago, when a stone-age housewife from southern England walked across the land bridge that then connected Britain to mainland Europe. Whilst staying for two weeks in a prehistoric hotel at the Lascaux Caves in what was later to become northern France, she had an affair with a hairy Neanderthal waiter. The waiter promised to write to her every day when she went back, but never did. And it's not surprising, as writing wasn't invented until 20,000 years later.

2 ANYONE who cops off with one of their fellow holidaymakers on an 18-30 holiday may be surprised to learn that, according to British law, they have NOT actually had a fling. The Foreign Travel Sexual Relationships Act passed by Edward Heath's government in 1974 defines a fling as *"…a series of between 2 (two) and 14 (fourteen) acts of sexual congress to include full or partial intromission, in a country outside of the United Kingdom's jurisdiction, with a person or persons resident in that country."*

3 FEW people realise that this country's longest and most successful marriage began as a holiday fling. On a two-week break on the Mediterranean island of Mykanos in 1946, a young Princess Elizabeth caught the eye of a Greek table-wiper by the name of Philip Stavoropoulos. Despite the opposition of her father, King George VI, the relationship blossomed into love and the couple were eventually married at St Paul's Cathedral to the delight of the whole nation.

4 THE oldest British woman ever to embark on a holiday romance was Phylis Mould of Redditch. In 1976 at the age of 102, she travelled to the Costa Brava for a 2-week all-inclusive package holiday. At breakfast in the hotel, a 19-year-old Spanish waiter named Amello took a shine to her and the pair began an affair. The relationship, however, was short lived as Phylis dumped Amelio after a week and started banging Felipe - a teenager she had spotted playing the castanets in a local Flamenco bar.

5 DURING World War II, food, clothing and petrol were all strictly rationed. And they weren't the only things. Between 1939 and 1945, rules were imposed on women travelling to Spain, restricting them to having it off with no more than three waiters during their holiday.

AS CYNDI LAUPER famously sang, *Girls Just Wanna Have Fun.* And the moment they set foot on foreign soil, the fun begins. There isn't a woman in Britain who, after leaving her husband or boyfriend safely at home and jetting off to the Costa Blanca, hasn't embarked on a torrid two-week dalliance with the first swarthy Latino who gives her the glad eye as she books into her hotel.

But despite this, how much do we really know about these casual foreign affairs? Here are…

10 FLINGS YOU NEVER KNEW ABOUT HOLIDAY ROMANCE

6 HOLIDAY romances are not just enjoyed by humans - they are also a feature of the animal kingdom. Migrating birds such as swallows often fly to warmer climes in the summer, spending two weeks getting poked off the exotically-plumaged native species before flying back home to resume their humdrum lives.

7 IT'S EASY to tar all Spanish waiters with the same brush and assume they are all constantly copulating with visiting British girls. In fact nothing could be further from the truth, because one of them isn't. Ricardo Cortez, known as El Desafortunado - The Unlucky One - has been a waiter in Loret del Mar's Hotel Fabuloso for 37 years, and in all that time has failed to coax a single British woman into his bed. The nearest he got was in 1998 when a girl from Leeds agreed to meet him after his shift one night. Unfortunately for Ricardo, the date never materialised as the girl's hired moped left the road on a treacherous mountain pass in the afternoon and she was killed. Once again, El Desafortunado was forced to return to his room alone and pull himself off.

8 NEW evidence suggests that pioneering US aviatrix Amelia Earhart did not perish after ditching her plane in the Pacific Ocean in 1937 as previously thought. Wreckage from her Lockheed Electra plane has been found suggesting that she crash-landed on the remote island of Nikumaroro, where the only other resident was a waiter named Manuel - the sole survivor of the sinking of a Spanish cruise ship the previous year. Earhart is thought to have fallen for Manuel's Latin good looks and glib patter, embarking on a shallow physical relationship with him, before succumbing to a combination of malnutrition, beri-beri and insect bites a fortnight later.

9 PAULINE Musters, the world's smallest woman, also holds the world record for the smallest ever holiday romance. In 1982, she booked a week's holiday at hotel in Playa De'n Bossa where, by coincidence, the cocktail waiter was the world's shortest man, Calvin Phillips. With her inhibitions loosened by a double sangria the size of a thimble, Musters fell for Phillips's glib patter and agreed to have sex with him. He took her back to his room, no bigger than a shoebox and made love to her on a mattress the size of a slice of bread. With his penis the size of a grain of rice.

10 HOLIDAY romances have formed the basis of countless books, movies, plays and songs. That film - not *Educating Rita*, but the other one like it - is just one example, but there are many, many more too numerous to mention.

Lothari ~ OH, NO!

Lover recruitment fiasco hits Spanish holiday industry

THE CEO of a Madrid-based service provider was last night facing calls to resign after his company failed to fulfill its contractual obligations with the Spanish government.

GroupoQuatro signed a £500m deal to recruit, train and supply 200,000 Latin lovers to seduce British women at Spanish resorts during the 2012 tourist season. But with just days to go before the start of the summer holiday rush, it became clear that the company had failed to meet its targets.

underestimated

Speaking to the Spanish press, GroupoQuatro chief executive **Umberto Ceveca** admitted that his company had underestimated the scale of the task. *"We simply didn't leave ourselves enough time to complete the procurement process,"* said Ceveca. *"But we have nevertheless managed to recruit and train a significant proportion of the workforce we initially undertook to provide, including around 60,000 swarthy waiters, 10,000 saturnine table-wipers and almost 2,000 sexually delinquent barmen."*

But his words cut little ice with GroupoQuatro's critics, who claim that the labour force as it stands will be ill-prepared for the task of pleasuring the expected summer influx of tipsy British women.

"These men have been hired from job centres around Spain," said Spanish opposition MP **Maria Esposito**. *"Many of them have no experience of coaxing naive foreign girls into bed, and half of them can't even speak the language of love."*

"Many don't even have a moustache or snakey little hips and tight 'bolillos'," she added.

Faced with the last-minute shortfall, the Spanish government has been forced to turn to the army to make up the numbers. All leave has been cancelled and thousands of troops have been drafted in to work in hotels at resorts throughout the country. Spanish armed forces chief **General Juan Gonzalez** was critical of GroupoQuatro's poor performance, but was confident that his men would rise to the occasion.

"Spanish soldiers are extremely well trained and disciplined," he said. *"Whether it's a war zone or an erogenous zone, my men get in, deploy their weapons, and get out."*

It Happened to Me!...

You tell Take-a-Shit about YOUR holiday romance memories

Latin lover surprise

TaS I left my husband Eric at home last year whilst I went on a girls-only holiday to the Costa Brava. Whilst I was there, I had a passionate affair with a man called Enrique who was a waiter at the hotel we were staying at. He was a wonderful, sensitive lover, nothing like my boring man back home, with whom sex had become a chore. The last day of the holiday was very tearful as I bade farewell to my Latin lover. Imagine my surprise when Enrique tore off his moustache in front of me to reveal he was my husband! Eric explained that had been masquerading as a waiter in order to put some spice back in our relationship.

Audrey Colostrum, Luton

TaS I must be the luckiest woman in the world, because I have sex with a swarthy Spanish waiter every night of the week. It's Manuel out of Fawlty Towers and I'm married to the actor what plays him.

Ada Sachs, Torquay

Lothario shock

TaS Three weeks ago I returned from a holiday in Calla Torrida, where I had enjoyed a brief but passionate fling with a man called Fernando, who was a waiter at a restaurant called Casa Paella on the harbour front. He told me that I was more beautiful than all the stars in the sky, and he had never felt this way about anyone before. However, last week, my doctor diagnosed me with crabs that I must have picked up whilst abroad. I feel so sorry for Fernando. He had clearly caught them off a lavatory seat, as he told me I was the first woman he had ever been with.

Sandra Wegs, Eastbourne

TaS I go back to the same hotel in Benidorm every year and each time I have a

WIN!

*Each letter we print wins a delightful West Highland White terrier with 3 legs and no eyes, **worth £100!***

passionate affair with a waiter. The trouble is, I am finding it very difficult to remember which ones I have already had a fling with. It is hard to tell them apart as they are all very dark and handsome and have a big moustache. Also, they all dress as waiters and all of them speak with a foreign accent. I don't want to inadvertently have an affair with anyone twice, as I like the novelty. I asked the hotel manager if he could issue his staff with name badges to help me remember which ones I have had intercourse with. He said he would, but it didn't really help as at least four of them were called Pablo, and there were several Alphonsos, Marios and Pedros.

Iris Dunbar, Leeds

Romeo revelation

TaS Two weeks ago I returned from Calla Torrida in Spain. On my holiday I went for a meal at a restaurant called Casa Paella, and I fell in love with the waiter, Fernando. What's more, he fell head over heels

in love with me, telling me that I was more beautiful than all the stars in the sky. However, this morning I went to the doctor and he told me that I have somehow contracted pubic lice whilst in Spain. I can only think I must have caught them off a toilet seat. I could not have caught them from Fernando as I was the first woman he had ever been with.

Janet Higgs-Boson, Surbiton

TaS Last year my wife and I went on holiday to the Costa del Sol where we stayed in a lovely hotel. However, I was rather annoyed to see one one the waiters openly flirting with my wife as he served us. I was even more appalled when I later found out that my wife had begun an affair with him and had been meeting him for sex. I was extremely cross, but then it occurred to me

that what's sauce for the goose is sauce for the gander. To teach my wife a lesson, I started having an affair with the waiter myself. The last day of our holiday was very tearful as we both prepared to say goodbye to our Latin lover. He has promised to write to us both, and as soon as he can he is going to come over to England and marry us.

Leonard Frottage, Lincoln

TaS Every year I go to Loret del Mar and have a fling with a waiter or barman. They always promise to write to me when I get back home, but in eight years, the Spanish Royal Mail has not managed to deliver a single one of their letters. Their postal service must be even worse than ours.

Edna Poultry, St Giles

Waiter disbelief

TaS Last week I returned at the end of a lovely holiday in Calla Torrida. My stay was made even more memorable by the fact that I met the most wonderful man, Fernando, while I was there. He was a waiter in Casa Paella, a little restaurant by the harbour, and he swept me off my feet. He told me I was more beautiful than all the stars in the sky, and that I was the only woman he had ever been with. However, since I came back my pubic mound has been itching like mad, and I'm wondering if I should go to the doctor.

Majorie Felcher, Tring

Holiday Law

*with **Quercus Petraea***

I SPENT A WEEK in Majorca this summer. While I was there I had a shallow, physical affair with the porter at my hotel. We met every afternoon in the service stairwell or boiler room for sex. However, on checking out of the hotel, I was appalled to discover that I had been CHARGED £140 for the affair. When I booked my holiday package, I was under the impression that my stay was 'all inclusive'. As a result, I had a heated argument in the foyer with the manager who insisted that 'a bit of the other' was an extra, like phone calls or the mini bar. In the end I was forced to pay up as he refused to give me back my passport until the bill was settled. Can I claim this back off my holiday insurance?

Mrs Keith, Yootle

Yes you can. The hotel manager was most definitely wrong on this occasion. Anything additional to your all-inclusive arrangement, such as out-of-hours room service or pay-per-view films, must be signed for if they are to be added to the bill as an extra when you check out. Unless your swarthy lover got you to sign a receipt at the end of each hurried liaison, then under EU law your fling is also deemed to be 'inclusive' to your package. Provided you can still produce your hotel bill, and that you took out ABTA-recognised travel insurance prior to departure, you can claim back up to £30 per scuttle for a maximum of 14 scuttles over a single two week-period, and up £50 for STD treatments, undergone whilst abroad or within three weeks of returning to the UK.

FOR or AGAINST

*Each week **Take-a-Shit** asks you if you are For or Against something. Simply send text to **018118055** followed by the word **FOR** if you are for the thing, or **AGAINST** if you are against the thing. This week...*

HOLIDAY ROMANCES

Texts could cost your standard text rate but some may be considerably higher. And most will be even higher than that. And don't forget, you can text as many times as you like.

Last week's For or Against was **LITTER**

FOR: 51%
AGAINST: 49%

SIR MERVYN KING

LUNCHTIME AT THE BANK OF ENGLAND

OOPH! THAT WAS AN ENORMOUS HELPING OF BEEF STROGANOFF TODAY, OLIVE!

GOVERNOR £

AND I PROBABLY SHOULDN'T HAVE HAD ALL THAT RICH CHOCOLATE GATEAU FOR PUDDING!

I'D BETTER NIP INTO MY PRIVATE LOO AND "MAKE A DEPOSIT"

WC

MY BOWELS COULD DO WITH A BIT OF "QUANTITATIVE EASING" AFTER ALL THAT FOOD!

GNNN...

SPLOOSH

GOOD LORD! WHAT A MONSTER STOOL!

THAT CHOCOLATE GATEAU CERTAINLY PROVIDED A SUBSTANTIAL RETURN ON MY INVESTMENT.

OH CRIKEY! WOULD YOU BELIEVE IT?

THERE'S NO TOILET PAPER!

I'LL JUST HAVE TO USE SOME OF THE BANK DEPOSIT SLIPS OUT OF MY DESK DRAWER!

THE COAST IS CLEAR — NOW GO! GO! GO!

WADDLE

YELP! HERE COMES MY SECRETARY!

QUICK, GRAB A HANDFUL OF DEPOSIT SLIPS THEN DASH BACK INTO THE LOO!

AH SIR MERVYN, THE BANK'S COURT OF DIRECTORS WOULD LIKE TO SEE YOU...

CRAB-LIKE SCUTTLE

THEY ARE CONCERNED ABOUT THE CURRENT FINANCIAL CRISIS AND WANT REASSURANCE THAT YOU ARE MAINTAINING A CAREFUL AND PRUDENT ECONOMIC POLICY.

YES, YES, BRING THEM UP TO MY OFFICE.

WIPE WIPE WIPE

WAIT A MINUTE, THESE AREN'T DEPOSIT SLIPS ... I'VE BEEN WIPING MY BOTTOM WITH FIFTY POUND NOTES!

I MUST'VE GRABBED A WAD OF NEWLY-MINTED CURRENCY, BY MISTAKE!

GASP! THE COURT OF DIRECTORS WOULD BE HORRIFIED IF THEY KNEW I'D USED OUR BANKNOTES AS BOG ROLL!

THEY'D THINK I WAS A RECKLESS ECONOMIC WASTREL!

I'D BETTER JUST FLUSH AWAY THE EVIDENCE...

KER LUNK!

HELP! THE CISTERN'S BUST— IT WON'T FLUSH!

I NEED SOME KIND OF STICK TO POKE IT ALL DOWN THE U-BEND...

OHO!

AFTERNOON GOVERNOR

WC

COULD YOU SIGN FOR THIS DELIVERY OF GOLD BARS PLEASE?

I NEED TO BORROW ONE OF THESE BARS...

IT'S AN EMERGENCY!

I'LL TRY AND PUSH THE BE-SHITTED FIFTY POUND NOTES DOWN UNDERNEATH THE TURD

JAB JAB SQUELCH

THEN AT LEAST THEY WON'T BE VISIBLE

WAH! MY MONSTROUS POO IS SO DENSE THAT THE GOLD BAR IS STUCK FAST!

PULL TUG

I CAN'T GET IT OUT!

NOW IT LOOKS LIKE I'VE BEEN WIPING MY ARSE ON GOLD BULLION, AS WELL!

THAT WON'T REASSURE THE COURT OF DIRECTORS THAT I'M A THRIFTY AND PARSIMONIOUS ECONOMIST!

MY ONLY CHANCE IS TO POUR A LOAD OF WATER OVER THE WHOLE LOT!

MAYBE THAT'LL FLUSH IT ALL AWAY

SIR MERVYN WILL SEE YOU IN A MOMENT, CAN I OFFER YOU A GLASS OF CHAMPAGNE WHILE YOU WAIT?

CHAMPAGNE?!

IT HARDLY SEEMS APPROPRIATE TO BE DRINKING CHAMPAGNE IN THESE TIMES OF ECONOMIC AUSTERITY!

FRUGALITY SHOULD BE OUR WATCHWORD! WE'RE ALL IN THIS RECESSION TOGETHER, YOU KNOW!

AH, THOSE BOTTLES ARE JUST WHAT I NEED, TA!

GRAB!

WC

HA-HAR! DOWN THE PAN YOU GO!

THIS'LL GET RID OF ALL THAT SHITTY MONEY AND GOLD!

AH! ERM...

OH BOLLOCKS!

MAJOR MISUNDERSTANDING

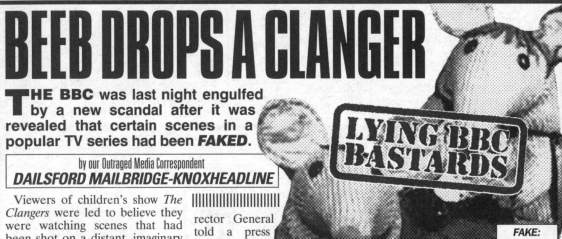

BEEB DROPS A CLANGER

THE BBC was last night engulfed by a new scandal after it was revealed that certain scenes in a popular TV series had been *FAKED*.

by our Outraged Media Correspondent
DAILSFORD MAILBRIDGE-KNOXHEADLINE

Viewers of children's show *The Clangers* were led to believe they were watching scenes that had been shot on a distant, imaginary planet far, far away across the vast emptiness of space.

However, red-faced bosses have now been forced to admit that the programmes were actually filmed in a converted **COWSHED** in **WHITSTABLE**. Worse, the clangers shown in the footage had been **KNITTED** from **WOOL** and were made to appear to move using trick stop-motion photography.

whistle

Furthermore, the BBC admitted that their noises had been "recorded later" using a Swanee whistle.

As a storm of protest gathered, shame-faced BBC chief Mark Thompson begged licence-payers for forgiveness. The weeping Director General told a press conference: "On this occasion, we have allowed our usually high standards to slip. It was never our intention to deceive the public, and we are truly sorry."

"I beseech the British people to give us one last chance," he sobbed, whilst wringing his hands in anguish.

titfer

But Thompson's weasel words cut little ice with the public. Furious London licence-payer Paul Dacre, 63, told us: "This latest scandal is the last straw. The BBC must be closed down with immediate effect, and all recordings of their programmes should be burnt on a big bonfire."

arsehare

And outraged *Clangers* viewer Maureen Braindead, 58, fumed: "I'm an utter moron and I believe in the literal actuality of every single thing I see on the television."

"I lack the basic cognitive skills necessary to understand the complex editorial and creative process that is involved in the production of a programme, and consequently feel badly let down by the BBC, an institution that used to have my full trust and respect," she added.

FAKE: Clangers were made of wool.

McFly on the Wall

TEEN pop sensations *McFLY* yesterday posed for photographers on Hadrian's Wall in a bid to raise public awareness of Britain's Roman antiquities.

"This stuff is like millions of years old or something," said the drummer.

"Yeah, it's really cool," agreed the guitarist, the other one and the other one.

The band told reporters who had travelled to Northumberland that they would one day love to walk the entire 76-mile length of the wall, which stretches from Land's End to John O'Groats, but at the moment they were all too busy with other projects to bother.

~ Reuters

Drunken bakers

35

LETTERBOCKS

Viz Comic
PO Box 841
Whitley Bay
NE26 9EQ
letters@viz.co.uk

STAR LETTER

★ **I AGREE** those orca whales in SeaWorld should be given human rights and set free. Except, of course, for that one who killed his trainer a couple of years ago. He should get the electric chair. They can't have it both ways.

Graeme Parkinson, e-mail

☐ **WHY DO** people make such a fuss about birds flying south in the winter? Everyone slags pigeons off but at least they stay here and put up with the cold like the rest of us.

Terry Corrigan, e-mail

☐ **DURING** the 1970s, I was a teacher at a private preparatory school in the south of England. I installed hidden cameras in the changing rooms so I could watch the boys to make sure there was no bullying or horseplay in the showers. These days people would no doubt put two and two together to make five and I'd be hauled over the coals and called every name under the sun. People's dirty minds sadden me.

Lettsworth Plywood Cirencester

☐ **THEY** say the Royal family earn all their millions of pounds because they bring an awful lot of tourists into this country. Well my brother's a coach driver, and he fetches thousands of the bastards in every day from Heathrow. He only gets paid about twelve grand plus tips and what he finds down the back of the seats.

Frank Hardboard, Camden

☐ **MY** husband says that lesbians were invented in ancient Greece or some such nonsense. But I am sure they were invented early in the twentieth century because Queen Victoria famously said that they didn't exist. Surely we can't both be right?

Dolly Clueless, Penge

☐ **A CASH** machine has just charged me £2 for a transaction but still told me to cover my PIN to prevent me from being robbed. Pretty ironic if you ask me.

Steve H, e-mail

☐ **"LET** not your left hand know what your right hand is doing" says the Bible. Well most of the time my right hand is having a wank. And I can't keep it a secret from my left hand because that's usually holding the sock.

Jason Wristwhiskers Newcastle

☐ **I WAS** wondering if any of your readers been given stupid names by 'out of their minds' parents. To get you started, mine called me Zond, the bastards.

Zond Flint, e-mail

☐ **SO** Sir Fred Goodwin has been stripped of his knighthood and is now just plain Fred Goodwin. Well frankly I don't think that's enough for this dreadful man. He should also be stripped of Fred and Goodwin as well so that he has to walk around with no name at all. That will teach him not to be such a rubbish bank manager.

Kaja, Googoo

☐ **DURING** the 1970s, I was a teacher at a private preparatory school in the south of England. I used to regularly inspect the

Have Your Say... ABOUT That Greek Bailout

EVERYONE agrees that the Greek economy is in free-fall, and now the finance ministers of the European Union have agreed a further multi-billion Euro rescue package in an attempt to keep the ailing country afloat. But is it a good thing or is it a bad thing? Nobody knows, for the simple reason that nobody has a fucking clue what the fuck's going on. Nevertheless, we went out on the street to see what the Great British public had to say on the matter...

"**ON A** recent holiday in Corfu, my wife and I went out to a restaurant. At the end of our meal, the manager gave us both a free glass of Metaxa brandy. It was a lovely gesture, so I think we should do everything we can to help out the Greeks in their hour of need."

Herbert Pocket, jeweller

"**GREECE** is full of ancient statues from Greek and Roman times, such as the Venus de Milo, Michelangelo's David etc. I've seen on Flog It!, Bargain Hunt and Dickinson's Real Deal where this sort of stuff is worth hundreds of pounds. If you ask me, the Greeks ought to put some of their valuable treasures up for auction before deciding to come round the rest of Europe with their begging bowl in their hand."

Justine Rumpelstiltskin, florist

"**IT'S NO** wonder the Greek economy is in such a state when they spend all their money building parthenons. They can't come cheap, and that's before they put the roof on."

Rance Pleasurecraft, quantity surveyor

"**I BET** they wish they still had a few of their philosophers kicking about. If Aristotle, Plato and Archimedes put their thinking caps on, I'm sure they'd come up with a solution to Greece's economic problems lickety-split."

Frank Mucus, circus clown

"**WHAT'S** the point of us handing over money to the Greeks? They won't be able to spend anything we send because they've got Euros and we've got pounds."

Paul Lewis, radio presenter

"**THE** other day I visited my local Greek deli for lunch. I couldn't believe it. After we've lent his country a billion pounds, the Greek shopowner had the bare-faced cheek to charge me £1.50 for some spanikopita. The ingratitude of these people beggars belief."

Dutch Holland, gynaecologist

"**SWITZERLAND** is the economic powerhouse of the world, and they make proper cheese. Perhaps if the Greeks pulled their finger out and made some proper cheese instead of that crumbly smegma they sprinkle on their salads, they wouldn't need bailing out quite so often. It's certainly worth thinking about."

Pelham Woodlouse, traffic warden

"**THE** problem with Greece is that it's got no celebrities. Except for Nana Mouskouri and Demis Roussos, and they're both dead. Perhaps if the country produced a few more stars, it might start to feel better about itself and decide to pull its socks up."

Keith Glans, sewage worker

"**MR** Glans (*above*) ought to check his facts. Contrary to what he says, Nana Mouskouri and Demis Roussos are both very much alive, although come to think of it, I'm pretty sure Demis Roussos was born in Egypt, so he probably doesn't really count as Greek."

Cissie Hymen, jazz trumpeter

"**THE** Greek government should take a leaf out of my thrifty old grandmother's book. After she got married, she put a penny out of my grandad's pay packet into a biscuit tin each week. Greece should do the same, and take a penny out of each bailout and put it in a tin for a rainy day. The Greek finance minister Mr Popazogalou, or whatever his name is, would be surprised how quickly the money builds up. When my granny died she had nearly ten pounds in her tin."

Agnes McBagpipes, retired teacher

THERE'S A LITTLE PLAQUE ON YOUR TEETH.

GUSTAV MAHLER WAS BORN HERE 1860

TOP

WALKERS. Save a fortune on expensive waterproof clothing by simply spraying yourself with WD40 before you go out.
Stuart Lucs, e-mail

HOMEOWNERS. Save money on heating this winter by laying electric blankets under all your carpets. Hey Presto! Instant underfloor heating throughout your house.
Mister Shifter, Jersey

RACEHORSES. Try rolling over on your backs every now and then. That might stop those angry little Irishmen from hitting you with sticks all the time.
Dan Segar, e-mail

BEFORE phoning the police to tell them you have a kangaroo in your garden, check it's not the next door neighbours' greyhound taking a dump.
Andy Pandy, e-mail

WORKERS. If you are last to leave your workplace at night, pretend you are in the finale of a sitcom by reaching for the lights, then turning and looking round the office one last time before smiling, then switching the lights off and walking out.
Money D, e-mail

MAKE your own Siamese cat by getting 2 regular cats and simply glueing their heads together.
Alex Upchuck, e-mail

toptips@viz.co.uk

WHY doesn't Jeremy Kyle have some nice, middle class people on his show for a change? They could calmly discuss their adultery over glasses of Pimms and hopefully both families could rent a villa in The Dordogne afterwards, to resolve any issues. It would be much better viewing.
Terry Corrigan, e-mail

WHAT is it with teachers? They complain that kids lead sedentary lives and don't get enough exercise, then they tell them off for running in the corridors.
Oliver Bitter, Hemp

WHATEVER happened to verrucas? When I was a kid, half the class couldn't go swimming because they had veruccas, but these days, you never hear about them. If you ask me, it's high time they brought good old veruccas back.
Sid Boggle, Fircombe

DURING the 1970s, I was a teacher at a private preparatory school in the south of England. Every morning after prayers the boys would be encouraged to swim naked in our outdoor dipping pond. I myself would join them, smearing myself with oil and encouraging the young scamps to treat me like a slide when entering the water. I would use my erection to stop them slipping in too quickly, urging them to grab hold of it as they whooshed down my greased torso. A great time was had by all, but I dare say that these days I'd probably be hauled over the coals and called every name under the sun. I sometimes wonder what sort of a world we are making for ourselves.
Lettsworth Plywood Cirencester

---

boys' tassels to make sure everything was as it should be in the prepuce, glans and scrotum department. In thirty years at the school, I never found a single child who needed to be referred to a doctor for tassel treatment, but had I done, I am sure their parents would have been very grateful to me for my vigilance. These days I'd probably be hauled over the coals and called every name under the sun. The way this world is going really saddens me.
Lettsworth Plywood Cirencester

I JUST shoplifted a packet of Antony Worrall Thompson brand stock cubes from Waitrose. I'm sure he would appreciate this small gesture of support.
Lee Viathan, e-mail

FOR 25 years my 'Uncle' Stan used to come round to my parent's house every Saturday and bring me and my brother a comic each, a large bar of Bourneville chocolate for dad and a pack of 10 Embassy Mild for mum. And he wasn't even a real uncle. If anyone has a more generous uncle who isn't actually related to them, then I'll eat my hat. If I can find one.
Richard Evans, Colwyn Bay

SO apparently it's called 'dogging' if you watch a couple having sex in a car parked in a secluded layby, but what is it called if you see some geezer wanking while driving a black Audi A4 along the M74 near Abington on 14th January 2012?
Mike Tatham, e-mail

I'VE just seen an American soldier on the telly wearing camouflage trousers and a high-viz jacket. Can anyone think of a more pointless outfit?
Mike Bogbrush, e-mail

THE NAME OF THE PET

WE NEVER asked you to write in and tell us how your pets got their names, but you did anyway, in your droves. Here's a selection of the best we never wanted to receive...

● **I AM** a trainspotter, and I employ an organised, tabulated system for naming my pets. My present dog, for example, is called DBm3. The first letter indicates that it is a dog, the second that it is black, the lower-case 'm' denotes its gender and the number tells me that it is the third pet I have owned. I bought it after the tragic loss of my cat, CWf2.
T Potter, Powburn

● **I STUDIED** history at Cambridge, and I named my budgerigar Perkin Warbeck after the pretender to the English throne of Henry VII. He claimed to be Richard Duke of York, son of Edward IV, and one of the Princes who were supposedly murdered in the Tower of London. I called him this because, when people ask me how he got his name, it is a good way of introducing the fact that I studied history at Cambridge into the conversation. By the way, I got a starred first.
Lambert Simnel (Oxon), London

● **WHILST** on holiday in Turkey, I saw a dancing bear in a market place. Its owner told me it was named Paddington, after the hero of the 1970s children's stories. However, unlike the real Paddington, who was a charming, whimsical and inquisitive little creature who wore a duffle coat and kept marmalade sandwiches under his hat, this thing was psychotic, covered in open sores, half-starved and had had all its teeth and claws pulled out. I just had to laugh at the comical mismatch!
Augusta Prodworthy, Bellshill

● **I'VE** got two goldfish that are absolutely identical. In fact, they might even be twins. As I am unable to tell them apart, I call them both Dave.
Jim Pubes, Jizzholm

● **LIKE** Mr Pubes (above), I've also got a goldfish. I call mine Goldie, because it's got big, fishy lips and reminds me of the actress Goldie Hawn after she had them collagen implants.
Sineadobhain O'Dddhaairddh, Liverpool

● **WHEN** I was a boy, my parents gave me a puppy for Christmas. They asked me what I was going to call him, and I told them I was going to think about it. In the end, however, I never got round to thinking of a name. I've had him fifteen years now, and there's no point calling him anything at this point, as you can't teach an old dog new tricks. If I need to attract his attention, I just throw something at him, such as a shoe or a stone.
Dafydd Llappgoggylliog, Holyhead

● **I HAVE** a pet kangaroo, and like all male kangaroos he has a bifurcated (split in two) penis, that is to say a pair of big bellends. I call him Stingbono. My brother's also got a pet kangaroo, which he calls Morrisseynoeledmonds.
Bruce Hogan, Alice Springs

● **I CALLED** my dog a name that lots of people used to call their dogs in the old days. However, it seems that these days you're not allowed to use that word any more. When I shouted my dog in the park the other day, I was arrested and charged with inciting racial hatred. Now I suppose I shall have to change his name from that name to something else, such as Rover. It's political correctness gone mad.
B Barrage, Redditch

● **I'VE** got five pedigree Pekingeses, and thinking up good names for that many dogs is no easy task. The first one is called Jin-Hua, which means Golden Flower, the second one I named Zhi-Zhe, which means Wise Man. However, you only get two goes on the internet Chinese translator before they make you pay for it, so the other three are called Fido, Butch and Scruffy.
Iris Fogg, Cataract-on-Sea

★ **HAVE** you got a funny or cute story about how your pet got its name? Write in to the usual address and tell us. There's a free dog for every one we print. Mark your envelope 'My Pet's Name.'

TWO SHORT PLANKS!

OK. THAT'LL BE £199.99. CAN I INTEREST YOU IN OUR 3 YEAR EXTENDED WARRANTY FOR ONLY £99.99?

WHAT DO YOU THINK?

GO FOR IT! DEFINITELY!

YES PLEASE.

HURRY UP! THIS IS REALLY HEAVY!!

PUSH! SHOVE!

EXIT PULL

I'M TRYING! THE DOOR'S STUCK THOUGH

Sucker DJs

Gullible BEEB Jocks Fall Foul of Smooth-talking Hustlers

OUR FAVOURITE radio presenters seem to have the gift of the gab, chatting effortlessly for hours on end each day. Filling their airtime with inane chit-chat and glib banter comes naturally to them, and they make it sound easy. So you'd be forgiven for supposing they would be the last people on earth to fall for the silver-tongued patter of a confidence trickster.

SHOCKING EXCLUSIVE!

But that's where you'd be wrong, because DJs seem even more prone to handing over their hard-earned cash to conmen, hucksters and hustlers than the rest of us. And the problem is now so rife that BBC radio bosses are running special courses to help their stars of the air waves spot the scam artists before it's too late.

A Radio 2 source told us: "I'm afraid that radio DJs are easy meat for unscrupulous tricksters, and a culture of conning has developed in the corridors of broadcasting house."

"Only last week, a man wandered into the building and set up a 'Find the Lady' stall outside popular mid-morning presenter **KEN BRUCE**'s studio."

shuffled

"As Ken was going in to do his programme, he saw a woman trying her hand at the game. He didn't recognise her, but the BBC is a big employer, and he assumed that she was a producer off another station or a researcher. The chap running the stall bet her £5 that she couldn't find the Queen amongst three cards face down on his table. He shuffled them around quite slowly and she spotted the picture card first go. The stallholder gave her £50 there and then and she wandered off."

"Intrigued, Bruce decided to try his luck and handed over a fiver. He watched intently as the cards were mixed up and then confidently pointed to the queen. Needless to say it was no surprise to anyone but Ken when the card was turned over and turned out to be the three of clubs."

"Ken seemed a little angry with himself for picking the wrong card as he went in his studio. He is very used to telling contestants they have got it wrong when doing his popular mid-morning Popmaster quiz, but he certainly didn't like it when the boot was on the other foot."

globetrotted

According to the source, Bruce was determined to win his money back, and took every opportunity throughout the rest of his show to nip out and have another attempt at finding the lady.

"Every time he put a record on, during the news bulletins or when Lynne Bowles was doing the traffic, Ken would quickly nip out and put another fiver down on the stall. By the time Jeremy Vine came on, he must have been about £300 out of pocket."

Eventually someone spotted what was going on and called security, but by that time the bunco artist and his female stooge had scarpered. It

Beyond our Ken: Bruce didn't cotton on he was being conned.

Bad Investment: Fool Lewis and his money were soon parted.

is believed that the same pair later fleeced several other BBC radio presenters including Radio 4's Eddie Mair, 5Live's Peter Allen and the cast of The Archers.

fraudsters

'Find the Lady' is the oldest trick in the book, but fraudsters move with the times and are always quick to exploit any new technological advance. And one radio presenter who learned this to his cost was Moneybox Live's **PAUL LEWIS**.

In his stultifyingly dull weekly Radio 4 broadcast, Lewis is at pains to advise listeners how best to look after their money. But he failed to take his own advice after receiving an e-mail purporting to be from a Nigerian Prince. The so-called royal claimed to have £6 million stashed in a British bank, but needed five grand paying into his account in order to get access to it. He promised Lewis a £2 million cut of the booty if he lent him the five grand. Eager

to cash in on such a lucky financial opportunity, Lewis wired the money back immediately.

When he didn't hear anything for a couple of weeks, the presenter merely put it down to red tape holding up the release of his cash. However, his heart sank when he received a second e-mail shortly afterwards, this time from the police, informing him that he had been the victim of a sophisticated internet hoax.

heart

However, Lewis took heart from the news that the cops were on the trail of the hucksters. They explained that if he paid a further £10,000 into the criminals' bank account, then officers would be lying in wait to arrest them when they went to withdraw the money. Keen to get his money back, Lewis wired off another £10K.

Needless to say, the second e-mail had also been a hoax, and the Radio 4 personal finance guru never saw a penny of his £15k again.

> **"Police explained that if he paid a further £10,000 into the criminals' bank account, then officers would be lying in wait to arrest them when they went to withdraw the money"**

WHAT DO YOU THINK OF THE PLAY?

IT'S A LITTLE PEDESTRIAN.

Scene of fraud: Broadcasting House or possibly Television Centre, yesterday.

MEDDLESOME RATBAG

Egg on face: Pentagenarian youth presenter Westwood duped.

Hairy Con Flake: DLT taken in by anthropomorphic lupine trickster.

It's not particularly surprising when older people become bamboozled and get taken for a ride by con artists. But you'd expect someone young and savvy, like 1Xtra's **TIM WESTWOOD** to have his wits about him. But even 'The Big Dog' found himself heavily out of pocket after falling for an obvious scam.

panic

The hip-hop disc-spinner was approached in the BBC canteen by an old woman who told him that she was selling a goose that laid golden eggs for £2000. Bishop's son Westwood had long hankered after a necklace made of solid gold goose eggs, and £2000 for a bird that could provide him with the ultimate bling accessory looked like the bargain of the century.

He handed over the money there and then, and arranged to meet the old woman in the BBC car park later that day.

terrorist

At the arranged time, Westwood turned up to find her waiting for him with a cardboard box under her arm. She handed it over with strict instructions not to look inside until after she had gone. He did as she said, but when he opened the box he didn't find a goose, but a scrawny ex-battery farm chicken with half a beak and no feathers. Needless to say, it didn't lay any eggs, golden or otherwise, and in fact it was dead by the time the hapless hip-hop DJ got it home.

"Tim was extremely embarrassed by the whole affair," a close pal told us. "He prides himself on being streetwise and down with the kids. But by falling for such an obvious con he has shown himself up as a right dick."

But Westwood can console himself with the thought that he is not the first DJ to fall foul of swindlers. In the mid 1970s, Radio 1 breakfast show presenter **DAVE LEE TRAVIS** became the victim of a sting whilst delivering food to an elderly relative.

shak

The DJ was taking a basket of cakes to his grandmother who lived in a cottage in the woods, when he encountered a smooth-talking wolf. Unbeknown to DLT, the animal had put on his grandmother's clothes after eating her and was now attempting to lure the self-styled 'Hairy Cornflake' close enough to the bed to suffer a similar fate.

Travis was only saved from the scam by a quick-thinking woodcutter, who spotted what was going on and killed the lupine hustler with one blow of his axe.

MACAW BLIMEY!

Street-Porter coughs up big parrot

TV HARRIDAN Janet Street-Porter was recovering at home last night after coughing up a parrot during an awards ceremony. The media fishwife was hosting the glitzy Independent Financial Adviser of the Year prize-giving at London's Grosvenor House when she brought up the exotically-plumaged bird.

Audience members looked on as the toothy termagant appeared to have difficulty breathing and stopped halfway through her introductory speech. She then began making guttural choking sounds whilst thumping herself in the chest and shaking her head violently from side to side.

noises

"These horrible hacking noises were coming out of her mouth for about twenty minutes, but we thought it was just part of her speech," said onlooker Mycroft Prepuce. "It was only when she started coughing up balls of brightly-coloured feathers that we realised something was wrong."

Shortly afterwards, the cockney virago, 65, did a huge belch and

SCREECHING BIRD: Street-Porter had parrot lodged in craw.

the 3-foot blue and yellow parrot flopped out of her mouth and onto the dias. "It was a little bit distressed after its ordeal, flapping around and screeching," said Prepuce. According to witnesses, once she'd hockled it up, a clearly-shaken Street-Porter finished her speech and handed out the prizes.

alphabetical

A spokesman for the indecorous presenter said it was possible she had accidentally swallowed the parrot whilst making a television programme in the 1980s. "Janet remembers interviewing an aviary attendant at a zoo and something flying into her mouth during the broadcast," the spokesman told us. "It now seems likely that this bird had been lodged in her throat ever since."

donkeys

The parrot was last night said to be resting at a bird rescue centre in the west of England. Head of the Swindon Parrot Sanctuary Fenwick Psittacosis told us: "It was in quite a bad state when it arrived, but we'll nurse it back to health until it's well enough to be humanely destroyed."

41

Terry's Towel Talk

Frank Towel Chat with Chelsea Skipper and Towel Fan John Terry

" Hi, readers, John Terry here. Now you probably know me best for OBSCURED ON LEGAL ADVICE and OBSCURED ON LEGAL ADVICE AGAIN. But when I'm not getting up to those sorts of shenanigans, which I wasn't, I'm an obsessive fan of towels. I love towels of all shapes and sizes. And so do you, judging by my post bag this week. So it's time for the ref to blow his whistle and get this towel-tastic page underway. "

● **LAUNDERING** towels is a heavy job and I can't understand people who insist on washing them after every use. I like to make sure each towel gets thoroughly used. First, I use it to dry myself after I come out the bath, then the following day, it is used as a hand towel by the bathroom basin. Then it goes down onto the floor to serve as a bath mat. After that, we use it to dry the dog, and finally my husband uses it to masturbate into whilst watching a pornographic film. Then it's back in the wash.

Ada Shortbread
Cromer

● **I CAN'T** see why women hang towels out to dry after they have washed them. They are only going to get wet again when they are used. Honestly, I will never understand women.

Harold Laburnum
Luton

● **I THINK** towels are a waste of money. After a bath, I just hang naked from the washing line in our garden for a couple of hours until I'm dry. If it starts to rain, my wife brings me in and sits me on a wooden clothes horse in front of the gas fire for a bit.

George Rhubarb, Tring

● **MY WIFE** and I were recently on holiday in a Spanish hotel, and on the first morning we went down to the swimming pool bright and early. It came as no surprise that the Germans had beaten us to it and put towels on all the sunbeds to stop us from using them. That was bad enough, but when we returned to our room, we found that they had been in there too and put towels in our bathroom, preventing us from using that, too.

Stan Hogweed, London

● **I'VE ALWAYS** found drying myself with a towel a bit of a chore. So I've speeded up the process by fastening a looped length of towel to my belt sander and running it over myself after a bath. I'm dry in half the time with my 'Power Towel'. I've also put a towelling 'tyre' on the disc of my angle grinder which makes short work of drying that hard-to-reach buttock cleft area.

Mick Bingo, Hull

● **WE HAVE** two sets of towels in our house, a pink set for myself and a blue set for my husband. It's not that I'm in favour of gender stereotyping, it's just that the the thought of drying

TOP TOWEL TIPS

SAVE money on laundering towels by booking into a cheap hotel, taking all your dirty towels with you and putting them into the bath. Then simply check out, taking all the lovely clean towels from your room with you. You'll save even more money if you sneak out in the middle of the night without paying.

H Freemantle, Hull

INSIDE of shoes wet? Simply put on a pair of terry-towelling socks and walk around for a few minutes until they are dry.

Ada Oatcake, Luton

my face with the same towel that my husband drags across his cock and balls when he comes out the shower turns my stomach.

Dolly Bartram
Totnes

● **THE HISTORY** Channel is very keen on programmes about the Tudors, World War II, the Greeks and Romans and all that stuff. But they never show any programmes about the history of towels. Perhaps they should rename the station The History of Everything but Towels Channel.

Tim Campton, London

● **I REGULARLY** watch *How It's Made* on the Discovery Science Channel. It offers a fascinating insight into how countless everyday things we take for granted are manufactured, from

You Ask, We Answer ...about towels

My father used to say someone had 'Thrown in the towel' when they had given up doing something, must in the same way that a boxing trainer throws a towel in the ring to stop a bout when his fighter is getting beaten. It seemed a very odd expression and I always used to wonder where it came from.

Angela Dundee, Las Vegas

● *The phrase 'throw in the towel' dates back to the middle ages and is a corruption of the expression 'throw in the trowel'. When medieval builders finished a castle, they believed that the devil entered their trowel and would bring bad luck if used on another* building. They would go to the top of the tallest turret and throw it in the moat.

Why is it that tea towels are made of flat cloth, but bath towels are made of fluffy, looped cloth? They are both used for getting water off things, so why the difference?

Bartram Kuntztrich, Tring

● *Tea towels traditionally have pictures printed on them, such as the Queen, a picture map of Cornwall or RSPB garden birds. If they were printed on fluffy material, the pictures would come out fuzzed, possibly leading to the misidentification of a Cornish town crest or garden bird. Typically, bath* towels on the other hand, are printed in one colour, such as blue, or red, so this being printed blurred is not so noticeable.

Do real-life Arabs wear tea towels on their heads tied with a snake belt like we used to in school Nativity plays, or do they buy a special headgear for that purpose? If they do, then what do they dry their pots on, and what do their children wear when they are shepherds in the school Nativity?

Alex Cheemonger, Leicester

● *To answer your questions in order. Arabs wear a special cloth on their heads called a Keffiyeh, which is made of linen like a tea towel, only slightly larger. Secondly, Arabs dry their pots on tea towels like the rest of us, or an old Keffiyeh, which their mum has cut down into a more manageable size. And thirdly, Arab children do not perform Nativity plays as Christmas is not celebrated as it falls in the middle of their summer which is not very snowy.*

candles to car tyres, and baseball bats to training shoes. Everything, it would seem, except for towels. In 234 episodes, not once has the manufacture of towels been covered. Perhaps the show should be renamed *How It's Made Unless It's a Towel*.

M Charles, Croydon

● **I SUBSCRIBE** to all the adult channels offered by my service provider. Television X, Xtreme TV, Red Hot Mums, the lot. It costs me in excess of £200 per month. And whilst there are plenty of shows featuring women in various states of undress, and indeed coitus, there are never any shows about towels or towel-related issues. I'm thinking of canceling my subscriptions.

Maurice Day, Fulchester

● **I KEEP** bees, and I have a little towel to dry them with if they get caught in a shower while they're outside

collecting honey. I used to use a hairdryer, but they are quite hairy, and it tended to fluff them up into little black and orange Afros.

Hector Ming, Clifton

● **INSPIRED** by Live Aid and my love of towels, I've been collecting old towels for charity for nearly thirty years. In that time I have amassed around 10,000 towels of all shapes and sizes. The trouble is, I have yet to find a charity that wants them, and half of them are sitting in a pile in my mother's garage,

with the other half under a tarpaulin next to her greenhouse. Oxfam are constantly banging on about children starving in Africa, but when I offer them 10,000 used towels they simply don't want to know.

Frank Mint, Cheam

● **WHEN** mobile phones came out in the 80s, they were the size of a housebrick. These days, they can be slipped into the smallest pocket without spoiling the line of one's clothes. So why is it that towels are the same size now as they were thirty years ago? Come on, towel scientists, pull your fingers out.

L Johns, Peebles

● **WE WERE** given a beautiful Egyptian cotton bath towel as a wedding gift forty years ago. It must have cost around six pounds, which was a lot of money in those days. But the quality was wonderful, so much better than the towels you buy these days. I would like to say that I'm am still using it after all these years, and it is still as good as the day it was bought. However, on our honeymoon, my husband used it to dry his ill-wiped anus after a bath, and we had to burn it.

Mabel Scrotum, Rhyll

● **I AM A** trainspotter, and I have adapted my skills to develop a tabulated system for drying myself after a bath involving initial letters of body parts and coloured towels. A beige towel is use to dry my back, buttocks and barse, a taupe towel to dry my toes, testicles and top lip, a fawn towel to dry my fingers, face and feet and so on. When I have dried a particular part of my body, I record the fact in a notebook to prevent my accidentally drying it a second time, which would be completely pointless.

T Potter, Powburn

ANTIQUES TOWEL SHOW

with antique towel expert
Arthur Wainscotting

MY MOTHER died this morning and whilst going through her things, I came across a tea towel with a picture of Henry VIII and his six wives on it. I believe she bought it in a gift shop at Hampton Court Palace in the 1980s. I was just wondering whether it actually belonged to Henry VIII, and if so, how much it would be worth.

Ernest Crumbhorn, Stoke

...Without seeing it, it is difficult to say whether or not what you have is a genuine Tudor tea towel. The provenance is good, since I have been to my local library and discovered that Henry VIII did indeed live at Hampton Court Palace, and what's more, he had six wives. The tea towel is potentially a very exciting find and if put in the right auction, could fetch as much as a million pounds. However, it could be a later Stuart copy, in which case you could halve that figure. If it has been used to dry pots or clean motor cycle parts, it could be devalued further.

....

I'VE GOT a large blue beach towel that used to belong to my grandmother. When I was a boy, she told me that it was the towel that Captain Webb took to the beach with his trunks rolled up in when he swam the English Channel in 1875. I'm not sure if it's true, because she was a terrible liar and used to say she was a Landgirl, when in fact she spent the war shacked up with a fishmonger in North Shields.

Ted Cummerbund, Tynemouth

...Captain Webb had many towels, and they come up for auction from time to time. The last one sold at a specialist Towel Auction at Christies with the hammer coming down just shy of £300,000. Unroll the towel to see if his trunks are still there, and if they are, you have yourself quite a find.

Miriam's Towel Problem Casebook

Kirsty's Towel Dilemma ~ Day 32

Kirsty and Dave had been going out for nearly a year and had taken the big step of buying a flat. One night they sat down to choose their bathroom towels...

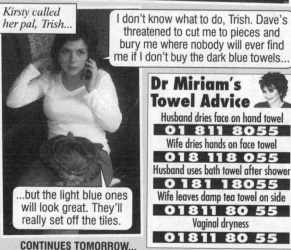

Kirsty called her pal, Trish...

CONTINUES TOMORROW...

Dr Miriam's Towel Advice

Husband dries face on hand towel
01 811 8055

Wife dries hands on face towel
018 118 055

Husband uses bath towel after shower
0181 18055

Wife leaves damp tea towel on side
01811 80 55

Vaginal dryness
01811 80 55

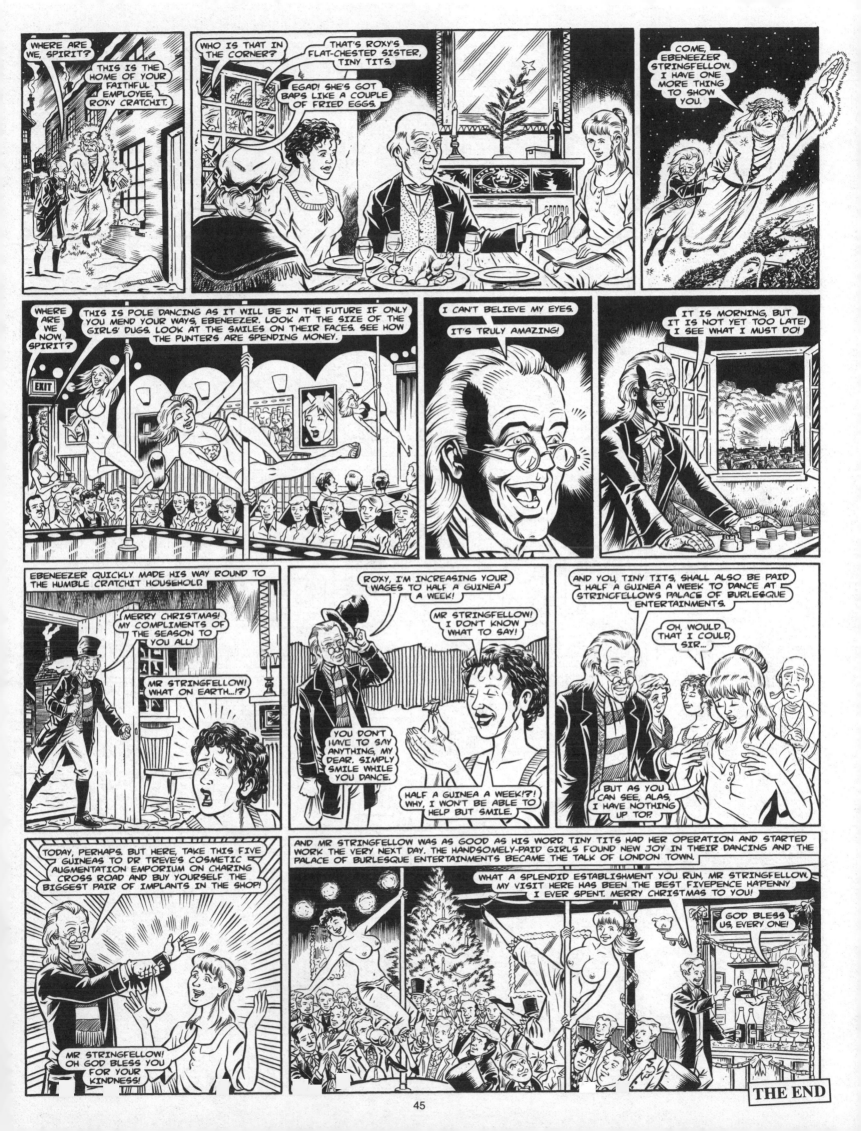

CHARLES DICKENS

BLESS MY SOUL!

IT WOULD APPEAR THAT PROSTITUTION IS AN ENDEMIC SOCIAL PROBLEM HERE IN VICTORIAN LONDON!

I SHALL SET UP A HOME FOR FALLEN WOMEN, SO THAT I MAY HELP TO SAVE THESE POOR UNFORTUNATE CREATURES FROM THEIR LIVES OF DEPRAVITY.

AND I'VE BRUNG YOU SOME MORE WHORES TO SAVE, MISTER DICKENS.

SPLENDID! SHOW THEM IN, CONSTABLE BRAMBLESQUEERS, AND I SHALL START SAVING THEM FORTHWITH!

'PON MY WORD! THOSE FALLEN WOMEN ARE ALL GAGGING FOR A SPOT OF REDEMPTION!

PRIME MINISTER WILLIAM GLADSTONE (1809-1898)

SLAVER! DICKENS WON'T MIND IF I OFFER ONE OR TWO OF 'EM A BIT OF CHRISTIAN CHARITY.

THIS STRUMPET IS SO MORALLY INTEMPERATE THAT SHE IS SIZZLING HOT!

I'LL POP HER ON THE WINDOWSILL TO COOL BEFORE I SAVE HER

WHA-?! IT'S PRIME MINISTER GLADSTONE!

ARF ARF! DON'T WORRY MR DICKENS - I'LL GIVE THIS POOR WRETCH A RIGHT GOOD SAVING!

HURL!

DONG!

TRY THIS FOR "HARD TIMES" YOU PROSSIE-PINCHING P.M.

YOW!

YOU CAN FIND YOUR OWN FLOOZIES TO RESCUE, MR GLADSTONE!

I'LL BE SAVING THIS LOT MESELF, TA VERY MUCH!

I'VE GOT TO GET INTO THAT HOUSE AND REHABILITATE A DEMIMONDE OR THREE!

SQUEAK SQUEAK

BALLOONS

THIS "BUXOM WHORE" DISGUISE SHOULD DO THE TRICK.

ALAS KIND SIR, I AM A POOR TRAMPLED LILY, REDUCED TO WORKING IN A BROTHEL OF ILL-REPUTE.

PRAY LET ME IN, THAT I MAY ESCAPE FROM THAT LIFE OF MORAL TURPITUDE.

HANG ABOUT! ONE OF YOUR BREASTS IS MAKING A WHISTLING NOISE....

PHWEEEEEP

...LIKE THE SOUND OF AIR ESCAPING FROM A BALLOON!

AHEM! THAT'S RIGHT... I AM SO DESTITUTE THAT I CAN'T AFFORD TO LIGHT A LAMP IN MY BROTHEL...

THUS I WAS COMPELLED TO TEACH MY TITS TO WHISTLE SO THAT THE PUNTERS WOULD BE ABLE TO FIND THEM IN THE DARK

I FIND YOUR "TALE OF TWO TITTIES" RATHER UNCONVINCING...MR GLADSTONE.

POP! POP!

JAB

EEK!

NOW BUGGER OFF AND KEEP YOUR PHILANTHROPIC URGES AWAY FROM MY HARLOTS!

SQUEAL!

BOOT!

SHORTLY

HEH HEH! I'LL LOWER MYSELF IN THROUGH THE SKYLIGHT, INSTEAD.

DICKENS HOME FOR FALLEN WOMEN

TROLLOP SALVATION, HERE I COME!

QUIETLY DOES IT!

Bless these whores

I'LL GIVE THIS TART A BIT OF MORAL GUIDANCE WHILST DICKENS ISN'T LOOKING!

OO-ER! THE SLUTTISH FEATHER IN HER HAT IS TICKLING MY NOSE!

I'M GOING TO SNEEZE! AAH-AAHH-AAAH...

CHOO!

YIKES! NOW THAT'S WHAT I CALL "GREAT EXPECTORATIONS"!

AH MR DICKENS, WE ARE PLEASED TO HEAR YOU ARE ENGAGED IN THE CHARITABLE ASSISTANCE OF UNFORTUNATES

GOSH! IT'S QUEEN VICTORIA ON A VISIT!

PLOP!

WHERE ARE THESE FALLEN WOMEN WE HAVE HEARD SO MUCH ABOUT?

WOW! HER MAJESTY HAS SLIPPED ON GLADSTONE'S "PHLEGM BRÛLÉE"

SHRIEK!

SKID!

GURR! PHLOB ON THE FLOOR AND MAKE US FALL ON OUR ARSE, WOULD YOU?

HO HO! THAT'S ONE "FALLEN WOMAN" GLADSTONE WILL HAVE TO SAVE HIMSELF FROM!

TOOT! TOOT!

The Leveson Inquiry gravy train is leaving the station... and it's full of *OUR* cash!

THE ONLY WAY IS ETHICS: Lord Leveson is chairing inquiry into press behaviour.

IT'S BEEN one of Britain's longest-running public hearings. **THE LEVESON INQUIRY** into press ethics was supposed to be a forthright examination of media standards, and high-profile stars have queued up at the Royal Courts of Justice to give evidence and bad-mouth the so-called dirty deeds of the tabloids.

But while no stone has been left unturned when it comes to lurid tales of phone hacking, invasion of privacy and police corruption, a far bigger scandal has been unfolding right under Lord Justice Leveson's nose. For we can now reveal that celebrity witnesses attending the hearings have been taking the opportunity to fleece hard-working tax-payers of literally **HUNDREDS** of pounds.

A 2-week investigation by *Viz Comic* has revealed how celebrities:

● **CLAIMED for taxi rides to and from the Royal Courts of Justice**

EXCLUSIVE!

● **QUAFFED** expensive bottled water whilst giving evidence

● **SAT** on luxury chairs costing up to £150 each

Four Weddings & a Funeral actor **HUGH GRANT** was the first to complain about press intrusion into his private life. And the reason why became obvious when we hacked into the floppy-haired star's mobile phone and heard him BOASTING to a pal about how he was living high on the hog courtesy of the Leveson Inquiry.

We phoned Notting Hill-based caterers D'Arcey Zeff Artisan Cupcakes and asked them what their most expensive buffet would cost per head. We were shocked to discover that millionaire Grant could have been merrily munching his way through a lunch costing a cool £35 without having to put his hand into his own pocket.

Talk about Love Actually! Who wouldn't love an expensive snack ... all courtesy of the hard-working British tax-payer!

KER-CHING! £35!

GOTCHA!

The call HUGH GRANT didn't want you to hear

CALLER: ...*What time have you got to be there [The Leveson Inquiry] for, then?*

GRANT: I think I'm on... it's about ten thirty I think... Yeah, ten thirty.

CALLER: *Right... Meet you for lunch? Say one... one-ish?*

GRANT: Lunch, yeah...actually, I don't know... (inaudible)... I'm not sure what time it's... might be done by one. I don't know. Probably just stay here and grab a sandwich during the break, actually. There's a sort of... they put food... there's a buffet for the witnesses.

CALLER: *Right.*

GRANT: Yeah. So I'll probably just, you know, grab something there. A sandwich and a coffee or something.

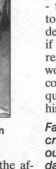

A-HA!: We caught Coogan taking taxi.

Called to give evidence in the afternoon, **STEVE COOGAN** missed out on a free lunch, but he made up for it in other ways. Despite living a mere hour-and-three-quarters' walk away from the Royal Courts of Justice - an easy stroll for a young, fit man - the *Alan Partridge* joker decided to travel in style and was seen arriving outside the hearing in a shiny black cab - a journey which would leave the average passenger with little change out of £18!

tip

But when our reporters turned Coogan's bins over and went through his rubbish later that night, they found no taxi receipts for his journey. And it was obvious why - they had clearly been handed in to the Leveson Inquiry expenses department. Even more sickening, if the cabbie gave Coogan a blank receipt, the millionaire funnyman would doubtless have added on the cost of his tip as well as a couple of quid for himself before submitting his claim.

Fare's fair, Coogan! Before you criticise press ethics, perhaps you ought to look at your own standards. You can't claim the moral high ground when you're lining your pockets with £25 of OUR cash!

KER-CHING! £25!

Translated into thousands of languages in millions of countries and made into a series of blockbuster movies, **JK ROWLING**'s bestselling Harry Potter books have made her wealthier than the Queen. Yet amazingly, when the author arrived at the Leveson Inquiry to bleat about press intrusion into her private life, she was already thinking

ROWLING IN IT: Harry Potter stories have made author a billionaire.

of schemes to make herself even richer.

For when Rowling left her luxury Edinburgh mansion that morning, she was snapped by a *Viz* photographer who had been hiding in a tree in her garden all night. And his long-range telephoto shots prove that she was empty-handed when she set off for the Royal Courts of Justice.

bin

Nothing unusual about that, you might think. Yet when Rowling appeared later that afternoon to give evidence before Lord Leveson, she was clearly seen using a biro to make a series of notes on a writing pad. Where had her pen and paper come from? Assuming she didn't use a Hogwarts spell to magic them up, there's only one conclusion we can draw. They were provided for the billionaire writer completely free of charge, courtesy of Joe Public!

£5.99's worth of stationery for an afternoon's work? It's a wizard wheeze that even Harry Potter would be proud of!

KER-CHING! £5.99!

We took our damning dossier of evidence to Parliamentary Culture Committee member Louise Mensch, who was shocked by what we uncovered. She told us: "This is a scandal that will sicken and horrify every right-minded person in Britain."

heavily

And the country's best-looking MP, although that's not saying much, went on to outline a four-point plan to ensure the situation could not happen again. "In any future inquiries we should slash costs by making witnesses walk to court and go to Greggs for their dinners," she said.

"And they should get a single sheet of paper with an Argos biro for making notes and have to bring their own chairs to sit on," she added.

Clarkson sparks new storm

HIS outspoken comments about India, strikers and Mexicans have already caused outrage at home and abroad. Now JEREMY CLARKSON looks set to walk into another storm of controversy following his latest tirade.

CARELESS TORQUE: Motormouth Clarkson disgusted onlookers with 4-letter tirade.

The outspoken *Top Gear* host found himself under the spotlight again last night after a foul-mouthed rant about the price of Mars Bars, crisps and cigarettes. The 51-year-old petrolhead made the offensive comments in a newsagents shop in Chipping Norton, leaving passers-by agog.

HEARD

Standing by the till, Clarkson was heard to say: "Eight pounds nine? Bl*mey, everything's going up at the moment, isn't it."

According to witnesses, after his four-letter outburst Clarkson paid for his purchases and left the shop, leaving newsagent Ranjit Patel, 61, stunned and shocked.

Last night, chairman of the British Confectionary Manufacturers' Association George Fillings slammed Clarkson's remarks. "It may be just a laugh to him, but irresponsible comments of this sort can cost people their jobs," he fumed.

FLOCK

And Chief of the UK Crisp Council Simon Obesity was equally scathing. He told us: "Once again Clarkson has put his mouth into top gear before engaging his brain. Crisps have actually come down in price in the last twelve months."

"So not only were his words offensive, they were plain wrong," Obesity added.

But the strongest condemnation came from British Cigarette Board spokesman Frank Lungcancer. "Clarkson should save his vitriol for the government. He clearly doesn't realise that nearly eighty percent of the price of his cigarettes goes to the exchequer in tax," he said.

ANAGLYPTA

"Ill thought-out comments of this sort could actually stop people smoking," he added.

In the wake of Clarkson's outburst, the BBC was deluged with angry demands for the petrolhead motormouth, who earns more than £2 million a year, to apologise and be sacked.

But the complaints were dismissed by *Top Gear* spokesman Andy Smoketyres. "Jeremy's a larger-than-life character, and everything he says has to be taken with a pinch of salt," he told us.

WOODCHIP

"His comments about the price of Mars Bars, crisps and cigarettes were tongue-in-cheek and were not intended to be taken seriously," he added.

But Smoketyres's weasel words cut no ice with peasants who live near Clarkson's palatial Cotswolds home. Local news last night reported hundreds of Chipping Norton residents armed with staves, pitchforks and flaming torches, angrily marching on the presenter's £10 million mansion.

A spokesman for the ill-educated lynch mob told reporters: "Burn him. Burn Clarkson." His comments were greeted with loud cheers from the rabble standing around him.

"Burn him now," the spokesman added.

McFly in the Ointment

TEEN pop sensations McFLY were yesterday rushed to hospital after accidentally falling into a giant vat of ointment whilst opening a new factory on Teesside.

The band were standing on one end of an industrial see-saw at Redcar Unguents Ltd. when a 10-ton weight fell from an overhead gantry, catapulting them into a 20,000 gallon tank of balm.

The band were swiftly hauled out of the viscid emollient and sent to nearby Middlesbrough Infirmary for check-ups.

A spokesman for the band assured anxious fans that the accident should not have any effect on plans for McFly's 2013 tour.

"The accident should not have any effect on plans for McFly's 2013 tour," he assured anxious fans. ~ *Reuters*

JOKE: GRADE-E

Oooh, Matron

Infamy! Infamy! They've all got it in for me

'Ere, stop messin' about!

ARE YOU CHECKING IN ANY BAGS TODAY SIR?

NO, I'VE JUST GOT SOME CARRY ON LUGGAGE

letterbocks

PO Box 841,
Whitley Bay,
NE26 9EQ

STATE OF NORTH BORNEO
ONE CENT 1

★ STAR LETTER

★ **HOW** is it that when there is a film premiere, the people going to it are the stars who were in it, the director, and the producers? You'd have thought they'd already have seen it.

Alan Heath, e-mail

DOES anyone know if friendly Lancashire TV steeplejack Fred Dibnah is going to be back on our screens anytime soon? I know he's been dead nearly 8 years, but I really did used to enjoy his programmes. It's about time the BBC made some good use of our licence money for a change and brought Fred Dibnah back to life so he can make some more shows about blowing up chimneys and polishing a traction engine.

Reg Watervole, Bolton

* *WE rang the BBC but they said there were no plans at present to re-animate the corpse of Fred Dibnah.*

WHERE are these tramps getting a cup of tea for 10p? Even a small cuppa in Costa costs you the thick end of two quid. Once again it seems it's one price for a cup of tea for tramps and another for the rest of us.

Cynthia Gleet, Hamp

I'M proud to say I've signed the petition against gay marriage. I'm very fond of my wife, and it's ridiculous that this government expects me to divorce her in order to marry some big muscly man with a bushy moustache. It's political correctness gone mad.

Brigadier Lethbridge, Cumbria

IT'S about time this government brought in a coherent pricing policy for dogs. Pet shops charge hundreds of pounds for tiny puppies weighing less than a pound, yet you can get a fully-grown 2-stone dog for a fiver from the RSPCA. It seems the more dog you get, the less you have to pay for it. Any butcher who operated that pricing policy on his sausages would soon go out of business.

Harry Ampere, Frome

WELL unlike Mr Watervole *(above)*, I absolutely hated Fred Dibnah's programmes. In fact I would happily pay twice my present licence fee to see a programme presented by someone who was the complete opposite of Fred Dibnah, such as the posh, unfriendly Brian Sewell, in which he polishes a chimney and blows up a traction engine.

John Innesnumberfive, Glasgow

MY 92-year-old husband was on his deathbed after a long illness, and I asked him whether, looking back over his long and eventful life, he had any regrets. "The only thing I regret is that I never won anything," he told me. I squeezed his hand. "Yes you did," I smiled. "You won my heart." "No," he said. "I meant something where you're presented with a cup or a cash prize, you stupid old bitch." And those were the very last words he ever spoke to me.

Edna Frogspawn, Yeovil

FURTHER to my earlier letter about being forced to undergo a so-called "marriage" to one of these gays. I would just like to point out that the thought of consummating such a union on my "honeymoon" fills me with revulsion and horror. Has the Prime Minister really thought this through?

Brigadier Lethbridge, Cumbria

I'M A keen ornithologist and I would quite like to see an ostrich wearing stockings and suspenders. I'm not prepared to dress one up myself, as I understand that they can be quite aggressive, but if any Viz readers have tried it, I'd be very interested in seeing some photographs.

Rev J Foucault, Truro

PS Before you ask, I'm not interested in rheas, emus or cassowaries.

SEVERAL years ago, I was waiting for a train at Derby Railway Station. However, as it arrived at the platform I was filled with a terrible sense of foreboding. Something in my head kept telling me not to get on that train, so I sat down on a bench and waited for the next one. I thought no more about my experience until I picked up a newspaper the next day and read the headline: "Local Train Arrives Without Incident". Needless to say, my blood ran warm.

Dafydd Spearmint, Mansfield

I'VE been suffering terribly lately with septic piles, double incontinence, an anal fistula and three weeping boils on the shaft of my penis. I haven't been able to get them treated because I've got a lady doctor, and I don't want her to get all turned on when she's examining me. I'm not a piece of meat.

Reg Fowlage, Tipton

WE read a lot in the press these days about the conditions in Japanese Prisoner of War camps, but I was in one between 1942 and 1946 and it really wasn't that bad. I had three square meals a day, a comfortable bed to sleep in, and there was nothing that the guards wouldn't do for me. Having said that, I was the camp commander.

Yoshimo Nakimura, Tokyo

SO I hear that the Queen has been sat on the throne for 60 years. I know how she feels. I've also had a curry from the Curry Capital (formerly the Rupali Restaurant), Bigg Market, Newcastle-upon-Tyne. All I can say to her majesty is: Keep calm, it will eventually pass.

Will the Badger, e-mail

Thought for the Page

With Radio 4 Gobshite

ANNE ATKINS

I SAW in the newspaper today an advertisement for double glazing, which offered two replacement windows for the price of one.

And that made me think. For Jesus is rather like that double glazing, isn't he? He lets light into our lives, and He keeps us warm when it's cold outside.

But Jesus's offer is even better, for He doesn't just give us two windows for the price of one, He gives us three. And they're not windows; they're loves. The love of the Father, the Sun and the Holy Ghost.

The advertisement also said that if I bought my replacement windows now, I'd pay nothing till the end of May 2013. Once again, Jesus beats that promise hands down. For when you accept His offer of unconditional love, you won't have anything to pay - not only till the end of May 2013 - but not ever! It's all free.

Those windows were guaranteed for 10 years. But God's love lasts till the end of time.

So what's the catch with the double glazing offer? Examine the small print at the bottom of the advertisement and you'll see that labour isn't included.

And what's the catch with Jesus's offer?

Examine the small print in your Bible and you'll see that there isn't one. Except that God watches everything you do, 24 hours a day, and if you even think about doing something that displeases him he'll throw you into a lake of burning excrement for all eternity.

YOU COULDN'T LEND US A TENOR, COULD YOU?

WHEN I moved house recently, I took a friend's advice and put butter on my cat's paws to prevent it roaming and help it find its way back to its new home. However, it didn't really help as the first time I let it out it slipped off the roof and broke its neck.

Elsie Farad, Kippax

FURTHER to my previous letters about the prospect of consummating my forthcoming gay marriage. The thought of having to force myself between some naked man's buttocks - possibly four or five times or more on our "wedding" night, before allowing him to do the same to me, is a prospect that I frankly do not relish. I'll do it, but only because I respect the laws of this country. I'm not happy about it, though, let me make that perfectly clear.

Brigadier Lethbridge, Cumbria

CHRISTMAS is my favourite time of year, and I always start getting excited about it as soon as Easter is out of the way. I've already brought my box of decorations down from the loft, but I've not started putting them up yet as it's still probably a bit too early. Nevertheless I'm already counting down the days to the festive season. December 25th simply can't come soon enough for me. I don't know why I like it so much, as all my family have emigrated to New Zealand, and I always spend Christmas Day on my own, crying.

Doris Dimetoxyamphetamine, Weatherfield

FURTHER to my letter on page 37 about my dear old 'Uncle' Stan who visited my family every Saturday bringing gifts for all of us. I'd like to state for the record that I lied, and Stan actually brought me and my brother Dave comics for just 22 years and not 25 as I claimed. The shame of this mistake will haunt me forever.

Richard Evans, e-mail

FURTHER to my previous letters regarding my forthcoming so-called "same-sex marriage" (which won't be a real marriage in my eyes, I can tell you), I was wondering if any readers could recommend a suitable lubricant for use during anal sex. I am looking for something which might perhaps heighten the sensations in order that I might at least experience some small modicum of pleasure during this whole sorry, sordid business.

Brigadier Lethbridge, Cumbria

NAME THAT TOON

THE GOVERNMENT recently announced ambitious plans to build a brand new TOWN between Birmingham and Coventry. But what should the proposed connurbation be called? We went out on the streets to get a few suggestions from the Great British public...

...**I THINK** it should be called something modern, like Spaceopolis 2000 or Megacity X. And instead of old-fashioned boroughs, they should divide it into numbered sectors such as Alpha 4, Delta 5 and Gamma 8, and everyone who lives there should have to wear a silver suit.
Gordy Mellerstain, Upholsterer

...**THEY** could call it Lymeswold, and then we could all pretend it's where the pretend cheese of the same name comes from.
Melrose Clintmain, Transgender prostitute

...**IT'S** about time one of our towns got named after a planet on Doctor Who, for example Tetrapyriarbus, Shadmoch or Metabilis 3.
Dido Griffoth, Junk captain

...**WHAT** about Titmarshville, Titmarshford, Titmarshston or Titmarsh-on-Avon, in honour of TV gardener Alan Titmarsh?
Fenton Nesbitt, Proctologist

...**THERE** are nearly thirty places in Britain called Newtown, none of which are particularly new any more. This genuinely new town between Birmingham and Coventry should be named Newtown, and all the old Newtowns could be given new names, such as Sparrowsford, Trilling Magma, Foreskin-on-Thames or Bont.
Mrs Warrenford, Burlesque dancer

...**THERE** are no places in Britain beginning with the letter X, so I think the new town should be called Xylophone Town, X-ray City or Xenophobia-under-Lyme.
Lampton Ladykirk, Glockenspielist

...**THEY** should run a competition and get the people who live there to name the new town. The winners would get a fortnight's holiday somewhere else, and £200 spending money.
Stenton Pitcox, Human cannonball

...**I WOULD** call it either Birmentry, Covingham, Cirmingham, Boventry or Wankbridge.
Gary Flatus, Lord Mayor

...**IT'S** about time this country recognised its greatest actress, Dame Judi Dench. The new city should be called Dame Judi Dench.
Preston Fishwick, Unemployed

What would YOU call Britain's newest town?
Text your suggestions to Radio 2's Jeremy Vine on 88291

Yes – 'We have no bananas!'

Prog rockers bereft of musatoid fruit

1970s progressive rockers **YES** last night announced that they had ran out of bananas. A spokesman for the band said they had ate their last one and there was none left in the bowl on the side. They said they had appealed to their mam to get them some more, but she wasn't going to get them any yet.

Mrs Yes insisted she wasn't going to go out to the shops specially just for bananas as they should of made the first lot last longer instead of eating them all straight away.

Big

She said she was doing a big shop tomorrow and she would get some then, but when she did they weren't to just eat them all again.

She told them: "Just go easy on them. Try and make this lot last a bit longer than them others I got."

"I don't mind you eating them," she continued. "As long as you're not just eating them for the sake of it."

Philadelphia

And Mrs Yes appealed to the band to why not eat some

EXCLUSIVE

of the other fruit that was still left in the bowl on the side.

"There's some nice apples and oranges in there that you haven't even touched," she told bass guitarist Chris Squire. "If you don't eat them soon they'll go off and I'll end up having to throw them out as usual."

But a spokesman for Atlantic Records told us the band was only interested in bananas. "They don't like apples and oranges because they've got skin on and all pips in," he told us.

Knob

"I suppose they might eat them if their mam peeled them and took the pips out," he added.

TOP

SAVE money on expensive computer printer ink refills by simply tracing what's on your screen onto greaseproof paper.
Jim Nicebiscuits, Dundee

REFORMED criminals. Remind yourself of the old days by staring at people through the tines of a fork.
Paul Wilson, Manchester

MAKE your neighbours think your dog's got solar panels by gluing several old microwave oven doors onto the south-facing roof of its kennel.
Will Watt, Malvern

FOOL your friends into thinking you are a keen grower of limes by planting a lemon tree in your garden and painting the resulting fruits green.
C. Marrs, e-mail

INSECURE men. Make your penis appear bigger by hanging a magnifying glass from the end of your tie.
Paul Morgan, e-mail

MAKE people think you fell asleep at a house party by shaving one of your eyebrows off and drawing a cock on your face.
Peter Crompton, e-mail

WESTERN Foreign Ministers. Give a foreign government that you don't like that extra air of evil by referring to it as a "regime".
Mike Tatham, e-mail

F1 FANS. Bring back the good old days of Grand Prix racing by dangling cigarette packets in front of your television in front of races. Marlboro, Mild Seven and John Player are particularly evocative.
B Ecclescake, Monaco

TIPS

I LIKE YOUR HAIR.

I'VE HAD IT CUT INTO A BOB.

LET'S PLAY BLOCKBUSTERS!

ERM.. OKAY... WHAT WAS KING CANUTE TRYING TO DO ON THE SEASHORE?

EASY. HE WAS TRYING TO HOLD BACK THE WAVES

YES. YOU'VE GOT THE IDEA...

...THEN ALL THE BELLS AND LIGHTS GO AND I DOCK YOU MORE POINTS.

EH!?.. WHAT THE FUCK **FOR?**

WELL... BECAUSE CANUTE WAS ACTUALLY TRYING TO DEMONSTRATE THAT HE **COULDN'T** HOLD BA.....

DOCKING **POINTS** OFF ME WHEN I GOT THE FUCKER **RIGHT**, TOM

IT'S A FUCKING **FIX** THIS QUIZ IS... THIS PUBLIC SCHOOL TWAT HAS GOT IT SET SO HIS LA-DI-DA MATES WIN ALL THE PRIZES.

NO, ROGER...

...THERE AREN'T PRIZES, ROGER. IT'S JUST A BIT OF FUN

I DON'T CARE, TOM. IT'S THE PRINCIPLE OF THE THING. HE'S TALKING SHIT

HE'LL BE TELLING ME BATS AREN'T FUCKING **BLIND** NEXT, YOU'LL SEE

WELL, AS A MATTER OF FACT, ROGER, MEMBERS OF THE ORDER CHIROPTERA HAVE REMARKABLY **GOOD** VISION

WHAT DID I SAY?

I TELL YOU WHAT, TOM, IF HE TRIES TO CHEAT ON THE SHOW I'LL STRAIGHTEN HIS FUCKING NOSE FOR HIM...CAMERAS ON ME OR **NOT'**

ROGER

MNNYAH! I SAY

I **DO** APOLOGISE, STEPHEN. ROGER HASN'T BEEN WELL LATELY AND HE'S A LITTLE TIRED

MNNYAH!

I CAN'T BELIEVE ANYONE COULD BEHAVE IN SO LOUTISH A MANNER

I FIND IT ALL TOO, TOO UPSETTING

THERE, THERE, MR' FRY...JUST RELAX

NO...I SHALL NOT STAY TO BE SO INSULTED BY A BOORISH, ILL MANNERED BILLYWIFFLE

I SHALL PACK A CRUMPLED LINEN SUIT AND GO TO BELGIUM AGAIN

SLAM!!

WELL DONE, ROGER. ON AIR IN 10 MINUTES AND NO PRESENTER

BOLLOCKS! YOU'VE GOT ME, TOM

I CAN PRESENT A QUIZ SHOW IN MY SLEEP...IN FACT, I THINK I **HAVE DONE** A TIME OR TWO...

AND WE'LL GET RID OF **THIS** LOAD OF RUBBISH AN' ALL, TOM... **I'LL** WRITE THE QUESTIONS

10 MINS LATER...

...NOW WE MOVE ONTO THE ROUND WHICH WE CALL GENERAL IGNORANCE...SO FINGERS ON BUZZERS...

WHICH BRITISH POP SINGER ONCE HAD A PINT AND A HALF OF SEMEN PUMPED OUT OF HIS STOMACH AT HIS LOCAL HOSPITAL?

BZZZZZZZZ'!!

SEAN?

MARC ALMOND

A-ROOO-GA! A-ROOO-GA! A-ROOO-GA!

MARC ALMON

OH, DEAR DEAR, SEAN...

...YOU FELL INTO OUR LITTLE TRAP THERE. THE MARC ALMOND PINT AND A HALF OF SEMEN STORY IS SADLY AN URBAN MYTH...

NO...IT WAS ACTUALLY **ROD STEWART**, AND I KNOW THAT FOR A FACT BECAUSE A MATE OF MINE USED TO GO OUT WITH THE SISTER OF ONE OF THE NURSES WHO PUMPED HIS STOMACH

ANYWAY, ONTO THE NEXT QUESTION

WHICH FORMER BLUE PETER PRESENTER ONCE TURNED UP AT CASUALTY ON CHRISTMAS EVE WITH A MILK BOTTLE JAMMED UP HIS ARSE?

the NUMNUTS

IT'S NEARLY TIME FOR THE ANTIQUES ROADSHOW, CEDRIC

OH GOODY! I'LL SWITCH ON THE TELLY, DEAR.

IN CEDRIC'S TESTICLES

HUH! WE'RE NOT INTERESTED IN THE ANTIQUES ROADSHOW!

SPUNK TANK

BOLLOCK DEPT.

HAVE A WANK

SUGGESTION BOX

I'LL GET OUR MAN TO TOSS HIMSELF OFF OVER SOME INTERNET PORN, INSTEAD

ACTUALLY DEAR — ON SECOND THOUGHTS I'M JUST GOING TO GO ON THE COMPUTER IN THE SPARE BEDROOM FOR A MOMENT

ANTIQUES ROADSHOW

I JUST NEED TO... ERM... CHECK MY EMAILS.

HEH HEH! NOW TO LOOK AT SOME FILTHY M-PEGS AND HAVE A CRAFTY SHERMAN!

JIZZ PRESSURE IS AT THREE POINT FIVE, SKIPPER!

HOLD IT STEADY, LADS.

COCK DEPT →

I'LL RUN UP TO THE COCK DEPARTMENT AND TELL NOBBY TO ACTIVATE THE BONE-ON MECHANISM.

OK NOBBY, CRANK THE SHAFT UP INTO A SEMI-ON! OUR MAN WILL START MASTURBATING IN FIVE MINUTES!

COCK DEPT

FLACCID LOB ON PINK STEEL

KLEENEX

WAH! I'VE SKIDDED ON ONE OF THESE DISCARDED TISSUES!

SLIP

COCK DEPT

FLACCID LOB ON PINK STEEL

NOBBY, I'VE WARNED YOU ABOUT LEAVING YOUR USED HANKIES LYING AROUND ON THE FLOOR!

WOW! I'VE SWITCHED THE BONE-ON MECHANISM TO FULL POWER!

COCK DEPT!

FLACCID LOB ON PINK STEEL

CLUNK

COO! WHERE DID THIS RAGING DIAMOND-CUTTER COME FROM?

SPARE BEDROOM

I MUST BE IN DIRE NEED OF EMPTYING MY YOGHURT POTS!

WHOOPS! I FORGOT WE HAD THE WIFE'S MOTHER STAYING WITH US!

SHRIEK!

SPARE BEDRM

CEDRIC! HOW DARE YOU BARGE IN HERE POINTING THAT THING AT ME!

PERHAPS THIS WILL COOL YOU DOWN, YOU FILTHY BEAST!

SCOOSH!

YARGGH! FREEZING SODA WATER!

HELP! THERE'S A TIDAL WAVE OF SODA WATER COMING DOWN THE HOG'S EYE!

COCK DEPT

FLACCID

SHORTLY

THE BONE-ON MECHANISM IS COMPLETELY WATERLOGGED!

COCK DEPT

FLACCID LOB ON PINK STEEL

GENITAL REPAIRS

IT'S GOING TO TAKE A FEW DAYS BEFORE I CAN GET IT WORKING AGAIN.

THAT SOAKING HAS TAKEN ALL THE LEAD OUT OF MY PENCIL.

I MAY AS WELL GO AND WATCH THE ANTIQUES ROADSHOW.

BAH! NOW OUR MAN CAN'T WAX THE DOLPHIN FOR DAYS!

IT'S ALL NOBBY'S FAULT FOR LEAVING HIS WANKERCHIEFS LYING ON THE FLOOR!

OOYAH! THERE'S NOWT WORSE THAN BEING DEPRIVED OF A BARCLAYS AFTER YOU'VE GEARED YOURSELF UP FOR ONE...

POUND POUND

MY TESTICLES ARE THROBBING LIKE MAD!

OPEN THIS DOOR, NOBBY! COME OUT AND TAKE YOUR PUNISHMENT!

BOLLOCK DEPT

WANK BANK PORN STORAGE VAULT

POUND POUND

OO-ER! NO THANKS!

GOLD BAR-GAIN!

24-carat cock-up at the Bank of England sees £½million ingots flying off shelves for just £4.26

THERE were red faces at the Bank of England last night after a pricing blunder saw **GOLD BARS** being sold for just £4.26. The heavy bullion blocks, which normally retail for almost half a million pounds each, were being snapped up by shoppers eager to bag a bargain after news of the sale of the century spread across social network sites.

By lunchtime, the hashtag *#goldbarsforafiver* was trending worldwide on Twitter and police had to be called to Threadneedle Street to control excited crowds outside the bank's gift shop, where the mispriced bars were on sale.

Bank bosses blamed an inexperienced assistant for putting the wrong barcode onto the 12.5kg bricks of precious metal. A spokesman told us: "A part-time member of staff who was unfamiliar with the labelling machine inadvertently priced the gold at way below its actual value."

"The mistake was only spotted after several thousand bars had been pur-

BULLION FOR YOU: Ingots were snapped up by public.

chased by members of the public," he added.

queues

Long queues quickly formed at the tills as excited buyers clamoured to snap up the bargain-priced ingots.

Cabbie Frankie Racist managed to bag himself ten bars at the knock-down rate. The Lewisham-based 62-year-old told us he was over the moon with his purchases. "I've got four-and-a-half million quids' worth of gold for less than fifty sheets," he beamed. "That's a result in anyone's book."

28-year-old unemployed mother of nine Tracey Bile said she was delighted with her purchase of thirty gold bars, representing a market value of nearly fifteen million pounds. "I heard about it on Twitter, so I brought all the kids down the shop and we carried three each to the till," she told us. "I ended up spending the whole week's benefits on them, but it was just too good a deal to resist."

wrestes

"I'm going to buy myself some mink coats and send all the kids to Eton," she added.

But one person who wasn't celebrating was the Bank of England's red-faced governor Mervyn King. "This mix-up has wiped nearly three billion pounds off the value of the bank," he told us.

But Sir Mervyn wasn't all doom and gloom. "On a more positive note, we've created nearly 400 new millionaires today, which is yet more proof that this country's economy is booming," he said.

"I've Got Your Number!" *says mobile expert Jock*

Got it all figured - mobile number expert Jock

...But what does YOU<u>R</u> number reveal about <u>YOU</u>?

MOBILE PHONES. We've all got one, we take them with us everywhere we go, and most of us can't imagine how we ever lived without them. But these modern miracles of communications technology are more than just devices for letting our loved ones know we're on the train, playing Angry Birds or looking up quiz answers in the pub toilets.

For believe it or not, every mobile number is actually a window into the mind of the person who owns it. Each digit is like a piece of a psychological jigsaw. And once they are pieced together, these fragments make up an astonishingly detailed picture of their owner's innermost personality traits.

JOCK HEARTBURN ran a successful cellphone accessory store on Glasgow's Shipbank Lane Market for several months. And, before taking early retirement when the market was closed down by police, the 58-year-old former van driver's dealings with the general public and their phones gave him a uniquely privileged insight into the way mobile numbers reveal the hidden psychological truths we would probably rather keep under wraps.

leatherette

Jock told us: "I didn't just sell leatherette cases and knock-off chargers on my stall. I also offered a box-breaking and unlocking service for people who had perhaps found a handset somewhere and needed to change the password so they could use it."

"The more punters I dealt with, the more I realised that the numbers of the mobiles I was unlocking were unlocking something themselves - each one was like a key to the innermost secrets of its owner's personality."

"I told my customers: You might not like what your mobile number says about you, but you can't deny it's one hundred percent true," Heartburn continued. "For the numbers never lie."

3 is a Magic Number

TWO'S COMPANY and three's a crowd, or so the old saying goes. But three is also a magic number ... especially when you find yourself in bed enjoying a threesome with a pair of pneumatic blonde bimbos! And if your phone number contains a 3, it's odds-on that a red hot troilistic orgy of just that sort is your ultimate secret fantasy. And here's the good news ... making your dream come true is easier than you might think. Remember, what's sauce for the goose is sauce for the gander, so simply find two birds who also have 3s in their mobile numbers. Suggest a sexy three-way romp to them, then lie back and enjoy the ride!

Celebrities with 3s in their mobile number: *Hugh Hefner, Robin Askwith, Mick Jagger, Lembit Opik*

Lucky 7

IN MANY CULTURES, 7 is regarded as the luckiest number, and this property is reflected in the fortunes of those who have it in their cellphone number. If you are one of these people, you should do the National Lottery on a regular basis, as well as splashing out as much as you can afford on scratchcards, the gee-gees and internet bingo. Or why not consider a career change to gold prospector, diamond miner or high-roller at the Las Vegas crap tables? Thanks to your lucky number, you're practically certain to hit the jackpot every time!

Celebrities with 7s in their mobile number: *Bill Gates, Alan Sugar, Richard Branson, Michael Carroll, Lord Lucan.*

13 - Unlucky for Some

TWELVE APOSTLES joined our Lord Jesus at the table for the Last Supper, and ever since then 13 has been regarded as a harbinger of ill fortune. So if you find the digits 1 and 3 in your mobile number, you will suffer bad luck on a daily basis. As you go about your business, watch out for falling chimney pots, banana skins, upturned rakes and roller skates carelessly-discarded at the top of the stairs. And at holiday time, if you see someone with 13 in their mobile number boarding the same plane as you, get off and catch a later flight, because that one's going to crash. It's a comforting thought, however, that this combination of figures is extremely rare, affecting a mere 1% of phones.

Celebrities with 13 in their mobile number: *Rod Hull & Emu, Captain Schettino, Marc Bolan, Princess Diana, Dodi Fayed, Henri Paul.*

69's Special

IT'S A SCIENTIFIC fact that the most highly-sexed people have 69 - or "soixante neuf" to give it its full French name - in their mobile number. So fellas - if a girl gives you her number and you find this saucy combination of figures somewhere in it, you're in for a two-way oral sex feast!

Celebrities with 69 in their mobile number: *Pamela Anderson, Ben Dover, Paris Hilton, John Prescott.*

On its own, number 1

IF YOUR MOBILE number contains the figure 1, this indicates that you are a loner who keeps yourself to yourself and shuns company. You prefer to lead a friendless, solitary life as far away from the hustle and bustle of the modern world as possible, perhaps working as a lighthouse keeper, hermit, Arctic explorer or Apollo Command Module pilot. Chances are that when you eventually die, your corpse will lie undiscovered for several months, until neighbours concerned about the smell coming from your house alert the police.

Celebrities with 1s in their mobile number: *Gilbert O'Sullivan, Marlene Dietrich, Dame Ellen Macarthur, Eric Carmen, Mr Trebus.*

Number 2s - Trouble Brewing

DO YOU FIND yourself constantly suffering gyp from your bowels - either uncontrollable, explosive diarrhoea and flatulence or bouts of constipation lasting for weeks on end? Do you find defecation painful, and is there often blood in the bowl after you have stooled? Chances are it's because you have a 2 as part of your cellphone number, leaving you constantly plagued by problem foulage down below and round the back. To alleviate your symptoms, try changing your SIM card to one with a different set of digits. If this doesn't work, you should go and see your doctor immediately, as you may be experiencing the early symptoms of colorectal cancer.

Celebrities with 2 in their mobile number: *Esther Rantzen, Simon Cowell, Dappy out of N'Dubz, Dizzy Gillespie.*

The keys that unlock your deepest secrets

*Use this scientific interactive guide to check out what your mobile number says about **YOU!***

666 - the Phone Number of the Beast

IT DOESN'T TAKE a genius to guess the personality of someone with this diabolical combination of digits on their cellphone. Owners of mobiles branded with the numerical sign of Beelzebub are evil incarnate and should be given as wide a berth as possible. Fortunately, 666 only occurs on one phone in every thousand, but with sixty million handsets in the UK, that's still a frightening 60,000 sociopathic thieves, murderers and *Deal Or No Deal* presenters at large on our streets. If you find yourself with this combination on your phone, ask a priest to exorcise your infernal SIM card before burning it on his altar and disposing of the ashes in a consecrated dustbin.

Celebrities with 666 in their mobile number: *Fred West, The Kray Twins, Pol Pot, Harold Shipman, Jeffrey Archer*

"The sort of things you say say a lot about the sort of people people are, says a lot about the sort of person you are," says Dr Raj Persaud.

Media Shrink Lifts the Lid on Media Shrinks

Belief that the type of shoes you wear says a lot about how creative you are indicates you are ambitious and enterprising, says Persaud.

THESE DAYS, you can't open a magazine without reading a feature by a pop-psychologist analysing some aspect of people's personalities based on what car they drive, what food they eat or what breed of dog they own. But what do these space-filling articles reveal about the kind of person who writes them?

Formerly-disgraced-now-undisgraced daytime telly psychiatrist **Rajinald Persaud** believes it is possible to tell a lot about someone by examining the sort of pseudoscientific hokum they peddle in the popular press.

"It really is a complete giveaway," Dr Persaud told us. "For instance, someone who believes that the colour you paint your front door says a lot about your sex life is probably an extrovert who loves parties and loud music."

"On the other hand, an adrenalin junkie who lives for thrills is more likely to maintain that a person's choice of socks reveals their secret phobias," he continued.

"Something like that, anyway. You know the sort of thing," he added.

Big Size 9s

9 IS THE LARGEST single digit on the keypad, and if your phone number includes it then it means you're big down under. And by that we don't mean famous in Australia, we mean well-endowed in the trouser department. And by that we don't mean you've got a lot of money to spend in the menswear section of Marks & Spencer, we're talking about your meat and two veg. And by that we don't mean your Sunday dinner, we mean you've got enormous genitals. Of course, if you're a woman, that might not be such welcome news.

Celebrities with 9 in their mobile number: *Burt Reynolds, Stephen Pound MP, King Dong, Robert Plant, Jordan.*

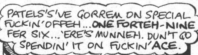

Finbarr Saunders & his DOUBLE ENTENDRES

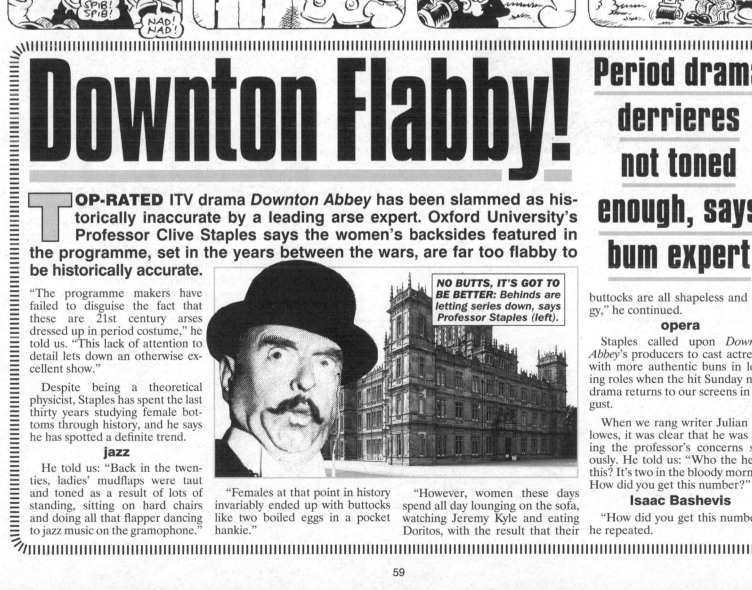

Downton Flabby!

Period drama derrieres not toned enough, says bum expert

TOP-RATED ITV drama *Downton Abbey* has been slammed as historically inaccurate by a leading arse expert. Oxford University's Professor Clive Staples says the women's backsides featured in the programme, set in the years between the wars, are far too flabby to be historically accurate.

"The programme makers have failed to disguise the fact that these are 21st century arses dressed up in period costume," he told us. "This lack of attention to detail lets down an otherwise excellent show."

Despite being a theoretical physicist, Staples has spent the last thirty years studying female bottoms through history, and he says he has spotted a definite trend.

jazz

He told us: "Back in the twenties, ladies' mudflaps were taut and toned as a result of lots of standing, sitting on hard chairs and doing all that flapper dancing to jazz music on the gramophone."

NO BUTTS, IT'S GOT TO BE BETTER: Behinds are letting series down, says Professor Staples (left).

"Females at that point in history invariably ended up with buttocks like two boiled eggs in a pocket hankie."

"However, women these days spend all day lounging on the sofa, watching Jeremy Kyle and eating Doritos, with the result that their buttocks are all shapeless and saggy," he continued.

opera

Staples called upon *Downton Abbey*'s producers to cast actresses with more authentic buns in leading roles when the hit Sunday night drama returns to our screens in August.

When we rang writer Julian Fellowes, it was clear that he was taking the professor's concerns seriously. He told us: "Who the hell is this? It's two in the bloody morning. How did you get this number?"

Isaac Bashevis

"How did you get this number?" he repeated.

Downtools Abbey

The Haves and the Have-nots: Cast members strike over unequal pay.

THE FILMING of the latest series of smash ITV drama Downton Abbey has been disrupted after angry actors walked off set. Talks over pay and conditions broke down when performers playing domestic staff in the hit show complained of unfair treatment.

Trouble arose when writer Julian Fellowes insisted the pay of actors in the series, which pulls in eleven million viewers each week, should accurately reflect the wages of the characters they were playing. Fellowes told *TV Quim* magazine: "In the interests of realism, I feel it is important that the domestic staff are paid exactly what they would have been paid back in the 1920s."

bitter

"It may lead to resentment, but back in the olden days when Downton Abbey is set, the below-stairs employees were often very bitter about their lot. If I can foster this emotion in the actors and it comes out onscreen, then that will be fabulous," he gushed.

Historic Drama Stars Strike over Pay & Conditions

By Our TV Correspondent
Fanny Akimbo

Actor Carter: 120-hour week.

But the controversial decision to cut pay has led to unrest amongst the cast. Jim Carter, who stars as butler Carson in the show, was privately said to be "fuming" after his pay was slashed to a mere 15 shillings (75p) per episode. And other actors have fared even less well, with Sophie McSheara who portrays scullery maid Daisy now on less than 6d (2½p) for a 40-hour week of rehearsals and shooting. Meanwhile Hugh Bonneville, their onscreen employer Lord Grantham, is coining it in on a salary estimated at more than 15,000 guineas for each show.

mild

Quentin Bumboy, spokesman for actors' union Equity told us: "The behaviour of ITV has been completely disgraceful and my members are not going to accept it. We have walked out and we will stay out until the producers see sense."

Bumboy insisted the industrial action was not simply as a result of the pay cuts. "Working conditions for the below-stairs actors are atrocious," he continued.

"The shooting schedule for them starts at five in the morning, seven days a week, whilst the actors who play the aristocratic Granthams get to swan onto the set at eleven and have every weekend off."

"Joanne Froggatt who plays chambermaid Anna spent

Froggatt: paid 3p an hour.

five years at RADA and is a member of the Royal Shakespeare Company, yet she's expected to rise at half-past four every day and carry fifteen buckets of hot water up six flights of stairs so that

Downtor

THE FILMING of the latest series of smash ITV drama *Downton Abbey* has been disrupted after US guest star *Shirley Maclaine* was found to be infested with mice. Shooting on the hit show had to be halted numerous times when dozens of the small grey rodents were spotted scurrying out from under the veteran US actress's skirts.

Production was also held up after the mice repeatedly nibbled through electrical wires, causing lights to fail during key scenes. Eventually the situation became so bad that desperate producers brought a cat onto the set in order to bring the problem under control.

poison

A Downton Abbey insider who wished to remain anonymous told us: "We'd tried everything and nothing seemed to work. We'd put traps up Shirley's dress and poison in her knickers, but the mice were breeding faster than we could kill them.

"In desperation, we went to the local animal rescue centre and got a cat, and that seems to have sorted out the problem," Bonnevile added.

In the first morning alone Marmalade, a five-year-old ginger tabby, caught as many as thirty-five mice which had made their nest somewhere in the 78-year-old *Sweet Charity* star.

"Maggie Smith can have a bath," he said. "And she's expected to do that for less than half a crown a week."

"It's utterly appalling," he added.

Highclere: Industrial action.

Actors were last night mounting a picket line at the gates of Highclere castle, where the series is filmed. There were angry scenes and shouts of "Scab" as a busload of non-union extras from *Upstairs Downstairs* was driven onto the set to take over the parts of domestic staff.

noble

But Julian Fellowes remained unrepentant. "Some actors are born to play noble aristocrats whilst others are destined to play common parts below stairs," he told us. "It's simply the way of the world."

"If these bone idle troublemakers don't want to portray characters who slave in the scullery for a pittance and drop their aitches, then there are plenty of actors who will," he added.

Downton Shabby
Period Drama Bloopers *with Mark Commode*

WHEN FILMING a high budget series like *Downton Abbey*, no expense is spared getting every every last detail right. Costume and set designers take infinite pains to make the show look as authentic as possible. But no matter how careful the show's makers are, errors creep in. And even before the third series hits the airwaves, internet forums are already buzzing with continuity cock-ups, costume catastrophes and anachronistic word meaning error beginning with a's spotted by the show's eagle-eyed viewers.

Here are just a few of the most historically hysterical bloopers from past series of Downton Abbey...

● IN THE FIRST episode, the Earl of Grantham's American wife *Cora Crawley* is driven through a village on her way to Downton Abbey. The scene is set in 1912, yet double yellow lines are clearly visible on a sidestreet, and a house in the background has a television aerial fastened to its chimney.

● IN SERIES 1, episode 4, *Mr Carson* the butler is called to the main house after the *Dowager Duchess of Grantham* faints. As he leaves the pantry he is not wearing a hat, yet seconds later when he enters the drawing room he can clearly be seen to have a television aerial coming out of the top of his head.

● DOWNTON ABBEY is set in the years between 1912 and 1920, yet the house in which it is filmed - Highclere Castle - was built in 1679.

● IN SEVERAL episodes, the chauffeur *Branson* is seen polishing the bonnet of *Lord Grantham*'s car - an L-reg Ford Capri 1.3L. However, that model of car takes 205/60/13 tyres - a size that was not available in the 1920s.

● SET IN THE first two decades of the twentieth century, Downton Abbey is filmed with sound. However, the station who makes the show - ITV - didn't go on air until 1956, nearly thirty years after the first talkie movie - *The Jazz Singer*, starring Al Jolson - was made.

● DAME MAGGIE SMITH, who plays *Violet Crawley* the Dowager Countess of Grantham, was born in 1934, 14 years after the show is set, 22 years before the station that broadcasts it was founded, and 255 years after the house where it is filmed was even built!

● IN THE FINAL episode of series 2, *Lord Grantham*'s valet *John Bates* is seen packing a suitcase for his master's forthcoming trip to London. Not only is Bates wearing a digital watch, but he has a television aerial coming out of his head and there are double yellow lines painted on his trousers. Also visible in

the room is a modern "Keep Left" sign, a vapour trail from a jumbo jet and a poster of Dizzee Rascal.

Tabby

Cat drafted in to solve Maclaine mouse plague

Maclaine's agent Hymen Prepuce IV said he was surprised to hear his client had a mouse problem. Speaking from his office on Broadway, he told us: "This whole situation has got my noyves a-jangle."

"This goyl's been in the business sixty years and she's never once been overrun with voymin," he added.

Infested: Downton star Maclaine (main pic) yesterday with the cat (upper left) brought in to rid star (main pic) of mice (far left)

World Vest News

America: A deranged postman yesterday shot dead 55 members of the public in an Albuquerque fast food restaurant, before turning the gun on himself. New Mexico police later released details of the vest he was wearing under his uniform, which was a medium-size polycotton mix from the K-Mart Budget range.

Australia: A surfer off Queensland's Gold Coast was yesterday killed by a shark. Authorities were keen to stress that the 35-year-old local man - a father of 2 - had not been wearing a vest at the time of the attack.

Russia: Underworld kingpin Sergei Poliakov yesterday went on trial in St Petersburg, charged with multiple counts of fraud, blackmail and corrupting government officials. Standing in the dock to hear the charges against him read out, Poliakov could clearly be seen to be wearing a white cotton vest under his shirt. The case continues.

China: Rescue services in the Xingpao Province have finally made contact with 26 faceworkers who were trapped below ground 3 weeks ago following an explosion at the Ming-xo Coal Mine. All are said to be alive, in good spirits and wearing vests.

World Vest Network News

Plymouth Man Accosted in Bournemouth

A PLYMOUTH man was yesterday verbally and physically abused whilst on holiday in Bournemouth. The victim suffered minor injuries but was shaken by his experience.

The 48 year-old Plymouthian who has not be named told the *Bournemouth Clarion:* "I was on holiday for a week in Bournemouth. I was walking along the pier, a man slapped me in the mouth and told me to fuck off back to Plymouth."

T-shirt

"I was wearing a T-shirt that said 'I am from Plymouth' on the front, so that's probably how he knew I was a Plymouthite."

He continued: "I was very upset. Plymouth and Bournemouth have a lot in common. They both have 'mouth' in them. We should all be friends. We should build on our similarities, not our differences. Having the word 'mouth' in both our town names is a good foundation on which to build trust and friendship."

"Mouth-named towns should be building bridges, not walls," he said.

Attack: The Plymouthee, yesterday

The Plymoutharian was treated for minor cuts at the Royal Bournemouth Hospital before he fucked off back to Plymouth.

"Not because he told me to, but because my holiday was over, so I was going back to Plymouth anyway," he told reporters.

A-frame

The Plymouthwegian made it back to Plymouth, but he says his traumatic experience has coloured his view of Bournemouth. Speaking to his home paper the *Plymouth Crucible*, he said that he would 'think twice' about holidaying in Bournemouth in the future.

"I don't think they like the Plymouthish over there. I might have a fornight somewhere else next year, like Dartmouth, Weymouth, Great Yarmouth. Or Birmingmouth."

A Touch of Cl-Arse

M OVE OVER Shirley Maclaine, because an even bigger star is set to join the cast of period drama *Downton Abbey* when the hit show returns to our screens this Autumn.

Famous bumcheeks set to join hit show

Only this isn't a famous face ... it's a bottom. For the arse of society beauty Lady Marchmaine will be played by none other than the bootylicious tush of *Pippa Middleton!*

Actress Lynsey Baxter, who will play Lady Marchmaine in the Sunday night ratings winner, told us: "I'm very excited to be appearing in *Downton Abbey*, and the part of Lady Marchmaine is every actress's dream come true."

rump

"But it's an even bigger honour to have Pippa Middleton's pert rump bringing my character's buttocks to life," she added.

Producers took the decision to bring in Her Royal Hotness's famous caboose into the period

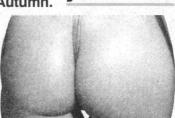

drama after criticism that the rear ends in the show were too flabby to be authentic.

lean

We rang writer Julian Fellowes to see if he was excited to be working with the future Queen's sister-in-law's booty. He told us: "Who is this? It's five past bloody two in the morning. How did you get this number. It's ex-directory."

"Call again and I'll go to the police," he added.

Letterbocks

Viz Comic, P.O. Box 841, Whitley Bay, NE26 9EQ

STAR LETTER

WHAT on earth is the point of giving air passengers life jackets that are designed to float in water? If you have to bail out of a plane, you'd be better off with a life-jacket filled with helium so you can float about safely up in the air until someone comes to rescue you. *Sid Flatus, Dudley*

THEY say that New York is the city that never sleeps, but I rang a random New York number at 4am their time and the bloke was fucking furious that I woke him.

Terry Corrigan, e-mail

CITY centre street mime artists are fucking hypocrites. They stand there all day miming about getting trapped in an invisible box and walking errant invisible dogs. But as soon as I walk up to them and mime pretending to get out a bulging wallet and placing a pretend £20 in their receptacle, I'm the most un-funny person in the world. I tell you, it's one law for mute, over-exaggerating street artistes and one for the rest of us.

Robert Doherty, e-mail

THEY say an elephant never forgets, but I watched one at the zoo the other day and he walked in his own shit and then did exactly the same thing again a couple of minutes later.

Ted Cardboard, e-mail

THE new Disney film *Mirror Mirror* claims to 'bring the Snow White Legend to life'. Does anyone know which part of the story in which a wicked Queen with a magical mirror uses a poisoned apple to kill her stepdaughter (only for a handsome Prince to kiss her back to life) is based on fact?

David Milner, Durham

I PLAYED hide and seek with my friend 30 years ago and he still hasn't found me.

Nigel Kelly, e-mail

ON a recent visit to Volvo's safety investigation department at their factory, I was shocked to see cars getting smashed up in 'crash tests'. If they drive this badly in the factory then I would hate to see one of them on the road.

Alan Heath, e-mail

I'D just like to warn any tradesmen that undertaking work on my house could precipitate a series of health-related catastrophes in either yourselves or your close family. There will be a very real chance you will be unable to complete the work due to hospital visits and funerals. Fear not though, such problems seem to resolve themselves upon the advent of your summer holidays.

Mike Tatham, Dundee

THE erstwhile Archbishop of Canterbury recently washed the feet of pilgrims. Should the new chap wish to modernise the C of E, might I suggest a fish pedicure.

Dr W Bassinger, Pimlico

YOU would think, wouldn't you, that with modern technology you could sign on remotely? I am now working on a building site in South Shields and it takes me a couple of hours to get to the dole office in Trinity Square, Gateshead and the foreman is beginning to get quite cross with me about taking time off. I tell you what, if this goes on much longer, then I think I might lose my job and if that happens I shall be certainly making an official complaint to the DHSS.

Bob, e-mail

AREN'T dreams amazing? Last night I had a dream that it was morning and time to go to work and when I woke up it was true!

T Bumpton, North Shields

KING KONG for a day...

WE ALL imagine what it would be like to be a 100 foot tall gorilla. But if our dreams came true and we got the chance to be a King Kong for 24 hours, what would we do? We asked the stars how they would spend their time if they were...

Bono, *Pop Arsehole*
King Kong was twenty times taller than the average man, which makes him about 40 times taller than me. If I were a King Kong for a day, I'd use my new size to do 40 times as much good for humanity as I normally do. Then I'd phone my accountant and see if it entitled me to pay 40 times less tax. Actually, I'd probably do that bit first.

Brian Sewell, *Art Critic*
I'm not aware of ever having watched the film King Kong, but I have seen gorillas in the zoo, and I would take my cue from them. Consequently, I should imagine I would spend the day as a 100-foot-simian eating vomit from the palm of my hand and throwing 10-foot-long turds at passers by.

Prince Charles, *Possible Monarch if he lives long enough*
I get really cross when I see modern architecture blighting the landscape of our towns. If I found myself transformed into a King Kong for the day, I think I would be unable to control my rage and would smash some architectural carbuncles, such as The National Gallery extension, the Lloyds Building, and that one what looks like a gherkin.

Brian Cox, *Synth band Astrologer*
The trouble with being a top physicist is that knowing everything about the stars and planets has taken away all of their magic. As a King Kong, I would be extremely simple, and this would rekindle my child-like fascination and sense of wonderment, and I would spend the time simply staring into the night sky, watching the vastness of the universe. Then when the sun came up I'd start frantically pulling myself off with my foot.

Nick Hewer, *Countdown Host*
If I were a King Kong, I'd immediately scale the outside of the Yorkshire TV studios, looking through all the windows with my giant eye until I found Rachael Riley's dressing room. Then I'd grab her and climb onto the roof of the building and sit picking her clothes off whilst she screamed in terror. Once I'd finished doing that, I'd angrily swat a few aeroplanes out the sky before plunging to my death in the carpark below.

TOP TIPS

CONVINCE people that you're in the cast of *Mad Men* by lighting up a fag in a doctor's waiting room and then grabbing the receptionist's arse.

Terry Corrigan, e-mail

WANT rid of old bedsheets? Just scrawl a random name and age - 'Happy 30th Tracy' works particularly well - and tie it to the nearest roundabout. Hey presto- the council will take it away for you a few days later.

Ross Heaviside, e-mail

COMBINE meal time with a bowel movement by sitting on the toilet the wrong way. This allows you to put your plate on the cistern and enjoy your dinner as you dispose of the last one.

Tim Chambers, e-mail

VIRGIN train commuters. Save money on electricity bills by taking your household appliances with you and use the plug sockets on the trains. Richard Branson is a billionaire, so he can afford it.

Eric Derek, e-mail

DR WHO. Missed the Jeremy Kyle Show by 2 hours? Simply go back in time 1 hour and watch it on ITV+1.

Nigel Forrage, e-mail

NEW hearing aid wearers. Remove your aid before having a tom tit. The straining can cause raised blood pressure in the ear leading to high pitched feedback.

P Townsend, e-mail

OWLS. Scare Christians by doing that twisty neck thing whilst reciting Latin text backwards and growling like a lion occasionally.

Tam Dale, e-mail

SPORTING equipment manufacturers. Minimise damage caused during freak hail storms by making golf balls a quarter of the size they are now.

Paul Hargreaves, e-mail

PEOPLE evading the Mafia. Don't hide in places like Chicago or Florida. Try somewhere more low-key like Gunnerton near Hexham, or Whitwood between Castleford and Rothwell.

T Thorn, Hexham

toptips@viz.co.uk

I NOTICED Jimmy Hill pretending to be some clouds yesterday. Do I win £5?

Paul Edmonds, via Twitter

I HAVE to say that the April Fool's Day headline on BBC Scotland - *"5 Nursing Home Deaths Probed"* - was not in the least bit amusing. If anything, it was a bit sad. Time to buck your ideas up Auntie Beeb.

Neil Shand, e-mail

WHEN my elderly father announced he was dating again less than a year after the death of our mother, our family were naturally concerned. However, our fears turned to alarm when Father revealed his new partner was not a woman at all but a string puppet, specifically 'Marina' from the 1960s Gerry Anderson series *Stingray* which he seems to have bought at a charity auction. Happily, in the last year, we have all grown to prefer Marina to our actual mother as she is better company in the evenings and much less racist.

Martin Belsize, Rochester

I WAS appalled by a recent visit to Madame Tussauds where I found the celebrities aloof and unfriendly. 15 minutes of fame and they think they can ignore the regular man on the street. I for one won't be watching celebrity jungle this year.

Nomis Nedleif, e-mail

WHY do gameshow hosts always say "You have been great contestants" when they lose?

Ross Kennett, e-mail

I'M A laboratory technician and I'm not allowed to smoke at work. Yet the beagles in my lab are actively encouraged to puff away on cigarettes all day. It's one rule for beagles and another for laboratory technicians.

Rance Butter, Knutsford

THEY say an area of rainforest the size of a football field is cut down every second. No wonder the Brazilians are so good at footy.

Martits, e-mail

I THINK if Jesus had concentrated a bit more on his job as a carpenter and less time performing miracles, he wouldn't have got into so much bother.

Jeff Blackboard, e-mail

MY name spelt backwards is eeL. Can anyone beat that?

Lee, e-mail

THERE has been much controversy surrounding the fact that some men on the Titanic lifeboats were dressed as women. I say so what? Haven't transvestites got as much a right to life as normal folk?

Terry Corrigan, e-mail

THEY say a leopard can't change its spots, but I saw one do it the other day at the zoo. Then again it might have been a different leopard as there were a few and they were running around a bit.

Stanley, e-mail

Tony Robinson's Tissue Time Team

Join Tony, Professor Mick and the twat with the feather in his hat as they dig back into the fascinating past of tissues.

Dear Tony and the Team,

● **DID** the Romans use tissues and if so, where did they keep them? I only ask because togas don't have pockets or sleeves.

Francine Hornby, Bath

✳ *ARCHAEOLOGICAL excavations at Vindolanda in Northumberland have unearthed tiny pieces of tissues dating back to the Roman occupation of the 2nd Century AD. It is believed that the soldiers guarding Hadrian's Wall kept the tissues stuffed into the tops of their sandals or in a small leather pouch hung around the neck. Every tiny fragment, each one smaller than a postage stamp, is worth more than £200.*

Dear Tony and the Team,

● **MY** wife recently found a tissue whilst digging in the garden. It looked very old and had the letter "B" written in the corner. We were wondering if it may have originally belonged to Boadicea, and if so how much it is worth.

Stanley Morgan, Epping

✳ *A GENUINE Boadicea tissue would be worth over a million pounds. However, the ancient Iceni Queen would probably have marked her tissues with "QB" for Queen Boadicea rather than a simple "B". This tissue is more likely, therefore, to have belonged to someone from history who went by a single name beginning with B, such as Beethoven, Botticelli or Bismarck. At auction it could fetch between £150 and £300 and you should probably insure it for £500.*

YOU'RE NICKED!

Pippa's nipsy facing long stretch

After her companion threatened Paris paparazzis with a fake handgun, bootilicious royal *PIPPA MIDDLETON* could be facing a 7-year spell in a French prison... *and her arse will be doing time with her.*

The pert buttocks could spend up to 23 hours each day locked in a cell, and royal watchers fear that they could emerge from their spell in chokey a shadow of their former selves. *But was the crime really so grave?* Should Britain's favourite farting clappers lose their liberty over what was at worst a bout of youthful high jinks following a boozy night out in the French capital? Or in this era of global terrorism, should all mud flaps be subject to the full force of the law no matter how peachy and toned? We went on the streets to find out what **YOU** thought...

...Pippa's buttocks were merely a passenger in the car. They were simply in the wrong place at the wrong time. By all means punish the gun waver and his passengers, Miss Middleton included, for their lack of judgement, but to incarcerate her cheeks too would be an appalling miscarriage of justice.

Bartram Crowther, traffic warden

...the law is the law and Pippa's cheeks have broken it. That said, I can see no useful purpose in locking them up. Perhaps they should perform some community service, cleaning war memorials, gardening for old people, or posing for a cheeky swim-suit photoshoot in Nuts.

Henry Frampton, pest controller

...I've spent time in prison, and let me tell you, a pretty pair of buttocks like Pippa's won't stand a chance. A bar of soap will be dropped in the shower and Miss Middleton will be forced to pick it up, leaving her innocent buttocks at the mercy of hardened criminals. Admittedly, it was a man's prison I was in, but I imagine the goings on are pretty similar.

Roy Weasles, burglar

...I am appalled by the thought of Pippa's young bottom being passed around in a filthy French prison from lesbian to lesbian, a mere plaything being used and abused for their enjoyment. Sorry, not apalled, I meant extremely aroused.

Mike Soapbox, glazier

...had the driver waved a gun at someone in the Isle of Man, Pippa's buttocks would be facing 25 lashes of the birch. Although I'm a staunch upholder of corporal punishment, I feel the use of sticks to be a little too savage, and perhaps 25 smacks from an open hand would be a more appropriate sanction. And I'm not one of these hypocrites who call for something to be done but are unprepared to do it themselves. So I'd like to put my name forward to spank her if she ever commits a misdemeanour in the Isle of Man.

Douglas Troubador, fireman

...justice is blind, and all our bottoms are equal before the law. Yet our prisons are stuffed to bursting with big hairy arses. The sad fact is that if you have a trim, perky tush and you wave a gun at someone, you are treated far more leniently than if you did the same thing, but had a big, mucky dirtbox.

Kier Starmer QC Queen's Counsellor

...Pippa claims that the gun that got pointed at the paparazzi was a fake, but it looked real enough to me, as does the bottom she is always waving at them. How do we know that that isn't a fake, too? She should be forced to have it examined by a doctor who would produce a certificate to testify as to its bona fides.

Dr Bill Shipton, buttock consultant

...I'm so worried about Pippa's arse going to prison, that I can't sleep. I was awake all last night, tossing in bed with images of her derriere going through my mind.

Bjorn Magnussen Punch & Judy professor

...the French have got a ruddy cheek, trying to put one of our princess's gluteus maximums behind bars after we saved them from the nazis. Perhaps next time we should let Hitler walk all over them.

Brigadier Lethbridge-Stewart Brigadier

TINRIBS

11-YEAR OLD TOMMY TAYLOR'S BEST PAL WAS A FANTASTIC ROBOT NAMED TINRIBS

AT SCHOOL. AH, MR SNODWORTHY. I'VE JUST BEEN WATCHING THAT RAY MEARS FELLOW ON THE TELLY.

2+2 =
2+3 =

AND I'VE DECIDED WE SHOULD TAKE THE PUPILS OUT INTO THE WOODS AND TEACH THEM THE ART OF 'BUSHCRAFT'.

COME ALONG EVERYONE, WE'LL CATCH A RABBIT OR A BEAR OR SOMETHING.

THEN WE'LL COOK IT FOR LUNCH, AS NATURE INTENDED.

HM. WELL THERE'S NO SIGN OF ANY RABBITS OR BEARS.

BUT WE COULD MAKE A TASTY STEW OUT OF THAT BLUEBOTTLE.

COME HERE, YOU DRATTED FLY!

BLAST! IT KEEPS DODGING OUT OF MY GRASP!

I CAN TRAP THAT BLUEBOTTLE, HEADMASTER — WITH THE AID OF MY ROBOT PAL'S ARMPIECE.

PANT GASP!

HI. I'M BARBIE. I LOVE YOU VERY MUCH.

I'LL JUST STICK TINRIBS'S INDEX FINGER RIGHT UP MR SNODWORTHY'S ARSE.

GEEP!

POIT!

LIKE SO!

THE BLUEBOTTLE WILL BE IRRESISTABLY ATTRACTED TO THIS SHIT-SMEARED FINGER..

THEN I SIMPLY CAPTURE IT IN ONE OF TINRIBS'S SOUP CANS!

GOT IT!

EXCELLENT BUSHCRAFT, YOUNG TAYLOR!

PUT THE FLY IN THIS SAUCEPAN OF WATER AND WE'LL HEAT IT UP TO MAKE A LOVELY STEW.

OH DEAR! IT'S HOPELESS TRYING TO GET A BONFIRE LIT — THE WOOD'S TOO DAMP!

HOW ARE WE GOING TO COOK OUR STEW NOW?

I HAVE AN IDEA HEADMASTER.

HERE'S A COUPLE OF PRETTY GIRLS OUT HIKING...

LOOK LADIES, THIS FINGER HAS BEEN UP OUR TEACHER'S BUM. HE'S OVER THERE!

EH?

SEE, THERE'S HIS POO ON IT!

UGH! THE DIRTY BEAST!

SPLENDID! MR SNODWORTHY'S INTENSE HUMILIATION IN FRONT OF THOSE GIRLS HAS TURNED HIS ENTIRE HEAD INTO A BLAZING STOVE!

BURNING EMBARRASSMENT

OUR BLUEBOTTLE STEW WILL SOON BE PIPING HOT!

BUT — HUH! IT JUST TASTES LIKE WARMED-UP WATER.

YOU'D BETTER ALL GO AND GATHER SOME NUTS AND BERRIES TO ADD A BIT OF FLAVOUR.

HI! I'M BARBIE. I LOVE YOU VERY MUCH.

WHAT'S THAT, TINRIBS? YOU'D LIKE TO GATHER SOME NUTS TOO?

HA HA! THESE ARE THE SORT OF NUTS A ROBOT LIKES TO EAT: METAL ONES!

THERE'S PLENTY OF THEM ON THIS OLD BICYCLE WHICH SOMEONE HAS DUMPED IN THE WOODS!

LET ME BORROW THIS BICYCLE, TAYLOR! I'M SICK OF THAT STUPID "BUSHCRAFT" NONSENSE.

SHOVE

I'M GOING TO CYCLE INTO TOWN AND FIND A MACCY D'S TO GET SOME PROPER FOOD!

WAH! SOME IDIOT HAS REMOVED ALL THE NUTS AND BOLTS FROM THIS BIKE!

CAUTION MUDDY BOG

IT'S FALLING TO BITS!

CRASH! SPOTCH!

CAUTION MUDDY BOG

GLUB!

GREAT SCOTT! THERE'S SOME KIND OF WILD PIG CRAWLING OUT OF THE MUD!

GRUNT!

CAUTION MUDDY BOG

QUICKLY CHILDREN — LET'S KILL IT, AND ROAST IT FOR OUR LUNCH!

SHORTLY— LOOK, HEADMASTER! I'VE STUCK THE PIG'S HEAD ON TINRIBS'S ARMPIECE, AS AN OFFERING TO ANY QUASI-SUPERNATURAL "BEAST" WHICH RESIDES IN THE WOODS!

MUNCH! GOOD IDEA, TAYLOR!

I WONDER WHERE MR SNODWORTHY IS? HE'D ENJOY THIS ROAST PORK!

BIFFA BACON

Panel 1: THIS IS A CANNY DROP O' LAGER, THIS, FATHA

Panel 2: AYE, IT'S NOT BAD... D'YUZ FANCY ANOTHER SPLASH, MUTHA?... ...SAY WHEN

Panel 3: B-DUNK!! B-DUNK! B-DUNK!! EH? ...WOT THE FRIG?

Panel 4: HOO, BIFFA! CAALL YER FUCKIN' DURG OFFAZ... IT'S SHAGGIN ME FUCKIN' LEG, MAN HUMP! HUMP!

Panel 5: IT'S GORRITS FUCKIN' LIPSTICK OOTAN EVERYTHIN' Y'WANNA GERRIT PUT DOON, BIFFA. IT'S FUCKIN' PORVORTED! KNACKA'S NEE FUCKIN' PORVORT. HE'S A MAN DURG! BIFFA IS A LUG

Panel 6: HE'S AANLY DEEIN WOT NATURE'S TELT 'IM

Panel 7: FUCKIN' 'ELL... HE'S SHAGGIN Y' FATHA'S LEG NOO!... EH!? HE'S ATTRACTED T' Y' HOR-MURNS, MUTHA

Panel 8: .THE DORTY FRIGGIN' PORVORT AYE! Y' DURG'S A FUCKIN' HUR-MUR-SEXUAL

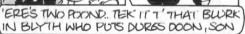

Panel 9: WUZ'LL HEV NEE ARSE BANDIT DURGS IN THIS HOOSE, BIFFA... IT'S AGIN NATURE AN' AGIN WOR FAITH AS CHRISTIANS... 'ERE'S TWO POOND... TEK IT T' THAT BLURK IN BLYTH WHO PUTS DURGS DOON, SON

Panel 10: SHORTLY... HOO, MISTAH... I'VE COME T' GET ME DURG PUT DOON TWO POOND, SON... BRING IT THROUGH T' THE SORGERY

Panel 11: WOT'S WRANG WI' IT? IS IT ILL, OR DIVVEN'T YUZ LIKE IT NEE MORE? NAH! IT'S A FUCKIN' HOM A HOM DURG, EH?

Panel 12: WELL Y' DIVVEN'T HEV T' PURRIT DOON FER THAT... I CAN TEK ITS BAALLS OFF FORRA POOND THAT'LL SORT IT OOT

Panel 13: SO... KEEP A TIGHT HURLD OF 'IM, SON. YUZ AANLY GET ONE SHOT AT THIS, Y'KNAA... ...IT MAKES 'EM GAN FUCKIN' RADGEY

Panel 14: CLANG!

Panel 15: FUCKIN' 'ELL, SON... THAT'S A CANNY HARD DURG YUZ'VE GOT THERE GRRRRR!

Panel 16: RIP! SNARL! GRRR! GROWL! GAAA!

Panel 17: SHORTLY... HOO! I THOUGHT WUZ TELT YUZ T' HEV THAT FUCKIN' FAIRY DURG PUT OOT IT'S FUCKIN' MISERY, BIFFA AYE!..THE BIG SOFT HEEMASEX SHITE! HOO... THEZ NOWT SOFT ABOOT THIS DURG...

Panel 18: .THE GADGY TRIED T' TAKE 'IS KNACKAS OFF...HE FUCKED 'IS CHISEL AN' RIPPED 'IM T' FUCKIN' PIECES GRR! PAT! PAT! WELL GIZ ME FUCKIN TWO POOND BACK THEN, SON

Panel 19: I CANNAT... I SPENT IT ON THIS! HARDEST DOG IN TOON

Panel 20: LATER... LERRIM FINISH, MUTHA... Y' DIVVEN'T WANT T' MAKE 'IM ANGRY... HEH! HEH! FUCKIN' BASTAAD

SEX, DRUGS and... ANTIQUES? It's certainly an unlikely combination, but according to a BBC insider it's been a way of life for the cast and crew of *The Antiques Roadshow* for years. And now, sacked roadie Seth Pipes is lifting the lid on the debauched backstage behaviour at the popular heirloom valuation programme.

"If viewers saw what goes on behind the scenes, it would turn their hair white," Pipes told us. "If it wasn't already white. Which it probably will be because they're the sort of people who watch *The Antiques Roadshow*."

"It's an absolute scandal. Life for those heirloom valuers is a never-ending merry-go-round of groupies, drugs, strong booze and high-jinks," he continued. "And it's all at the BBC licence-payers' expense."

China in his Shaky Hands

I remember one time, we'd set up the roadshow in the grounds of Belvoir Castle in Leicestershire. The show was going out live at 7pm, so there was a lot of work to be done, rigging the lights, plugging in the cameras and setting up the tables. About five minutes before the broadcast, the producer called me over to one of the trailers. I'll not say which veteran expert it belonged to, but suffice it to say that when he was on screen valuing the ceramics, he looked like butter wouldn't melt. But I knew him as the biggest hellraiser on the programme.

His antics on and off the set had earned him a well-deserved reputation as the Oliver Reed of the Antiques Roadshow (Indeed, I had it on good authority from a mate at Pinewood that Oliver Reed used to be known as the Henry Sandon of the movie industry!), but he certainly was a sorry sight now. He'd got the shakes and he'd got them bad, and there wasn't a drop of booze left in his caravan. The floor was littered with empty bottles and broken glass. Whisky, gin, window polish... you name it, he'd drank the lot.

BBC fixer spills beans on backstage shenanigans

Somehow, me and the producer carried him over to the set and propped him up at his table. Seconds later, the director shouted 'Action!' and we were on air. The first member of the public sat down and handed him a Georgian Toby jug. As he picked it up to start pointing out its characteristic brown salt glaze and firing marks, the camera zoomed in and it was obvious his hands were shaking. In fact, they were so blurred, the cameraman thought they'd gone out of focus. It was clear that if we didn't get some alcohol down him - and quick - he was going to break the handle off the jug, or worse, drop it and smash it into a thousand pieces.

Suddenly, I spotted a bottle of brandy on the next table. Without stopping to think, I grabbed it, pulled the cork out with my teeth and, while the cameras were pointing at the punter saying she'd never really thought about what it might be worth, emptied the contents into the jug. For the next five minutes, every time the director cut away to a queue of glum-looking people carrying clocks, or a long shot of the castle grounds, Sandon took the opportunity to take a hefty swig of the brandy.

Pretty soon, he'd glugged the lot and the tremors had stopped. He went

on to turn in a bravura performance that day, valuing several pot dogs and some plates and cups like the old pro he was. You'd never have suspected that mere minutes before the broadcast, the genial, bespectacled old buffer on screen had been lying on the floor of his caravan in a pool of his own vomit, shaking like a shitting dog.

It was only at the after-show wrap-party that the laughing director took me to one side and told me the brandy I'd snatched had been a bottle of vintage Napoleonic Cognac from 1789 that someone had brought in to be valued. My eyes nearly popped out of my head when he told me that at auction, it would probably have fetched something in the region of a million pounds, and it should have been valued for at least twice that for insurance purposes! Apparently, it had been passed down through the same family for ten generations. Now Henry had knocked it back in ten glugs!

Going Off for a Song

You might suppose that that sort of crazy behaviour is a recent development, but nothing could be further from the truth, let me tell you. *The Antiques Roadshow*'s always been well known at the beeb as party central, even from its earliest days. Back in the late seventies, when the show started, the presenter was Arthur Negus. With his shock of white hair, thick glasses and rumpled old suit, Arthur looked like everybody's favourite granddad.

And that's just what he was like off-set too... assuming your favourite granddad was a cross between Keith Moon, Rod Stewart and Peter Stringfellow!

To say Arthur Negus was a ladies' man would be the understatement of the century. The man was as sexually insatiable as a tomcat with two dicks, and when he wasn't eyeing up a bit of

eighteenth century furniture in front of the cameras, he was eyeing up a bit of twentieth century crumpet behind them. I remember this one time, we were doing the show from Rievaulx Abbey in Yorkshire. A stunning young blonde piece came along with a giant four-poster bed that had been in her family for years.

As luck would have it, she got caught in traffic and didn't arrive at the set til we'd all but finished shooting the show. There was no time to film Negus giving her heirloom the once-over, but he offered to give her a private valuation for insurance purposes ... if she'd bring it round to his trailer later on. When she turned up, Arthur got the surprise of her life, because it turned out she was a quadruplet, and she'd got her three equally gorgeous twin sisters to help her carry the bed across the car park.

Once they'd manhandled it through the caravan door, Negus started to examine it. He explained that it was a fine example of Rococo woodwork, running his fingers over its beautifully carved cabriole legs and fine mahogany dovetail joints. He told the ladies they had inherited a fine period piece, although he thought some of the turned finials may have been from a later period. One of them asked him if he could put a value on the bed, and a wicked glint appeared behind his thick glasses.

"I couldn't possibly tell you what it's worth without testing it out first," Negus grinned, licking his lips. The sexy quads didn't need asking twice, and within minutes they had all stripped off, jumped in the bed and Arthur was enjoying a fours-up... not for the first or last time in his illustrious career!

It was an open secret in the antiques world that Arthur was hung like a horse, and went at the women like an out-of-control auctioneer's hammer, driving them all to heights of ecstasy thay had never dreamed of. That four-

KING DONG ARTHUR: Heirloom expert Negus was donkey-rigged, says Seth.

tics ow!

ANTIQUES ROADIE: Pipes paints a lurid picture of life behind the scenes on popular show.

poster was 300 years old, and had been built of stout English oak by the finest craftsmen of the renaissance, but it simply couldn't stand up to the relentless punishment meted out to it during Negus's marathon five-way romp. By the time he had finished, the ageing antiques expert had satisfied the blondes a dozen times, and the bed had been reduced to a splintered pile of matchwood.

As the girls put their knickers on and made their way out of the caravan, Negus gave them the bad news. "In its present condition, I'm afraid this antique is worthless," he told them. "If you had looked after it better, it would have easily fetched something in the region of a million pounds at auction, and it should have been insured for at least twice that."

Gun Expert was Quick on the Trigger

That wasn't the only saucy scandal that happened on *The Antiques Roadshow*. All the experts constantly found themselves being offered sexual favours in return for inflated valuations for insurance purposes, and most of them were only too happy to oblige. They might have been antiques aficionados, but they were only human. If sex was being offered to them on a 17th century china plate, they'd have been mad to turn it down.

The Roadshow was visiting a cathedral down south somewhere, and a bloke and his missus had brought in a Civil War musket to be valued. They were directed to the militaria expert, who I shan't name to spare his blushes, and he gave their gun the once-over. He was explaining all about its history, but the couple were clearly only interested in how much they could sell it for. They kept interrupting him and trying to hurry him up, and their faces fell when the expert finally told them that they

could expect their antique firearm to fetch a mere £150 to £200 at auction.

The husband was clearly disappointed at the size of the valuation, but his wife had other ideas. "Let's see if there's something I can do to get it up a bit," she said as she climbed onto all fours and crawled under the table. Before long the antiques expert's eyes were popping out of his head and he was grinning from ear to ear. I'll not tell you exactly what the woman was doing under there, except to say she was sucking him off. Her ruse certainly paid off, as he started valuing the musket for ever-increasing amounts of money for insurance purposes as his excitement mounted. A thousand pounds ... ten thousand pounds ... the amount just kept getting bigger and bigger.

Then suddenly, the arms and militaria expert shot his bolt ... quite literally. At the peak of his sexual ecstasy, he must have accidentally pulled the trigger, because the 500-year-old flintlock firearm went off with a loud bang. There was a smash and a scream, as the musket ball hit a Ming vase that was being valued by Eric Knowles at the next table, breaking it into a thousand pieces.

Luckily no-one was hurt, but we later found out that that vase would have been worth a million pounds

at auction, and should probably have been insured for at least twice that!

Presenter was High and Dry

For an antiques expert, life on the road could be boring. The show went out at Sunday tea-time, and there was always a sense of building excitement as the crowds brought in their tin toys, paintings of cows and snuff-boxes, ready for them to be valued on air. The flipside was that there were six-and-a-half days every week when there was nothing to do, and I'm sorry to say that many of the show's personalities resorted to illicit substances as a way of recreating the buzz of the live broadcast. Luckily, most of them could handle it, but one or two got hooked.

This one time we'd rocked up in Leicestershire to do a Roadshow from Belvoir Castle. Halfway through the afternoon before the show, the director took me to one side and told me there was trouble with the presenter. Now, I'm not naming names, but it was an open secret that this particular Roadshow personality - a well-respected newsreader and former Rear of the Year - was a sod for the drugs. "She's run out of shit and gone cold turkey," said the director. "What are we going to do, Seth?

We're on air in two hours, and she's in no state to go in front of the cameras." Sure enough, I had a look through the trailer window and saw a sight I'll never forget.

The presenter in question was laying in her bunk, sweating cobs, shivering and scratching frantically at imaginary spiders under her skin. She was staring open-mouthed at a hallucination of Hugh Scully in a nappy crawling across the ceiling. It was clear she needed a big fix of drugs and she needed it fast.

Well I don't know whether you've ever tried to score a kilo of primo narcotics in Melton Mowbray on a quiet Sunday afternoon, but let me tell you it's not the easiest task in the world. Somehow I managed to find a pusher on the lower East Side of town, on the wrong side of the tracks between Burton Lazars and Thorpe Arnold, and scored a nice big bag of drugs. Then I high-tailed it back to the presenter's caravan.

As I went through the door, she grabbed the bag off me and emptied the drugs onto the table. She had all the paraphernalia set out ready, bongs, syringes, spliffs, silver foil and injection needles. But the one thing she didn't have was the one thing she needed - a spoon! As luck would have it, a member of the public was walking past carrying a silver-plated George III serving spoon. There was no time to explain, so I reached out the window and grabbed it.

Hungrily, she began devouring the pile of drugs, shoveling them into her face with the antique spoon. It must have been strong stuff, because it stopped her withdrawal symptoms in their tracks. Within moments, she had calmed down and become the calm, assured former presenter of *Crimewatch* that the public knew and loved. And not a moment too soon, because the programme was just seconds away from going on air.

I watched her step out of the caravan and take her place in front of the cameras. "This evening *The Antiques Roadshow* comes to you from the picturesque surroundings of Belvoir Castle, ancestral home of the Earls of Rutland," she said. It was hard to believe that just thirty seconds before, this consummate professional had been a crazed junkie, scoffing drugs like there was no tomorrow.

The spoon she had been using didn't fare quite so well. The drugs she had been eating with it had been so powerful that they had stripped every last bit of silver plate off it. When I showed it to silverware expert Alastair Dickenson, he shook his head sadly. "This spoon is worthless," he said.

"In pristine condition, it would have fetched a million pounds at auction, and I would have put a value of at least twice that amount on it for insurance purposes," he added.

NEXT WEEK *The time I was a focus puller on Songs of Praise. And focus wasn't the only thing I had to pull, I can tell you!*

BILLY BOTTOM and his zany **TOILET PRANKS**

RIGHT. I'M OFF FOR A BIG SHIT... I'VE GOT A RIGHT OLD SACK OF SPUDS IN 'ERE WAITIN' TO BE PLANTED
...AN' THAT CHOD BIN'S GOT MY NAME ON IT.

AW, **SHITE!** IT'S BLOCKED UP WITH **BANGERS AN' MASH!**

BLOODY 'ELL... THAT'S GOIN' **NOWHERE**, THAT LOT... IT'S A JOB FOR A PROFESSIONAL
FLUSH! FLUSH!

SO... IS THAT DYNO-ROD? ME BOG'S BACKED UP WI' TURDS AN' BUMWAD
SORRY, MR. BOTTOM
WE'RE VERY BUSY. IT'LL BE THREE WEEKS BEFORE WE CAN SORT IT OUT.

SLAM!!
THREE WEEKS!?... I'LL NOT LAST THREE BLOODY **MINUTES**...
TING!
...ME NIPSY'S GOIN' INTO BLOODY SPASM

SHORTLY... RIGHT... I'VE TIED ME SPUD MASHER TO A BROOM SHANK ...THAT'LL SHIFT THE BASTARDS.

PLUNGE! PLUNGE! JOUST! BLOIK!!
HNNG! HNNG!

SNAP!
EH!?

BUGGER IT!... NOW THERE'S A SPUD MASHER IN THE BLOODY EQUATION...

SHORTLY... MY SHOPPIN'S MAKIN' A BREAK FOR THE BLOODY BORDER... IT'S TIME FOR PLAN B...
...I'LL PUT A BIN BAG ON ME ARM, GO IN AN' THROTTLE THE BUGGERS.

SQUELCH! SQUELCH! SQUELCH! SQUELCH!
OH, AYE... I FELT ONE OF 'EM GIVE A BIT, THERE.

OH, **CACK!** THE BAG'S RIPPED... IT MUST OF SNAGGED ON THE SPUD MASHER...
CHRIST ALL BLOODY MIGHTY

THERE'S SHIT UP ME NAILS AN' ALL SORTS
NEXT TIME I'LL USE A THICK RUBBLE SACK

ANYROAD, I'VE GOT T' GET IT SORTED SHARPISH. I'VE GOT A MOLE AT THE COUNTER, AN' HE'S NOT TAKIN' NO FOR A BLOODY ANSWER

I'VE GOT A COUPLE OF AIR BOMBS LEFT OVER FROM BONFIRE NIGHT IN 'ERE...

IF THIS DON'T SHIFT THE BUGGERS, **NOWT** WILL

SLAM!

BANG!

BINGO! THAT'S DONE THE TRICK... A NICE, EMPTY PAN T' POACH ME EGGS IN

HEH! HEH!.. TIME TO RELEASE THE CHOCOLATE HOSTAGES...

HNNNG!.. HNNNNG!! HNNNNNG!!!

KNACKERS! WOULD YOU BELIEVE IT?... I'VE BAKED IT THAT LONG IT'S GOT **STUCK!**

SO... 'ERE WE GO... IF IT CLEARS TURDS OUT THE POT, IT'LL CLEAR 'EM OUT ME CACKPIPE...
FSSSSS!

BANG!!
OW!! JESUS H. CHRIST

OH NO! it's the PATHETIC SHARKS!

OOH, LOOK! REVELS! I ABSOLUTELY LOVE REVELS! CAN I HAVE ONE?

NO YOU CAN'T... GET OFF...THEY'RE MINE...≡MUNCH MUNCH≡

BUT THAT'S GREEDY. IT'S A FAMILY BAG, MADE FOR SHARING. YOU CAN'T HAVE A WHOLE FAMILY BAG TO YOURSELF.

WELL I CAN TOO, BECAUSE THEY'RE FOR SHARING WITH YOUR FAMILY AND WE'RE NOT A FAMILY...WE'RE A SCHOOL.

NO WE'RE NOT. SCHOOLS ARE FOR WHALES, BUT WE'RE A SORT OF FISH SO WE MUST BE A SHOAL.

ACTUALLY, THE COLLECTIVE NOUN FOR A GROUP OF SHARKS IS A "SHIVER".

WELL I THINK WE'RE A FAMILY, SO YOU SHOULD SHARE THOSE REVELS BETWEEN ALL OF US.

WELL WE'RE NOT. FAMILIES ARE BROTHERS AND SISTERS AND THINGS. WE'RE NOT BROTHERS...WE'RE NOT EVEN THE SAME SPECIES.

MY BROTHER GOT MADE INTO SOUP BY SOME BAD MEN IN JAPAN...

...BUT HE DIDN'T LIKE REVELS.

ANYWAY, I CAN'T SHARE THEM BECAUSE YOU MIGHT GET A PEANUT ONE AND IF YOU'VE GOT AN ALLERGY YOU'LL SUE ME.

THEY DON'T DO PEANUT ONES ANYMORE FOR THAT VERY REASON.

MY BROTHER WAS ALLERGIC TO CAT HAIR.

...YES, APPARENTLY THEY MAKE UP THE DIFFERENCE BY ADDING EXTRA MALTESER ONES TO THE BAG BECAUSE THEY'RE CHEAPER.

EEURGH! I HATE THE MALTESER ONES.

≡MUNCH MUNCH≡

MY FAVOURITES ARE THE ORANGE ONES, BUT THE TROUBLE IS THEY LOOK EXACTLY THE SAME AS THE MALTESER ONES.

YES, BUT ORANGE IS HEAVIER THAN MALTESER, SO YOU CAN TELL THE DIFFERENCE BY DROPPING THEM AND SEEING WHICH ONE HITS THE FLOOR FIRST.

WELL WHAT USE IS THAT? ONCE IT'S BEEN ON THE FLOOR IT'LL HAVE ALL GERMS ON AND YOU CAN'T EAT IT.

YES YOU CAN IF YOU PICK IT UP WITHIN FIVE SECONDS AND BLOW ON IT. THEY DID IT ON MYTHBUSTERS.

I DON'T LIKE THE COFFEE ONES EITHER. DON'T GIVE ME A COFFEE ONE.

I'M NOT GIVING YOU ANY.

NO. GREEDY GUTS HERE IS GOING TO EAT THEM ALL HIMSELF.

WELL I HOPE HE GETS A TUMMY ACHE.

THAT'S RICH COMING FROM YOU. YOU NEVER GAVE ME ANY OF THAT CRUNCHIE YOU HAD THIS MORNING.

I WOULD HAVE, BUT IT'S UNHYGIENIC TO BITE SOMETHING AND THEN GIVE IT TO SOMEONE ELSE TO PUT IN THEIR MOUTH. IT'LL HAVE ALL THEIR LURGEY ON IT.

YOU COULD HAVE BROKEN A BIT OFF AND GIVEN IT TO ME.

I DON'T KNOW HOW I'M SUPPOSED TO BREAK A CRUNCHIE IN TWO WHEN I HAVEN'T GOT OPPOSABLE THUMBS.

ANYWAY, IT WAS A FUN-SIZE CRUNCHIE. "JUST TWO BITES BIG"...THAT'S WHAT IT SAYS IN THE ADVERT.

I HATE CRUNCHIES. THEY TASTE ALL BURNT.

≡TSK≡ IT'S THE LAST REVEL IN THE BAG, AND JUST MY LUCK IT'S A TOFFEE ONE.

I CAN'T EAT THAT. IT'LL PULL ALL MY FILLINGS OUT.

OVER HERE! I'LL HAVE IT!

NO! ME!

I ASKED BEFORE YOU, AND IT'S FIRST COME FIRST SERVED.!

BUT TOFFEE IS MY FAVOURITE, SO I OUGHT TO HAVE IT..!

WHAT?! WHY?

WELL, I'D DERIVE THE MOST PLEASURE FROM IT.

YES, BUT YOU'VE ALREADY HAD A CRUNCHIE TODAY.

YOU'LL JUST WASTE IT.

NO I WON'T..!

STOP ARGUING! LOOK, I'M GOING TO THROW IT IN THE AIR AND THE ONE WHO CATCHES IT CAN HAVE IT, OKAY..?

I HOPE IT'S ME!

ONE...TWO... THREE...

FLICK!

PLOINK!

CHOMP!

OOPS.

GAK!

SHORTLY...

SHARK PATROL

HAVE THEY GONE YET?

NO, THEY'RE STILL THERE... BUT THEY WOULDN'T HAVE COME IF A CERTAIN PERSON HAD GIVEN US SOME OF HIS REVELS.

EURGH! I CAN'T BELIEVE I BIT THAT MAN IN TWO. I CAN STILL TASTE IT. HAS ANYONE GOT ANY MINTS?

YES, BUT YOU'RE NOT HAVING ANY. THEY'RE MINE.

MUNCH-MUNCH

OH, LORDY! IT'S... THE FAT SLAGS

'ERE, SAN... WOT Y'TAKIN' YER KNICKERS OFF FOR? BAZ IS SIGNIN' ON... HE WON'T BE 'ERE TILL THREE.

I KNOW, BUT THE WINDOW CLEANER WILL...

...AN' WE'VE GOT NO MONEY T'PAY 'IM... SO I'M GOIN' T' GIVE 'IM A BIT OF A **THRILL** INSTEAD...

...HE MIGHT LERRUZ OFF

OOH!... 'ERE HE IS... PULL ME CURTAINS OPEN SO HE GETS A GOOD VIEW...

ME BEDROOM **CURTAINS**

EH?

OH, RIGHT

!

IS HE GEDDIN' A GOOD LOOK, EH, SAN?

OH, AYE! HE'S GEDDIN HIS FIVER'S WORTH

WOT'S UP, TERRY?

THE BLONDE ONE'S LYIN' ON THE BED WI NO KNICKERS ON... AN' IT REMINDED ME... I'D LEFT ME BUCKET BEHIND

...AN' ME SHAMMY LEATHERS

ROGER MELLIE

THE MAN on the TELLY

MON...

TUE...

WED...

THUR...

EXCUSE ME, SIR...

FRI...

ROGER NATHANIEL MELLIE... YOU HAVE PLEADED GUILTY TO STEALING GOODS FROM THE FULCHESTER BRANCH OF FRESHCO'S SUPERMARKET

YOUR PRODUCER, TOM, HAS APPEARED AS YOUR CHARACTER WITNESS AND SPOKE MOVINGLY IN YOUR FAVOUR...

...THE FACT THAT YOU TURNED UP THREE HOURS LATE FOR THIS HEARING, HOWEVER, WILL **NOT** HELP YOUR CASE

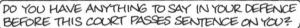

DO YOU HAVE ANYTHING TO SAY IN YOUR DEFENCE BEFORE THIS COURT PASSES SENTENCE ON YOU?

INDEED I DO, MY LORD...

INDEED I **DO**...

YOUR HONOUR... MEMBERS OF THE JURY... I CANNOT THINK WHAT WAS GOING THROUGH MY MIND WHEN I STOLE THOSE ITEMS... ONLY TIME WILL TELL WHY I DID WHAT I DID...

BUT THIS COURT CAN REST ASSURED THAT I WILL BE SEEKING PROFESSIONAL HELP FOR WHAT IS CLEARLY A TERRIBLE, TERRIBLE ILLNESS

BUT THAT ILLNESS ASIDE, I AM WELL AWARE THAT I HAVE LET **MYSELF** DOWN... I HAVE LET MY **FAMILY** DOWN... AND I HAVE LET MY **FANS** DOWN

BUT MOST UNFORGIVABLY, I HAVE LET DOWN THE MANY THOUSANDS... SNIFF!.. PERHAPS **MILLIONS** OF UNDER-PRIVILEGED, SICK AND WHEELCHAIR-BOUND KIDDIES... SNIFF!.. WHO RELY ON MY TIRELESS CHARITY WORK.

...KIDDIES LIKE LITTLE BILLY, HERE...

...BILLY HAD NEVER BEEN TO THE SEASIDE, YOUR HONOUR...

UNTIL HE WAS TAKEN TO SKEGNESS ON A ROGER MELLIE FOUNDATION SUNSHINE COACH...

...KIDDIES LIKE LITTLE ORPHAN SALLY, HERE... SALLY HAD NEVER RECEIVED A CHRISTMAS PRESENT UNTIL THE ROGER MELLIE XMAS SMILE PROJECT GAVE HER A TEDDY BEAR...

...KIDDIES LIKE LITTLE TOMMY, WHO WAS GOING BLIND UNTIL HIS VISION WAS SAVED BY THE ROGER MELLIE SIGHT FOR SORE EYES FOUNDATION

TAP! TAP! TAP!

THE LASER EQUIPMENT THAT RE-ATTACHED HIS LITTLE RETINAS WAS PAID FOR BY A CHARITY MARATHON RUN, DURING WHICH I SUFFERED A HEART ATTACK...

...YOUR HONOUR... IT WAS THE THOUGHT OF LITTLE TOMMY LIVING HIS LIFE IN DARKNESS THAT KEPT ME GOING TO THE FINISH LINE

...YES... IT IS **THESE** PEOPLE WHO I HAVE LET DOWN THE MOST... AND IT IS THESE WHO WILL SUFFER THE MOST IF I AM GIVEN A CUSTODIAL SENTENCE

SNIFF!

SHORTLY...

FULCHESTER COURTS

JUSTICE

DID YOU **SEE** THE TITS ON THAT STENOGRAPHER, TOM?... NOT FUCKIN' BAD, EH?

HERE YOU GO, KIDS... A TENNER A PIECE... NOW FUCK OFF BACK TO THE ARCADE

CHEERS, ROG

WELL, YOU DODGED A BULLET THERE, ROGER... FIFTY HOURS COMMUNITY SERVICE

HMM!

WE'LL GET THAT BLOKE FROM THE LOOKALIKE AGENCY TO DO IT... HE'S ONLY £2·50 AN HOUR

THAT WAS QUITE A SPEECH, ROGER. THERE WASN'T A DRY EYE IN THE HOUSE... IT WAS VERY IMPRESSIVE

IT SHOULD BE, TOM... I'VE GIVEN THE FUCKER OFTEN ENOUGH

GOT ME OFF MANY A DRINK-DRIVE BAN, THAT... **TWO** THIS CHRISTMAS ALONE

BEEP-IP! BEEP-IP!

OH, HANG ON... I'VE GOT A TEXT

WHO'S IT FROM THEN, TOM?

IT'S FROM THE BBC, ROGER.. THEY WANT YOU TO REVIVE A CLASSIC DAYTIME T.V. SHOW

SEE, TOM... NO SUCH THING AS BAD PUBLICITY... WHICH SHOW IS IT?

OH, CHRIST!

A WEEK LATER...

3...2...1... AND CUE ROGER!

Roger's **SUPERMARKET SWEEP**

HELLO!... GOOD MORNING AND WELCOME TO ROGER'S SUPERMARKET SWEEP!

EXCUSE ME, SIR...

IT'S THE DEBATE that's driving wedges into the heart of Britain's communities, sending divorce rates rocketing and splitting families asunder from Lands End to John O'Groats: Who is the greatest Armstrong?

IS IT MOON Man NEIL who to took one small step into the history books in 1969? Perhaps it's cyclist LANCE who pedalled his way into the record books by winning the Tour de France seven times. Or is it boy's action figure STRETCH who provided children with a few minutes of mild pleasure in the 1970s? Now it's time for the world's leading Armstrongs to go head to head to head in a three-way Armstrong Wrestling Contest that will decide once and for all...

WHO is the world's best ARMSTRONG?

Neil — NASA Astronaut and first man on the Moon

Lance — 7-times winner of the Tour de France

Round 1: TRAVEL

FEW PEOPLE have travelled further than Astronaut Neil, who drove his rocket Apollo 11 all the way to the Moon and back in 1969, a total of half a million miles - that's the equivalent of travelling to the Moon and back. But nagging questions remain as to whether the crew ever went into space at all, and many people believe that rather than the Moon, Armstrong and his cronies faked their whole mission on a Hollywood film set.

Score: 4

DURING his illustrious sporting career, cyclist Lance has put in more than half a million miles in the saddle - equivalent to pedalling all the way to the Moon and back. So you'd be forgiven for expecting a high score in this round. However, as his record of winning cycling's most coveted prize shows, Armstrong has only ever been to France, where he has competed in the famous Tour de race seven times.

Score: 3

Round 2: LIMB DUCTILITY

AS THE only man to walk on the Moon, Neil was one of the few people on Earth who experienced limb ductility. In the vacuum of space, Armstrong's arms and legs would have become considerably longer in the absence of gravity. However, whilst experiencing the high blast-off G-forces in his Saturn 5 rocket, his limbs would have become much shorter. In the end, the two effects would have cancelled each other out, so it's a mediocre score for the late lunar pioneer.

Score: 5

LIMB ductility would be a real disadvantage for Lance Armstrong. If there's one thing a racing cyclist needs, it's consistency of arm and leg length during a race. In a highly competitive sport where mere seconds can mean the difference between taking the yellow jersey and finding yourself at the back of the peloton, having to stop every few miles while his dad altered the height of the saddle and handlebars would spell disaster.

Score: 2

Round 3: BALANCE

THROUGHOUT his NASA career, Armstrong was notorious for having no sense of balance, even managing to fall over on the Moon where there is no gravity! Cape Canaveral boffins were forced to abandon plans for a Judge Dredd-style lunar motorbike when they found out it would be Armstrong at the controls. Instead they opted for a more stable four-wheeled Lunar Rover.

Score: 3

FIVE-SEVENTHS of the word balance is Lance, so you'd expect this Armstrong to have a good sense of it. And you'd be right, for the seven-times Tour de France winner can ride a bike which has extremely thin wheels for miles on end without falling off. Not only that, he can also do no hands and sit on the handle bars and pedal backwards. And do wheelies.

Score: 8

Round 4: DOPING ALLEGATIONS

IT'S A recorded fact that Project Apollo astronauts were routinely plied with drugs prior to blasting off on their week-long Moon missions. But they weren't ripped to their spaceman tits on squidgy black, crystal meth or anabollock steroids, they were simply drugs to bung them up, as NASA boffins had yet to develop a toilet which could cope with solid motions in the weightless vacuum of the lunar module.

Score: 7

THE WORLD of professional cycling is regularly rocked by drugs scandals, and throughout his career, Lance has not been immune from suspicion. And unluckily for him, despite never having taken any performance enhancing pharmaceuticals to aid his capabilities, he was recently banned for life and stripped of all his titles by the US Anti Doping Agency USADA.

Score: 5

Round 5: TOUR DE FRANCE WINS

ALTHOUGH he never officially competed in the famous French road race, astronaut Neil famously flew to the Moon and back in a rocket - a distance of 500,000 miles. That's the equivalent of pedaling 250 month-long Tour de Frances back to back ... in a week! Neil's prodigious feat is still unmatched in the field of professional cycling, so it's a giant leap in points for the late Moon-walker.

Score: 7

DESPITE crossing the finish line in first place an unmatched seven times, it's a disappointing "nil pwa" in this round for the multiple Tour de France winner. Following unfair doping allegations based on rigorous scientific analysis of blood samples, Lance has recently been stripped of his titles and his seven victories have been struck from the sporting records.

Score: 0

OH DEAR! Neil may have taken one small step for man on the Moon, but he was unable to take the giant leap he needed to win this competition, and gets brought back down to earth with a bump.

TOTAL 26

ON YOUR bike, son. Lance may have been King of the Mountains seven times, but sadly King of the Armstrongs is a title that will forever elude him as his bid to win falls as flat as one of his tyres.

TOTAL 18

Stretch
Elastic toy

A BAD start for Stretch, who rarely travelled anywhere except the short distance from the Argos shop to a child's house, and then a few months later from the house to the Oxfam shop, a total distance of perhaps 20 miles - equivalent to travelling 10 miles towards the Moon and back. However, as an inexplicably successful toy brand, Stretch Armstrongs were available in every country on the planet, making him the unexpected winner of this round.

Score: 7

THANKS to his limbs that could be drawn out to great lengths, one might expect Stretch to romp home the winner in this, his specialist round. However, the dictionary definition of ductile is "of a metal, capable of being drawn into a wire." Armstrong's admittedly stretchy limbs were made of silicone and polymers rather than metal and so were not technically ductile at all. Consequently, it's a big zero for the ductile-limbed action figure.

Score: 0

ALTHOUGH symmetrical, Stretch Armstrong is top heavy and has extremely small feet. Added to this, his non-Newtonian fluid-filled legs have no inherent rigidity, meaning he is unable to balance unaided for more than a couple of seconds at a time. However, the box he comes in has a flat, square base so it can be stacked on toy shop shelves, ironically making him the most stable of the three.

Score: 9

WITH HIS ripped physique, large jaw and invisible genitals, Stretch Armstrong looks like a prime candidate for steroid abuse. However, if you thought the flexible toy was full of exotic muscle-building chemicals and banned substances you'd be quite wrong, for squeaky-clean Stretch's rubber skin is actually filled with gelled corn syrup - a substance which athletes are allowed to consume perfectly legally.

Score: 2

TOUR DE FRANCE records only go back to 1905, when the race was won by French cyclist *Maurice-Francois Garin*. It's quite possible that Stretch Armstrong could have entered and won the competition on many occasions prior to that date; we will simply never know. In the absence of any evidence, it seems only fair to give him the benefit of the doubt, and he gets a middling score in this round.

Score: 9

HOORAH! Stretch pulls out to win by a short neck and two extremely long arms. When the historians of the future look back at the Chronicles of the Armstrongs, they'll see that Stretch went out on a limb to pull off the greatest victory of all time.

TOTAL 27

the REAL ALE TWATS

¡IVAN JELICAL

PRAISE JESUS!

EVANGELICAL CHURCH OF THE RISEN SAVIOUR OF THE HOLY VIRGIN SPIRIT OF THE IMMACULATE RESURRECTION

AS THE CIVIL WAR IN ZOBLAVIA RAGES ON, IT IS THE ORDINARY PEOPLE WHO PAY THE PRICE

HERE IN THIS VILLAGE ON THE ZOBLAVIAN BORDER, MEN, WOMEN AND CHILDREN ARE DYING OF HUNGER AND DISEASE

WITHOUT THE FOOD, WATER AND MEDICAL SUPPLIES WHICH THEY SO DESPERATELY NEED, THOUSANDS MORE CHILDREN LIKE THESE WILL CONTINUE TO DIE EVERY DAY...

GASP!

THOSE PEOPLE NEED PRACTICAL HELP RIGHT AWAY — AND AS CHRISTIANS, IT IS TIME FOR US TO **TAKE ACTION!**

WE MUST LOAD UP OUR VAN WITH ESSENTIAL SUPPLIES AND DRIVE OUT THERE IMMEDIATELY!

THOSE POOR BELEAGUERED PEOPLE OF ZOBLAVIA WILL BE OVERJOYED WHEN WE ARRIVE WITH A TRANSIT VAN FULL OF CHEAPLY-PRINTED BIBLES.

YES — IT WILL BE THE VERY THING THAT THEY NEED!

DO YOU THINK 250 BIBLES WILL BE ENOUGH?

HM! THE COUNTRY IS BEING DECIMATED BY STARVATION AND CHOLERA — WE'D BETTER TAKE 300 TO BE ON THE SAFE SIDE.

OK, WE'RE ALL LOADED UP...

ZOBLAVIA HERE WE COME!

OH NO! THE ENGINE WON'T START!

WHIRR-CLICK WHIRR-CLICK

THIS CALLS FOR IMMEDIATE ACTION!

LET US KNEEL AND PRAY...

OH LORD, IN YOUR BOUNTIFUL WISDOM, HEAL THIS VEHICLE THAT IT MAY WORK AGAIN...

THAT SOUNDED LIKE YOUR STARTER MOTOR GONE. COULD BE THE SOLENOID.

PLEASE! DO NOT INTERRUPT WHILE WE ARE AT PRAYER.

WE BESEECH THEE O LORD, HAVE MERCY ON THIS UNWORTHY VAN...

NO, HERE'S YOUR PROBLEM — LOOSE CONNECTIONS ON THE BATTERY TERMINALS. I CAN FIX THAT RIGHT AWAY...

...IN YOUR INFINITE BENEVOLENCE, BREATHE LIFE INTO THIS ENGINE, THAT WE MAY TRANSPORT THY GOSPEL OF HOPE TO THE HEATHEN...

THERE, THAT SHOULD DO THE TRICK! I'LL TRY THE IGNITION

THY WILL BE DONE, IN THE NAME OF THE FATHER, THE SON AND THE MICKIE MOST. AMEN.

VROOM VROOM!

THERE YOU GO!

HEAR THAT BRETHREN? THE LORD HAS HEALED OUR VAN!

HALLELUYAH! IT'S A MIRACLE!

PRAISE HIM!

NOW THEN, WHICH WAY IS IT TO ZOBLAVIA, DO YOU THINK?

DON'T BLOODY MENTION IT, THEN, UNGRATEFUL TWATS.

SCREET!

DO WE TURN LEFT OR RIGHT?

NEITHER! FOR DOES NOT PSALMS 27 VERSE 11 TELL US: "TEACH ME YOUR WAY, LORD. LEAD ME ON A STRAIGHT PATH"?

THEN LET US DRIVE STRAIGHT AHEAD, IN ACCORDANCE WITH HOLY SCRIPTURE.

VROOM! CRASH!

TINKLE!

WHAT A TERRIBLE ACCIDENT! THESE PEOPLE ARE SUFFERING FROM MULTIPLE BONE FRACTURES AND SEVERE FACIAL LACERATIONS!

GROAN!

I'M PHONING HELP RIGHT AWAY!

MOMENTS LATER

WOO-WOO-WOO! SCREECH!

OVER HERE! PLEASE HURRY!

DO NOT DESPAIR, BRETHREN AND SISTREN — FOR HELP IS AT HAND

CHRISTIAN EMERGENCY SERVICE

WE HAVE BROUGHT YOU BIBLES IN ABUNDANCE!

GASP! CROAK! BLEED!

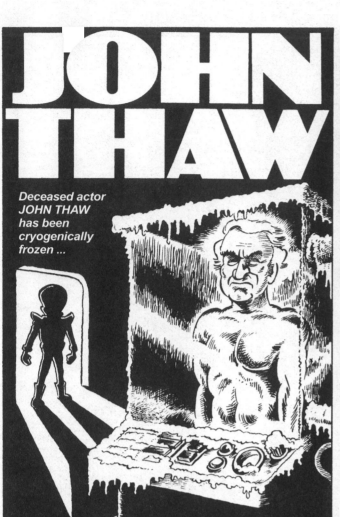

YOU'RE NICKED!

Shop-lift shame of our favourite stars

THE roster of stars who have been caught shop-lifting reads like a *Who's Who* of A-listers, including as it does **WINONA RIDER**, **LINDSAY LOHAN**, and many more who we are unable to name due to the laws of defamation. And now telly chef **ANTHONY WORRALL THOMPSON** has added his name to the roll-call of shame after being arrested for pinching a sandwich, a newspaper and three onions from his local supermarket.

Of course, only a tiny proportion of celebs ever get caught red-handed trying to secure a five finger discount. But what on earth drives stars to risk their hard-won reputations for a couple of batteries, a tin of salmon or a pot of discounted coleslaw?

In Worrall Thompson's case, could a combination of stresses in his personal life, business worries and the strain of flambéing Christmas puddings have pushed him over the edge, as he thinks? We may never know

the real reasons that the former *Ready Steady Cook* favourite succumbed to temptation at the self-service checkout, and it is utterly pointless to speculate when we are not in full possession of the facts.

So we asked former daytime TV shrink **DR RAJ PERSAUD** to speculate on our behalf. Just for fun, Dr Persaud has used his skill and judgement to prepare hypothetical case histories of a number of top stars, imagining what they might be caught stealing and explaining the underlying psychological causes of their fictitious kleptomania.

Of course, Dr Persaud would like us to make it clear that he is not for a moment suggesting that the celebrities named would ever shoplift. He assures us that in his professional opinion, in all likelihood they would not.

TROUBLE IN STORES: Stars could be driven to steal from shops, says Dr Persaud.

Case File No. 1

NAME... Professor Brian Cox

CRIME... *The suspect entered the newsagent's shop on the corner of Albany Road, Oldham at 8.35am. Inside, he asked the assistant for two ounces of Midget Gems, and while she was up the ladder getting the jar down, he was seen to help himself to two Twixes, a Lion Bar and three tubes of Fruit Polos, which he concealed in his anorak pockets.*

PSYCHIATRIC REPORT

THE SUBJECT is a successful scientist and high-profile television host and earns a salary in the high six figures. So what has caused him to steal a couple of pounds' worth of sweets?

To find out, we must go back to his childhood. It is quite likely that Cox was bullied at school due to his intelligence, possibly having his head forced into a urinal and being made to eat the pineapple disinfectant block.

It is also extremely likely that cruel wags in his class dubbed him "Sucker Cox" - a nickname that no doubt stayed with

him throughout university and his short-lived pop career as keyboardist with D:Ream, and almost certainly still continues to dog him during his working life at the CERN Large Hadron Collider in Switzerland.

This will have led him to harbour feelings of resentment against society, feelings that he now vents through stealing sweets from his local corner shop.

Also, as a particle physicist, Cox has repeatedly asserted his belief that atoms are made up mostly of empty space, and since the stolen items consist mainly of sweet atoms (and wrapper atoms), in his eyes they are made up of nothing and are therefore valueless.

Case File No. 4

NAME... John Sergeant

CRIME... *The suspect took a selection of expensive clothes, including shirts, coats, trousers and jumpers, into the changing rooms at a major London department store under the pretence of trying them on. He then proceeded to put on all the clothes and replace his own garments over the top, before attempting to leave and being collared by a security guard.*

PSYCHIATRIC REPORT

IF RETIRED BBC man Sergeant had spent years as a war correspondent, reporting from trouble spots around the world in a flak jacket and tin hat, his dishonest behaviour could be excused as a desire to reignite the adrenaline rush of danger he would have felt during his working life.

However, in actual fact, the closest the ex-chief political correspondent ever got to danger was the slight risk of tripping over his microphone cable whilst reporting from outside 10 Downing Street, so he cannot excuse his shocking theft attempt that way.

No, I believe that Sergeant

subconsciously feels that time has stolen his youth and beauty, leaving him with a face like a fried breakfast, and that by stealing these clothes he is in some way restoring the balance. Perhaps he feels that the theft will in some way harmonise the ying, yang, cheech and chong of his karma.

The danger is that, unless the *Strictly Come Dancing* favourite's dishonest behaviour is nipped in the bud soon, it will only get worse as he gets older and the ravages of time take an even more horrific toll on his features.

Case File No. 2

NAME... Ben Dover

CRIME... *The suspect was seen by a supermarket store detective placing a packet of six AA batteries, a bottle of Kia Ora and some Jaffa Cake Minis up his jumper, before attempting to leave the shop without paying.*

PSYCHIATRIC REPORT.................

DURING HIS twenty-year career as Britain's leading adult film star, Dover (charged under his real name of Gloria Honeyford) has had intimate relations with literally thousands of actresses.

In his films, women make themselves available to him at the drop of a hat; any kind of sexual activity (eg. ACDC, DP, DVDA, ESD or SBFC) is there for the asking. Dover has never had to try to get a "bird" between the sheets; in his mind women are just objects.

As far as he is concerned, there is no difference between six double-D women on a water-bed or six double-A batteries in a multi-pack; if he wants them, he simply takes them. However, while this may be okay when he's in front of the cameras on a porn set, it's definitely not acceptable behaviour in a supermarket.

Case File No. 3

NAME... The Krankies

CRIME... *The suspects were spotted acting suspiciously on CCTV at a service station in Fife. Whilst Ian paid for petrol, keeping the cashier occupied, his wife Janette was seen placing two sachets of car shampoo, a set of Allen keys and a headlamp bulb under her school cap.*

PSYCHIATRIC REPORT.................

THROUGHOUT THEIR entire show-biz career, the Krankies have continually pushed back boundaries and challenged accepted taboos. Before Boy George, Pete Burns and Marilyn Manson, Wee Jimmy was the original "gender bender", whilst his husband Ian defies convention every Christmas by "dragging up" as a pantomime dame and cavorting in front of a paying audience.

Not content with blurring the lines between the sexes, the Krankies recently shook polite society to its foundations when they came out as swingers, shocking their fans with lurid boasts about their steamy past. As far as they are concerned, stealing car accessories from a 24-hour garage is simply another one of society's taboos - ripe to be broken.

Hooked on the fandabidozi buzz of forbidden fruit, they are unable to resist temptation.

Sadly, they cannot be punished for their crime because Wee Jimmy is under the age of criminal responsibility, and were his hubby Ian to be imprisoned there would be nobody to get him ready for school in the morning.

Case File No. 5

NAME... Some woman off *TOWIE*

CRIME... *Some woman off TOWIE was spotted at a supermarket till, paying for several items. However, in the car park she was seen to remove a 4-pack of San Miguel lager, which had been concealed under a coat, from the bottom of her trolley. When challenged, she produced a receipt which showed that she had not paid for the lager.*

PSYCHIATRIC REPORT.................

A SUDDEN rise to fame of the sort experienced by some woman off *TOWIE* can have very strange effects on the mind, especially when it is coupled with low intelligence and a complete lack of talent.

Subconsciously, the subject feels undeserving of the fame that has been bestowed upon them, and has an irresistible urge to do something to justify their presence in the headlines, such as getting out of a taxi without no knickers on or, as in this case, being arrested for shoplifting.

TOWIE is a "dramality" show, in which the lines between fiction and reality are deliberately blurred. As a result, the subject is unable to distinguish between the real world, in which stealing is against the law, and the fictional soap opera world of Essex.

Case File No. 6

NAME... Madonna

CRIME... *The Like a Virgin singer was spotted acting suspiciously in the frozen desserts section of her local Iceland in Camden Town. She was taken into a back room by security staff and subjected to a search, whereupon she was found to have concealed two Cornettos inside a modified pointy-breasted basque.*

PSYCHIATRIC REPORT.................

AS SIGMUND Freud discovered, the cause of aberrant behaviour in an adult can always be traced back to childhood influences.

In this case, Madonna's up-bringing in a strict Catholic household, where ice-creams would have been looked upon as sinful, would undoubtedly lead to her crave them in later life.

Of course, she is a millionaire many times over and could easily afford to buy two Cornettos from Iceland, but by pinching them she is breaking one of the Ten Commandments by which she was raised - "Thou shalt not steal".

She is also a highly-sexed woman, and secreting the cold ice-creams in her bra will cause her nipples to harden with excitement. As her body warmth heats up the frozen treats, they will begin to melt, and cool rivulets of creamy white liquid will begin to trickle down between her pert breasts, heightening the guilty erotic charge of the theft even more.

In her fevered mind's eye, she will probably picture an authority figure - perhaps a priest or lawyer, but most likely a psychiatrist with glasses - punishing her for her crime by spanking her bare bottom before licking the melted ice-cream off her lithe body.

GILBERT RATCHET

I'M OFF TO THE ART GALLERY, READERS

ART GALLERY

THAT'S BECAUSE I'M A CULTURED SORT OF FELLOW, AND ALSO IT'S RAINING.

I'LL JUST STAND IN FRONT OF THIS PIECE OF MODERN ART

STROKE! STROKE!

RECLINING POPE

AND MY AUTOMATIC CHIN-STROKING DEVICE WILL GIVE THE IMPRESSION THAT I'VE GOT THE SLIGHTEST FUCKING NOTION WHAT IT'S SUPPOSED TO BE ABOUT.

SAY GILBERT, CAN I BORROW THAT GADGET FOR A MINUTE?

GOSH! IT'S BRIAN SEWELL!

I WANT TO IMPRESS THOSE HOT BABES, AND MAKE THEM THINK I'M ALL BRAINY AND KNOW ABOUT ART AND STUFF.

I'LL ADD AN EXTRA FEATURE TO MY CHIN-STROKER WHICH WILL IMPRESS THOSE GIRLS EVEN MORE

HMM... YE-E-ES HMM...

THIS TAPE PLAYER WILL EMIT INTELLIGENT "ART APPRECIATION" NOISES AS YOU CONTEMPLATE THE SCULPTURE.

NICE ONE, GILBERT!

STROKE! STROKE!

YES... HMM... HMM...

HMM YE-E-ES,

THOSE FOXY CHICKS WILL TOTALLY THINK THAT I UNDERSTAND ALL THIS SHIT

'SCUSE US, WE JUST NEED TO PUT THIS NUDE LADY PAINTING HERE

CLONK!

LOOK OUT - YOU'VE KNOCKED THE CHIN-STROKING ARM OUT OF ALIGNMENT!

CRIKEY! THE ART APPRECIATION NOISE MAKER HAS BEEN TURNED TO HIGH SPEED!

STROKE STROKE

MM! MM! MM! YES! YES! MM!

UGH! LOOK AT THIS BRUTE FIDDLING WITH HIMSELF IN FRONT OF A NUDE LADY PICTURE

STROKE STROKE STROKE

MM! MM! YES! YES!

HOW FRIGHTFULLY CRUDE AND UNSOPHISTICATED!

GURR! YOU'VE RUINED MY CHANCE OF IMPRESSING THOSE GIRLS!

OO-ER!

HERE'S WHAT I THINK OF YOUR STUPID MACHINE, GILBERT!

HURL!

TAKE THAT!

YIKES!

PROD!

WOW! MY CHIN-STROKER HAS GIVEN THAT MONA LISA A "THREE STOOGES" STYLE EYE-POKE!

GASP! WHAT HAVE YOU IDIOTS DONE TO OUR PRICELESS MONA LISA?

YOU'VE MADE HER LOOK ALL BOSS-EYED!

YOU'D BETTER GET THIS MASTERPIECE FIXED, OR YOU'LL BE PAYING FOR A NEW ONE

HER EYES ARE SUPPOSED TO FOLLOW YOU AROUND THE ROOM, NOT SQUINT AT HER OWN NOSE!

I'LL GET THE MONA LISA'S EYES TO FOLLOW YOU ROUND THE ROOM AGAIN.

ATLAS DOING HIS BACK IN WHILST ATTEMPTING TO LIFT THE GLOBE

FIRST I'LL REMOVE THE TESTICLES FROM THIS CAST IRON STATUE AND DRAW PUPILS ON THEM..

I'VE ATTACHED THE IRON "EYE-BALLS" TO THE MONA LISA'S FACE ON A PAIR OF SPRINGS

NOW I SIMPLY TIE THIS EXTRA POWERFUL MAGNET TO YOUR HAT - LIKE SO.

WHY, THAT'S AMAZING!

WHEREVER I STAND IN THE ROOM, THE PAINTING'S EYES SWIVEL ROUND TO LOOK STRAIGHT AT ME!

CRA-A-ACK

WELL DONE - YOU'VE RESTORED LEONARDO'S PAINTING TO ITS FORMER GLORY!

UH-OH! THAT POWERFUL MAGNET IS PULLING A STEEL GIRDER DOWN OUT OF THE CEILING!

CRASH

WAH!

YOW! THE WHOLE ROOF'S COME IN!

ARE YOU TWO RESPONSIBLE FOR THIS BIG PILE OF BRICKS AND RUBBLE?!

GULP! IT'S THE GALLERY OWNER - NOW WE'RE IN TROUBLE!

CONGRATULATIONS! IT'S THE FINEST EXAMPLE OF MODERN ART I'VE SEEN!

PLEASE ACCEPT THIS LAUREL WREATH AND SASH TO SIGNIFY YOUR ACCEPTANCE INTO THE ART WORLD

AND OOH BRIAN, FANCY YOU BEING A CELEBRATED ARTIST! YOU'RE SO CLEVER!

WAHEY! I'VE PULLED THESE BIRDS!

CHEERS GILBERT - TREAT YOURSELF TO A FIVER'S WORTH OF SWEETS

WHOOPEE! (SLURP!)

PIGEON FANCIER

"YAWN."

SHORTLY...

PECK!

PECK! PECK!

CRUNCH!

LATER...

RUB! RUB!!

COO COO

HOP!

CHOMP!

SHORTLY...

COO

CHOCS

CHOCS

SHORTLY AGAIN...
A&E

SIGH!

TAP! TAP! TAP!
MEET HOT PILFs IN YOUR AREA

86

88

"...OOH DEAR...WHERE AM I...? WHAT'S HAPPENED...?"

OI! THEM HANDS ARE SUPPOSED TO BE IN HER MOUTH, NOT HER MINNIE-MOO, YOU MUCKY PUP!

NITROUS OXIDE

OH, LORDY! IT'S... THE FAT SLAGS

SO WOT **IS** BODY MASS INDEX ANYROAD, TRAY?

IT'S THE PROPORTION OF FAT ON YER BODY IN RELATION T' YER HEIGHT. IT'S A MORE ACCURATE MEASURE OF IF YER OVERWEIGHT

OH, RIGHT.

ELECTRONIC SCALES

Y' TAKE YER WEIGHT, SEE, AN' Y' DIVIDE IT BY Y' HEIGHT SQUARED...

1.7m

AN' Y' SEE WOT THE ANSWER IS... BETWEEN 18 AN 25 IS NORMAL, 26-40 IS FAT, AN OVER 40 IS MILDLY OBESE

RIGHT, SO THAT'S YER WEIGHT... DIVIDE BY...1... POINT...7...SQUARED...

EQUALS...

TAP! TAP! TAP!

TAP! TAP! TAP!

WELL?

EEH!..IT SAYS Y BMI IS 43, SAN

43!?!...NO!...THAT CAN'T BE RIGHT!... **43!?!..**Y' MUST OF MADE A MISTAKE, TRAY.

OH, 'ANG ON... I SEE WOT I'VE DONE...I'VE PUT YER WEIGHT IN **STONES** INSTEAD OF KILOGRAMMES...

...LET'S 'AVE A LOOK, THEN...

272

THAT'S MORE LIKE IT

FANCY SOME CHIPS?

AYE!

MEET EDWARD, CONFESSO

RETIRED priest EDWARD KNACKERS spent a lifetime cocooned in the confessional, patiently listening to his parishioners as they unburdened themselves of their innermost secrets. But his church - St Fiacre's in London's Shepherd's Bush - was situated just a stone's throw from BBC Television Centre, and the guilty people who queued up to repent their mortal sins were often household names!

Confidential admissions of adultery, envy, theft and even murder... Father Knackers has heard them all straight from the lips of some of the biggest stars of stage and screen.

"When I became a priest I took an oath on the Holy Bible," Knackers told us. "I swore to uphold the sacred bond of trust between me and my parishioners. And for three decades, the sensational secrets vouchsafed to me by those penitent celebs were

IIIIIIIIIIIIIIIIIIIIIIIIIIIIIIIIIIIIIIIIIIIIIIIIIIIIII

strictly for God's ears only."

But now, following his retirement on the grounds of ill health, 63-year-old Edward is finally free to lift the lid on the secret sins of the household names who confided in him for more than thirty years. And in these exclusive extracts from his new memoir *In With the Sin Crowd* (Eggs-Benedict Books), he reveals the guilty confessions of a roll-call of famous faces that reads like an A-list of showbiz royalty.

THAT'S REPENTERTAINMENT: Father Knackers heard shocking confessions from showbiz A-listers.

Box was Last Resort for Ross

"Because of their hectic shooting schedules, television celebrities can often turn up to confess their transgressions at the oddest times of day. So I wasn't in the least bit surprised to see the familiar figure of **JONATHAN ROSS** making his way up the aisle one Friday, even though it was nearly midnight.

He expained he'd just been filming an episode of his top-rated BBC chat show, and he'd popped in to the church on his way home for a spot of sacramental absolution. I showed him to the booth, and he began to confess through the grille.

"Bless me Father Knackers, for I am guilty of the sin of Onanism," he told me. "I have been spilling my seed upon the ground and in a sock."

He went on to recount how he had become obsessed with the act of personal pollution, often onaning up to eight times a day or more. Self pleasure is a mortal sin, so I gave him the maximum penalty of three Hail Marys.

But instead of the contrite response I was expecting from the TV motormouth, all I could hear was the rustle of pages being turned, heavy breathing and what sounded like a small umbrella being put up and down very rapidly.

Puzzled, I peered through the confessional hatch to see what was going on. There was Ross with his trousers round his ankles, giving into fleshly temptation whilst eagerly leafing through a well-thumbed copy of Churns magazine. It seemed that even whilst in the confessional booth, the chat show king had been unable to control his base urges for long enough to receive the Lord's bountiful forgiveness.

Once he had shot his bolt, I confiscated the mucky book and doubled his fine to six Hail Marys. As I ex-

plained to him on the way out, the Lord takes a particularly dim view of celebrities wanking, especially when they do it on church property."

For the Glove of God

"Most confessions, steeped as they are in shame, guilt and remorse, are delivered in hushed whispers. As a priest, I often found myself having to push my ear right up against the grille in order to discern all the juicy details.

But one celebrity confessant was even quieter than most; 1970s glove puppet **SOOTY**, who arrived in my church on the arm of his long-

time friend and business partner Harry Corbett. As he stood outside the confessions box, Sooty leaned across and whispered into Corbett's ear. "What's that, Sooty? You want to absolve your mortal sins and beg the Lord God for forgiveness?" he said. Moments later the pair were settling down on the other side of the mesh and I was preparing to hear the fuzzy yellow bear's confession.

Pushing the kiddies' favourite puppet to his ear, Corbett repeated each of Sooty's shamefaced admissions through the grille. "What's that, Sooty? You want me to ask the priest to bless you father for you have sinned?" he said. "You've done what, Sooty? You've been having an affair with a married woman for the last twen-

THE ... OR!

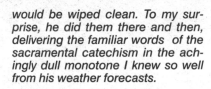

Celebrity priest spills beans on Beeb stars' guilty secrets

ty years? Eeh, you have been a naughty little bear, haven't you."

Then Corbett's tone changed and the colour drained from his face. "What's that, Sooty? You've been having regular sexual relations with who!?" he gasped. *"What's that? My wife?!"* The penitent cloth bear went on to confess - through Harry - how he had conducted a two-decade-long torrid affair with Mrs Ada Corbett right under her husband's nose.

Adultery is one of the worst mortal sins, so I immediately administered the Sacrament of Absolution and sentenced Sooty to whisper three Hail Marys into Harry's ear.

Corbett left that confessional a broken man, and only I knew why. For earlier that afternoon, he had been in church with his other puppet Sweep, who had confessed via a series of high-pitched squeaks to having a drunken one-night stand with Ada, as a consequence of which he believed himself to be the father of the couple's son Matthew."

Fish Out of Water

"Over the years I became quite blasé about famous faces turning up to confess their sins. Whether it was *BBC Breakfast*'s Bill Turnbull shamefacedly admitting to having impure thoughts about Susanna Reid, Sian Williams and Carol Kirkwood wrestling in some custard or Dick & Dom coming clean about coveting Ant & Dec's BAFTAs, it was all in a day's work at St Fiacre's.

So I wasn't at all surprised to see ITV weatherman **MICHAEL FISH** furtively making his way up the aisle. I guessed he was going to confess

feeling vainglorious after delivering a particularly accurate forecast of sunny weather in the west, turning to squally showers later. But the confession that came through the grille took me completely by surprise.

It turned out that Fish and several other high-profile weathermen had planned and carried out a violent, armed heist on a security van delivering wages to the ITV studios. Fish explained that none of them had needed the money - they had done it simply for the buzz and to break the monotony of talking about the weather all the time.

However, said Fish, the blag had gone badly wrong. A security guard had been coshed by John Kettley whilst raising the alarm and was now in a coma. Worse still, the gang's lookout Ian McCaskill had got caught in the crossfire and had taken a slug in the guts. The panicking weathermen had fled empty-handed and dumped their injured colleague outside St Pancras hospital.

Fish explained that he wasn't scared of the police. "We covered our tracks, alright," he told me. "And McCaskill won't sing. He's no rat." But what did frighten him was the wrath of God. He knew he had broken the Commandments against stealing, covetousness and taking the Lord's name in vain, and he was desperate for his sins to be forgiven so he could escape the eternal torment that he was certain awaited him in the afterlife.

I told him that if he said three Hail Marys, the slate

would be wiped clean. To my surprise, he did them there and then, delivering the familiar words of the sacramental catechism in the achingly dull monotone I knew so well from his weather forecasts.

As he was leaving, he asked if I would do him a favour. Reaching into his jacket pocket, he pulled out a revolver. "Could you get rid of this for me please, Father Knackers?" he said, wiping his fingerprints off the barrel with a handkerchief. I hid the gun under a pile of hymn books in the vestry until the next funeral I had to do, and then slipped it into the coffin."

Hot Under the Dog Collar

"You may think that listening to people confessing their sins all day might get a bit boring, but the job did have its perks. I remember this one time when curvy telly chef **NIGELLA LAWSON** came in to atone for the venial sin of gluttony. She explained that she'd crept down to the fridge in the early hours of the morning and helped herself to a selection of puddings out of the fridge.

As she described herself hungrily licking the cream off a big pie, plunging her hand into a moist trifle before coquettishly sucking her fingers clean one by one and sliding a banana in and out of her mouth, I felt the temperature in the confessions box start to rise.

Pretty soon, I was at boiling point. In fact, I had to pull my dog collar to one side to allow the steam to come out. I may have taken a sacred vow of celibacy, but I'm only flesh and blood. I'm ashamed to admit that listening to Nigella's husky voice describing these saucy goings on soon had me experiencing some impure thoughts of my own.

As soon as she had said her penance and left, I popped round to the other side of the grille to confess my own sinful behaviour to myself. Luckily, I was in a lenient mood that day, forgiving myself with just half a Hail Mary, suspended for two months."

Forgive us a Twirl

"One day I was relaxing in the confessions box, reading the paper when I heard unusually quick footsteps heading up the aisle. Peeking out of the door, I recognised dapper family entertainer **BRUCE FORSYTH** tap-dancing his way through the church.

"Good evening, Father Knackers. Nice to confess me, to confess me nice," he announced as I shook his hand. I'd always been a big Brucie fan, and I must say, the former Generation Game host was absolutely charming, merrily regaling me with anecdotes about his showbiz career and signing a hymn book for my neice. I told him how much I enjoyed Strictly Come Dancing and he promised to sort me out some tickets for the next series.

It's often a disappointment to meet your heroes in the flesh, but I have to say that Brucie was a real gent, with a twinkle in his eye and a smile for everyone.

Once inside the box, he confessed to keeping fifteen homeless women in a moth-infested pit in his basement. He said he'd starved them for two weeks before killing them and had then flayed their corpses to make himself a skin suit. I told him to say three Hail Marys.

And he was as good as his word. The *Strictly* tickets turned up in the post the very next day."

FATHER **KNACKERS** has only been free to share his showbiz confessional experiences since leaving the church in February. He told us: "I was sorry to say goodbye to my parish, but there had been a slight misunderstanding involving around 400 choirboys over a 30 year period."

"After discussing the matter with my Bishop, it was decided that I was ill and it would probably be best if I took early retirement," he added.

In With the Sin Crowd by Father Edward Knackers is available at all good bookshops, priced £1.99.

Letterbocks

Viz Comic, P.O. Box 841, Whitley Bay, NE26 9EQ • letters@viz.co.uk

STAR LETTER

SURELY 'fun size' Twix should be bigger than normal Twix? Based on this logic the less you eat of them the more fun it is. Come on Twix get your 'finger' out.

Fluff Freeman, e-mail

WHY doesn't Usain Bolt run marathons? If he can do 100m in 9.58 seconds he could do the whole thing in a little over an hour, which is about half the fastest ever marathon time. He's missing out on another potential world record here.

Matthew, Edinburgh

I JUST received an e-mail from Tesco telling me not to forget my dad on Father's day, 17th June. Well my dad died four years ago, and this thoughtless e-mail has brought the grief flooding back. No amount of money would compensate me for Tesco's heartless action, but perhaps £50 worth of vouchers to spend in their drinks section might go some way towards an apology. And double Clubpoints for a year would be nice.

Frampton Trimble Nottingham

SAY what you want about the Queen but watching this year's State Opening of Parliament, you've really got to give her some credit. I mean, how many heads of state could sit on a gold-plated throne, in a £1m hat a give a speech about austerity whilst keeping a straight face?

Paddy Milner, e-mail

I'M having a takeaway curry at the weekend. I never eat the little bag of warm greasy onions that they chuck in for free. If any *Viz* readers would like them, send me an SAE & I'll post them to you. If not I'll stick them in the *Friday Ad* or something.

Will West, e-mail

TELL you what, that Florence what's out of Florence & The Machine has a right gob on her. Jeez. Turn it down a bit love, some of us have got to get up for work in the morning.

Tim Rusling, e-mail

IS it a mere coincidence that the word 'nippy' (meaning 'a bit cold') sounds like it is derived from the word 'nipples', which just so happen to go hard when it is indeed a bit 'nippy'. I ask the questions that the governments don't want you to hear.

Anonymous, e-mail

HOW come when people claim to see ghosts they always see a grey lady or a headless coachman? It's never a clown or a trumpet player. Ghosts are so predictable.

Adam Hogarth, e-mail

MATURE CHEDDAR

DOES ANYONE MIND IF I PUT CLASSIC FM ON?

'DOCTOR heal thyself,' they say. My husband is a doctor and I wish he'd listen to this advice because he's had a cold for over 2 weeks now and his constant moaning about it is getting right on my tits.

Polly Evans, Colwyn Bay

WHY all the mystery surrounding the sinking of the Titanic? I saw the film and Yosser Hughes was driving the boat. An unemployable itinerant scouser behind the wheel was a bad call whichever way you look at it.

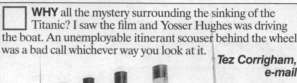

Tez Corrigham, e-mail

I HAVE never been a socialist and have no sypathy for The Jarrow Marchers or the striking miners of 1984-85. However, after watching an episode of Terry & June tonight, I am incensed that a hard working man can lose his job if his boss doesn't like his wife's casserole and is allergic to cats. I have since joined the Communist Party and will be moving to China as soon as my visa comes through.

TC Oregan, e-mail

WORKING for the Samaritans I hear tales of despair and anguish on a daily basis, and it can be quite depressing. But somtimes I get a housewife who calls to discuss her husband's strange, saucy bedroom requests, so it evens itself out in the end.

G Bennet, e-mail

I LOST the chance of a job because a shop-lifting conviction came up on my CRB check. It's alright for some though. How the fuck

did Nelson Mandela get a job as a president after all the bird he's done?

T Cardboard, e-mail

TOP

CLOWNS. Avoid embarrassing trips and falls by wearing shoes that fit instead of the usual, daft size 18 clowns' shoes.

Graham Hassall, e-mail

GIRLS. Mozzarella balls still in their packets make a great organic alternative to Silicone implants.

Dr Stuart Schneider, e-mail

CONVINCE strangers that you are from another planet by painting yourself green

Sting Declares War on Woodpeckers

LUTE-PLUCKING bellend *STING* yesterday declared war on woodpeckers, urging people around the world to shoot, poison or otherwise neck as many of the brightly-coloured birds as possible.

"Trees are the lungs of the planet," the environmentalist knob-end told reporters at a press conference on his private jet. "They breathe in greenhouse gases such as ozones and CFCs and they exhale pure carbon dioxide for us to breathe," he said.

"And I for one am not going to sit idly by whilst these woodpeckers eat all our trees," the pop arsehole said. "Quite simply, without trees, we will all die."

helicopters

He continued: "This may not be much of a deal for the average man in the street. But I have much more to lose than most, including seven enormous houses around the world, a fleet of high performance cars, helicopters and private jets."

"I'm not going to let some bark-chomping bird take it all my things away," he added.

Let's get rid of Yaffles, says Twat

But the chart-topping wankstain's comments angered bird lovers. RSPB Chariman Accrington Stanley hit back at Sting's claims that yaffles represented a threat to the world's tree stocks.

tumble driers

"Admittedly, an adult woodpecker eats five times its own bodyweight in wood every day," said Mr Stanley. "But you have to remember that they are made of feathers, so they don't weigh very much. This means that each woodpecker only eats its way through about two medium-sized trees during its life."

Sting in a crown, yesterday

"Sting should stick to singing or shut up. Preferably shut up," he added.

But the star, real name Donner Sumner, was last night unrepentant and said that his campaign was going full steam ahead. "I'm in the studio at the moment recording a charity single called *Kill the Woodpeckers*," he told us. "It's sung to the tune of *Feed the World*, but I'm having a bit of trouble fitting the word woodpecker into one note," he said.

"If anyone knows another word for woodpecker that's gone one syllable in it, could they get in touch," the tit-end added.

and continuously saying, "take me to your leader."

Sam Backhouse, e-mail

FOOTBALL fans. When thinking of accusing the referee of self-pleasuring, pause for a moment's self reflection to minimise the risk of any hypocrisy.

Stu Pot, e-mail

GREEN-fingered folk. Save money on expensive and pretty plants by painting weeds with old, unwanted tins of garish and bright-coloured paint.

Graham Hassall, e-mail

LADIES. Sick of men wanking into their webcams when you're looking for a date? Start doing it back to the dirty buggers and give them a taste of their own medicine.

Alya Bessex, e-mail

FOOL unattractive girls at nightclubs into thinking it's closing time by engaging them in conversation.

Ryan Collins, e-mail

LADIES. Prevent sexist workmen from shouting "get yer tits out" in the street, by having them permanently on display.

Pippa Rankin, e-mail

TV PRODUCERS. Why not start filming *Ready Steady Cook* a few hours earlier? That way the chefs won't have to rush so much at the end.

D Tennant, e-mail

SHOPLIFTERS. Walk backwards into shops so that if you get caught by store security, when the CCTV footage is rewound you can prove you had already left the shop before the crime was committed.

*A Shoplifter
HM Prison Bedford*

toptips@viz.co.uk

HOW about this for the shittest street party to celebrate Her Majesty's Golden Jubilee?
*Michael Robinson
e-mail*

AS I could hear my missus beginning her usual long weekly phone call to her mum, I decided to relax in a gentlemanly way on the computer upstairs. It then occurred to me that the filth I was viewing was simultanously travelling down the same pair of copper wires as their conversation about curtain material. Isn't technology amazing.

Stan Underpants, e-mail

DONALD Trump will never be taken seriously in the UK so long as he's named after a fart. And I'm afraid Vince Cable is sailing close to the wind too.

John Baird, e-mail

I THINK it's a disgrace that everyone on the BBC news who speaks in a foreign language is constantly talked over. Just because they only speak in German, Polish or Greek, the BBC think they have the right to interrupt them with someone speaking the so-called Queen's English. It's about time the fat cats looked into what our licence fee is being spent on.

C Moran, e-mail

TELL you what you don't see much of these days - politicians falling over on shingly beaches. No wonder the country's in the state it is. Come on MPs, get back to the beaches and go arse over tit. Let's make this nation great again.

Rob Hemsley, Rhyl

WATCHING *Saving Private Ryan* recently, it occurred to me that keeping the Germans guessing as to where the allied beach landings would be was a major factor in winning the war. Had Churchill and Roosevelt chosen Filey or perhaps Rhyl, the Germans would have been completely flummoxed and many lives would have been saved on that Longest of Days.

Terry Corrigan, e-mail

I WILL never understand my wife for as long as I live. She's deaf and I refuse to learn sign language.

A Hamster, e-mail

I THINK the next time David Cameron goes to Washington to meet President Obama he should forget all this NATO shit, world recession issues and Iran's nuclear development. They should just decide whether it is pronounced 'tomato' or 'tomayto.' This has dragged on long enough.

Mr T C, e-mail

HOW about a picture of some Chinamen pulling a massive pair of tits along the road on an ox-drawn cart?

John Highmore, e-mail

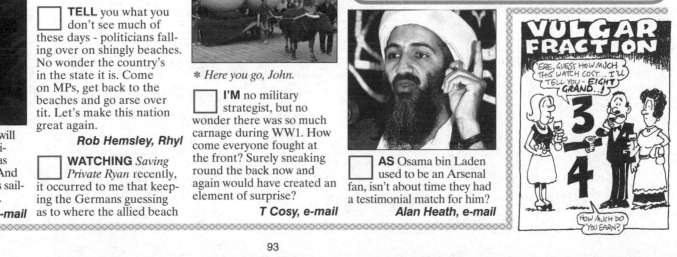

* Here you go, John.

I'M no military strategist, but no wonder there was so much carnage during WW1. How come everyone fought at the front? Surely sneaking round the back now and again would have created an element of surprise?

T Cosy, e-mail

WE ALL imagine what it would be like to be a 70s porn star with a 2-foot-long manhood. But if our dreams came true and we got the chance to be King Dong for 24 hours, what would we do? We asked the stars how they would spend their time if they were...

King Dong
for a day

Sting, *Pop Arsehole*
I'd use my 24-inch unit to raise awareness of the environmental issues affecting the planet. I'd write things like '*Save the Rainforests*' and '*Nuclear Power - No Thanks*' down the shaft so that when people saw my films, they would read the slogans as they watched it going in and out. Also, being an expert on tantric sex, my bongo ficks would last up to five hours before the pop shot, so I would have a long time to get my environmental messages across.

David Badiel, *Comedian*
It's well known that I suffer from insomnia. So if I was King Dong, I'd have a quick flick through my favourite jazz-mag *Anal Lust*. That way, I'd get a bone-on and go so light-headed that I would faint on the spot and get a lovely night's sleep.

Robin Askwith, *UK porn star*
I used to make saucy sex films where the viewer never saw my meat and two veg, just my arse going up and down between some bird's legs. If I were King Dong, I'd make a brand new film called *Confessions of a Driving Instructor With a Two Foot long Cock.* You still wouldn't get to see it, but my arse would go up and down six times further than in my previous films.

Rolf Harris, *Multi-talentless Aussie*
If I were King Dong for a day, I'd fit a shoe onto my bell end so as I could do my popular *Jake the Peg* act. Every time I needed to take a step, I would think of something sexy like ladies' knockers and my chopper would twitch forward one step. This would leave me both hands free to play the stylophone, shake a wobbleboard or paint an enormous shit picture.

Rowan Williams, *Archbishop of Canterbury*
I'm afraid having a 2-foot-long member for a day would make little difference to me as I already have one that long and it's been a curse to me all my life. At school, I was unable to do games in case I tripped over it, and at vicar college I was nicknamed '*Bellrope Williams*' and the other vicars used to put rude words to the hymns about my appendage.

AS Osama bin Laden used to be an Arsenal fan, isn't about time they had a testimonial match for him?

Alan Heath, e-mail

VULGAR FRACTION

'ERE, GUESS HOW MUCH THIS WATCH COST... I'LL TELL YOU - EIGHT GRAND..!

3/4

HOW MUCH DO YOU EARN?

ME FUCKIN' CHALFONTS!

HAVE YOU GOT ANYTHING CONCEALED IN YOUR UNDERPANTS, SIR..?

GRRRRR!

CALL YOUR DOG OFF! THEY'RE GOING TO EXPLODE!

!

SECURITY ALERT! SECURITY ALERT! UNDERPANT BOMB IN THE DEPARTURE LOUNGE! ALL UNITS! ALL UNITS!

AAARGH! AAARGH!

SHORTLY...

CONTROLLED EXPLOSION IN 5...4...3...2...1...

BOMB DISPOSAL UNIT

POLICE LINE DO NOT CROSS   NOT CROSS   POLICE

SPAWNY GET

IT'S MY LUCKY DAY, READERS... I'VE WON A TENNER ON A SCRATCHY

I'M OFF TO CASH IT IN...

ZOOB!

?

RAT'S COCKS! I'VE BEEN ABDUCTED BY ALIENS AND THEY'RE GOING TO PROBE MY ARSE. IT SEEMS LIKE MY LUCK HAS RAN OUT

BRACE YOURSELF, EARTHLING!

SHOVE!!

GAAA! ME JACKSIE!

WHILE WE WERE PROBING YOUR ARSE WE FOUND A MALIGNANT POLYP

OH, BOLLOCKS.

...WHICH WE REMOVED USING SPACE-AGE LASERS. YOU'RE COMPLETELY CURED

CHEERS... WELL I'LL BE OFF THEN.

NO! I'M AFRAID YOU CAN NEVER LEAVE... WE ARE TAKING YOU BACK TO OUR PLANET

GUARDS... SEIZE HIM!

YOU SEE, THE MALES ON PLANET BONGO ARE ALL IMPOTENT... WE NEED A HEALTHY MALE EARTHLING TO IMPREGNATE ALL THE FEMALES OF OUR PLANET

EURGH!

THE FEMALES OF OUR SPECIES DO NOT LOOK LIKE WE MALES... THEY LOOK EXACTLY LIKE YOUR EARTHLING WOMEN...

WOW!

DO NOT BE ALARMED...

...ONLY WITH BIGGER TITS

SO...

WAHAY!

*ME NEXT *THEN ME

READER'S VOICE

YOU SPAWNY GET!

CARDINAL MAURICE O'LOURDES the ARCHBISHOP of EDINBURGH

THE CARDINAL IS PREPARING FOR A PAPAL VISIT

I SHALL RETURN HERE IN ONE HOUR WITH THE HOLY FATHER.

IT'LL BE A BRAW HONOUR TAE HAVE THE POPE ROOND FER DINNER AT MA HUMBLE WEE ABODE!

NOW I SHOULD REMIND YOU THAT HIS HOLINESS CANNOT ABIDE *GAYNESS* OF ANY KIND.

I TRUST THERE WILL BE NO TALK OF "HOMOSEXUAL EQUALITY" AT THE DINNER TABLE TONIGHT.

CERTAINLY NAUGHT! AH'M NO' ONE OF THESE PANSY "LIBERAL" CLERGYMEN, YE KEN!

THE HOLY FATHER WILL NAE FIND A HINT O' GAYNESS IN *THIS* HOOSE!

WHY, AH'M EVEN HAVIN' THE TV TUNED IN TAE SKY SPORTS, SO WE CAN WATCH THE FOOTY WHILST WE EAT!

AND YE DINNAE GET MORE HETEROSAYKSHUL THAN THAT!

JINGS, AH'D BETTER GET CHANGED INTAE MA SUNDAY-BEST VESTMENTS!

THESE AWLD ROBES ARE TOO SHABBY FER DINNER WI' THE POPE!

OOH CARDINAL, I'M AFRAID YOUR BEST RED CASSOCK HAS FADED IN THE WASH. IT'S COME OUT PINK!

PINK?! AH CANNAE WEAR PINK! HIS HOLINESS WID THINK AH'M A RAVING JESSIE!

AH'LL JIST HAVE TAE QUICKLY GET MASELF A NEW CASSOCK!

IT'LL NEED TAE BE TAILOR-MADE SPECIALLY. WHERE'S MA PERSONAL ASSISTANT? PERKINS!

PERKINS, AH WANT YE TAE GET THE FINEST TAILORS IN THE TOON AND BRING THEM HERE IMMEDIATELY!

RIGHT AWAY YOUR EMINENCE!

CARDINAL, I CAN'T SEEM TO FIND SKY SPORTS, BUT I'VE FOUND THIS MOVIE CHANNEL...

Follow the yellow brick road...

OOH LOOK, IT'S "THE WIZARD OF OZ"!

SWITCH THAT OVER! WHIT'LL THE POPE SAY IF HE CATCHES US WATCHIN' THE WIZARD OF OZ?!

IT'S THE GAYEST FILM IN THE WORLD!

YOUR EMINENCE, I'VE BROUGHT YOU THE FINEST SAILORS IN TOWN, LIKE YOU ASKED!

EH?!

HM. I CAN'T SEEM TO CHANGE THE CHANNEL

I ASKED FER *TAILORS*, NOT *SAILORS*, YE CLOTH-EARED BARMPOT!

AH'M PREPARIN' A HETEROSAYKSHUL DINNER PARTY, NOT A TRIBUTE TAE THE MUSICALS O' BUSBY BERKELEY!

ABOUT THE DINNER, CARDINAL O'LOURDES. I'VE RUSTLED UP A NICE TRADITIONAL DISH FOR DESSERT...

...EXTRA-STICKY TOFFEE PUDDING!

OOH, I DIDN'T KNOW YOU WERE FRIENDLY WITH SAILOR-BOYS, CARDINAL!

LOOK OOT! YE'VE DROPPED THE PUDDEN IN MA LAP!

OCH, YE CLUMSY BESOM! NOO AH'LL HAVE TAE TRY AND CLEAN THIS STICKY TOFFEE OFF MA CASSOCK!

AND THE POPE IS DUE TAE ARRIVE ANY MOMENT!

HELP MA BOAB! WHIT ARE YE DAEIN' DOON THERE, MON?!

TRIP!

I'M STILL TRYING TO CHANGE THE TV CHANNEL, CARDINAL!

CRASH!

OOFYAH!

WID YE BELIEVE IT?!

THE EXTRA-STICKY TOFFEE HAS GLUED MA CASSOCK TAE YON SAILOR'S TROOSERS!

GRUNT! AH'LL JIST HAVE TAE UNSTICK MASELF BY JERKIN' BACK AND FORTH A FEW TIMES

UH! UH! A COUPLE MORE JERKS AN' AH'LL BE FREE...

MEANWHILE IN THE HALLWAY

CARDINAL O'LOURDES IS A STAUNCH DEFENDER OF TRADITIONAL CHRISTIAN FAMILY VALUES, YOUR HOLINESS.

JA, ZAT IS GUT. ZERE IS NOT ENOUGH TRADITIONAL VALUES IN ZE BRITISH CHURCH...

BRITAIN HAS ALLOWED ZIS WHOLE "GAY" BUSINESS TO GO TOO FAR!

EFFRYWHERE YOU LOOK ZERE IS GAYNESS — EVEN ON ZE TV SHOWS, LIKE "ARE YOU BEINK SERVED" VITH MR HUMPHRIES. DISGUSTING!

UH! UH! UH! AH'M FREE! AH'M FREE!

♪♪ we're off to see the wizard the wonderful wizard of Oz... ♪♪

CRIVVENS!

THIS IS NO' WHIT IT LOOKS LIKE, YER HOLINESS...

The Lives of the Saints

St. Ella of Artois

The Patron Saint of Strong Lager

IN THE Middle Ages a humble shepherd named Ella lived near Artois d'Aquitaine in northern France. The village was sorely afflicted by a terrible plague of boilers, pigs and hounds. The women were so ugly that the local men could not bring themselves to go courting with them. As a result, they were very sad, and their cods were like unto two tins of Fussell's milk.

ONE DAY, Ella went up into the hills to look for a sheep that had wandered from his flock. On a quiet pathway he came across a cask of strong lager that had fallen from the back of a passing tumbril cart. The day was hot and the shepherd was thirsty, so he stopped to quaff a pint of the beer. It tasted good and made him feel happy. *"Thank-you Lord for your bounteous gift of ale,"* he said.

REFRESHED and light of heart and head, he ventured forth into the town to seek company. In a tavern, he met a woman but was repulsed by her ugliness, for she did indeed have a face like a sack of spanners. But the Lord spake unto Ella, saying, *"Fear not. Trust in me and have another pint, for I move in mysterious ways my wonders to perform."*

ELLA DID as God had ordained, and as he drained his glass an amazing thing happened, for the woman no longer appeared quite as fugly as once she had, even though she still did look quite rough, to be fair. *"My God, thou hath wrought a wondrous change in this woman through the beer thou hast given me,"* he cried. *"Even though I still wouldn't touch her with Yours."*

BUT GOD bade the shepherd to keep drinking of the lager, and as he did, a miraculous transformation occurred. For the more he drank, the more attractive the woman became. Until yea, after the eighth or ninth pint, she was truly a stunner. Ella fell to his knees and raised his glass on high, crying out in a loud, slurred voice, saying *"Hallelujah, for I have pulled a gorgeous bit of muff."*

ELLA ENJOINED the woman to come back to his dwelling for a coffee and the rest, and lo, they knew each other like knives. After he had shot his bolt, the shepherd immediately fell into a deep sleep, waking only six times during the night to get up for a slash.

IN THE morning, Ella awoke and gazed upon the woman in his bed. But now she was no longer beautiful and once again had a face like a cow's arse. Even though his head was sorely vexed with a throbbing ague, Ella raised his voice unto the heavens, crying *"Christ Almighty. How did I manage to do that?"* And at that moment he knew it had truly been a miracle brought about by the beer.

EVERY Friday night in every town in Christendom, that incredible miracle of transubstantiation still occurs, when young men drink copious drafts of strong lager and cop off with Keira Knightley, only to wake up with Olive off *On the Buses* snoring away in their fart sack.

Next Week: St. Greavesie, Patron Saint of Football Pundits

Stick man North to take over Rail Franchise

VETERAN PORN star and money shot legend *Peter North* has expressed surprise and concern at the government's decision to award him the contract for operating and maintaining the West Coast mainline rail franchise.

North, 55, was not tipped as one of the front runners in the tender process, with the 15 thousand mile commute from Southern California touted as one of the main reasons.

balls

"Who the fuck is this? And what the fuck is the west coast mainline?" he asked reporters when told of the government's decision. "Listen, I'm in the middle of shooting here. I'm up to my goddam balls. Can you call back later?" he added.

After a 15 minute reverse-charge conversation, in which the details of the tender bid and operator's binding terms and conditions were explained in detail, the star of *Deep Throat This 20* and *The Sperminator* began to lose patience.

order

"Listen, I know nothing about running a goddam profitable rail franchise. My main experience is in having sex on camera for

Northern Line: Grumble star Peter set to take over rail franchise.

money and then delivering a voluminous money shot accompanied by a pleasurable groan," he said, before making an orgasmic noise and hanging up.

But despite North's concerns, the Transport Select Committee insist that the right choice has been made.

york times

"Mr North may not realise it but he ticks many of the boxes required in the tender approval process," said Transport secretary Justine Greening. "He is used to operating to a budget and he's certainly had a lot of experience on delivering on time," she quipped. "And he's got a big cock."

Pervert Jailed for Hamster Sex Act

Oddball: Drains and Hammond (inset)~terrified

A BERKSHIRE man was today sentenced to three years in a maximum security prison after being found guilty of pleasuring himself in what courts described as a *"sordid and dangerous manner."*

Oddball *Bartholomew Drains*, 41, was discovered naked and unconscious at his Windsor home last month, having inserted Richard 'The Hamster' Hammond into his rectum for a sexual thrill.

confused

Prosecution lawyer Shepton Vimgard QC told the court how on the afternoon in question, Drains had spotted Richard 'The Hamster' Hammond scurrying around outside the *Top Gear* studio in London. When no-one was looking, he gathered the bewildered 'Hamster' up in his hands and popped him into the glove compartment of his car. Once he'd driven home, Drains forced the terrified 'Hamster' into a heavily-lubricated condom and inserted him slowly up his anus.

grotesque

Vimgard added, *"For Drains, the feeling of a frightened and confused 'Hamster' scratching about blindly inside his rectal passage would have represented the height of sexual ecstasy."*

According to the prosecution, the 'Hamster's' horrifying ordeal lasted just over six hours. It was only after a physically exhausted Drains pulled the sodden prophylactic from the depths of his sphincter that the pint-sized petrolhead was able to breathe comfortably again.

A *Top Gear* source told reporters this afternoon: "Richard 'The Hamster' Hammond is delighted that this grotesque individual has been made to feel the full force of the law. He hopes this will serve as a warning for anyone else thinking of stuffing him up their arse in future."

99

OH NO! IT'S THE PATHETIC SHARKS

THE TIME: NOW! THE SITUATION: GRIM, AS AN ARCTIC RESEARCH VESSEL INVESTIGATES THE RAPIDLY CHANGING ENVIRONMENT...

THE ICE IN THE ARCTIC IS MELTING FASTER THAN SCIENTISTS HAD PREDICTED. ARILD HAALAND, YOU'RE IN CHARGE OF THIS RESEARCH TEAM,-IS THIS DUE TO GLOBAL WARMING?

OH YES. MOST DEFINITELY.

THE RAPID MELTING OF THE ICE IN THIS AREA IS UNPRECEDENTED BUT OUR RESEARCH INDICATES THAT IT IS ALL DOWN TO CLIMATE CHANGE AND...

WHO WANTED A SAUSAGE? SAUSAGES ARE READY!

ARE YOU SURE THE SAUSAGES ARE COOKED? I DON'T WANT THEM ALL PINK INSIDE LIKE THE LAST TIME!

OF COURSE THEY'RE COOKED! LOOK! THEY'RE DARK BROWN!

THAT DOESN'T MEAN THEY'RE COOKED ON THE INSIDE!

ER, DO YOU USUALLY FIND SHARKS IN THE ARCTIC?

IT'S VERY UNUSUAL! THEY TEND TO SWIM IN WARMER WATERS.

IT'S O.K! WE'VE GOT SOME OF THOSE PATIO HEATERS TO KEEP OUT THE CHILL!

YES, THEY MAKE THE ICE LOVELY AND WARM BUT THEY SINK WHEN IT MELTS!

HEY! STOP SPLASHING WITH YOUR BOAT! YOU'LL PUT MY BARBECUE OUT!

SOME PEOPLE HAVE NO CONSIDERATION FOR OTHERS!

ARE MY VEGGIE BURGERS DONE YET? I'M STARVING!

NOW LOOK WHAT'S HAPPENED! THE BARBIE IS RUINED! OH I'M SO FLIPPING MAD NOW, AND THAT'S SWEARING!

RUPERT IS LIKE GORDON RAMSEY WHEN HE'S VEXED!

I KNOW! TYPICAL TEMPREMENTAL CHEF!

WHAT ABOUT MY VEGGIE BURGERS?

JUST FOR THAT YOU CAN JOLLY WELL TAKE US TO THE NEAREST WILKINSONS SO WE CAN BUY ANOTHER BARBECUE KIT!

OH, I THINK I'VE PUT MY BACK OUT JUMPING ON BOARD LIKE THAT!

YOU'RE A MARTYR TO YOUR BACK, AREN'T YOU?

THIS IS INCREDIBLE! A SCHOOL OF SHARKS HAVE LEAPT ON BOARD THE SHIP! OUR LIVES COULD BE IN DEADLY DANGER!

I'VE BROUGHT ALONG THE REST OF MY BURGERS. CAN YOU COOK THEM FOR ME, MISTER?...

...BUT I DON'T WANT THEM COOKED NEXT TO THEIR SAUSAGES. I CAN'T STAND IT WHEN THEY GET ALL SAUSAGE JUICE ON THEM.

WHAT?!?! JUST GET OFF MY SHID!

OH IT'S LIKE THAT IS IT? I SUPPOSE WE'RE NOT GOOD ENOUGH TO BE SEEN ON THE DECK ARE WE?

IT'S JUST LIKE TITANIC! THEY WANT WORKING CLASS TO STAY DOWN BELOW!

ARE WE WORKING CLASS? HMM, I SUPPOSE SO, AS NONE OF US OWN A CAR!

BUT WE DID HAVE PATIO HEATERS, WHICH IS A BIT MIDDLE CLASS... ...BUT NO PATIO, ADMITTEDLY.

LOOK AT ME! LOOK AT ME! MY HEART WILL GO ON...

ME NEXT! ME NEXT!

GET OFF MY SHIP!

HANG ON, CAN ANYONE SMELL BURNING?

NOT ME, BUT THEN MY SINUSES ARE PLAYING UP AGAIN.

I ONLY WANTED TO COOK MY VEGGIE BURGERS!

I TOLD YOU TO LEAVE ALL THE COOKING TO ME! YOU'RE USELESS!

FIRE!!

DON'T PANIC! I CAN STEER A BOAT! I DID IT ON A Wii GAME ONCE. OR WAS THAT A PLANE? I FORGET.

CRASH!

SHORTLY...

YOU'D THINK THEY'D BE PLEASED THAT WE FOUND AN ICEBERG, CONSIDERING THE FUSS THEY MADE ABOUT THEM MELTING.

THE SPECIAL EFFECTS IN THE FILM WERE BETTER THAN THIS, WEREN'T THEY?

TCH. MY BURGERS ARE RUINED.

FELIX and his AMAZING UNDERPANTS

101

Yellow Lines ~ Don't Do It!

Just the ticket: Fistula adopts no-nonsense approach to traffic control.

NOBODY likes getting a parking ticket. Falling foul of a traffic warden is one of the petty annoyances that can drive even the most easy-going motorist to distraction. We might plead with them to give us the benefit of the doubt or beg them to grant us another chance; we may even try to slip them a fiver to look the other way. But would we go any further to escape getting a fixed penalty notice slapped on our windscreen?

Perhaps not. But the stars certainly would, and one man who has seen at first hand the lengths to which famous faces will go to dodge a parking ticket is London traffic warden **ALAN FISTULA**.

In more than thirty years at the frontline of parking enforcement in the nation's capital, Alan, 58, has put tickets under the wipers of countless Ferraris, Rollers and Bentleys belonging to an A-Z of showbiz royalty. And, he says, the celeb motorists he has encountered would do literally anything to avoid a fine!

In these exclusive extracts from his brand new autobiography, *A Park on the Wild Side* (Toasted Teacake Books, £8.99), Fistula lifts the lid on his extraordinary career as traffic warden to some of the best known stars of pop, stage and screen....

> There are many ways to fall foul of the 1995 London Metropolitan Parking Regulations Act (as amended). But to stay on the right side of the law, you simply have to use your common sense.

Sadly, common sense seems to be a quality lacking in the stars.

Chelsea

On one occasion, I recall seeing a Range Rover parked outside a gym in Chelsea. There was plenty of time left on the meter, but to my experienced eye, it looked like the rear bumper was possibly overhanging the end of the bay. That, of course, would be an offence, as the whole vehicle is required to be within the designated lines.

Fortunately, I always carry a large draughtsman's set square for just these occasions. I set it on the tarmac behind the car and slid it forwards until the vertical edge touched the bumper at its widest point. I was right. The

Street Life Secrets of Star Traffic Warden Alan

Range Rover was protruding beyond the regulation line by a full half inch. I took out my pad, licked the end of my biro and started writing out a ticket.

This is the part of the job I hate, but it's got to be done. Without rules and regulations, the city would descend into anarchy, with cars parked not quite within the limits of their sanctioned bays.

As I filled in the penalty code, I became aware of a woman standing next to me. It was none other than **MADONNA**, whom I immediately recognised thanks to the trademark pointy-titted basque she was wearing. The Range Rover was her car, and when I told her she was looking at a £60 fine (or £40 if she paid within seven days) she was none too happy.

hot cross

"When I saw you ticketing my car, I ran straight out to try and stop you," she explained in her familiar New York accent. *"I was in such a rush I never had the chance to take a shower."*

> ## "I was in such a rush I never had the chance to take a shower. How about I have one now, and you can watch"
>
> ~Madonna

"How about I go back in and have one now... and you can come in and watch," she said, fluttering her eyelashes seductively. *"Perhaps you could even soap my back for me."*

I'm a traffic warden of the world, and I knew what Madonna was offering. And the chance to rub soapy suds into the lithe body of the *Like a Virgin* singer is one for which most men would compromise their principles. But that yellow band round my hat stands for something, and I wasn't about to throw my integrity away for a few minutes of sordid, steamy sex with the world's most erotic star.

It wasn't the first time a beautiful woman had thrown herself at my mercy, and I'm sure it won't be the last. But I left Madonna in no doubt that it would have been more than my job was worth to ignore her parking misdemeanor. And the Material Girl looked True Blue as I slapped a ticket Into the Groove at the bottom of her windscreen.

Over the years, Alan's patrols have taken him to some pretty swanky areas of the capital. Indeed, it's not unusual to see him pounding the parking beat along streets where the price of the houses can run into tens of thousands of pounds. And it was along just such a thoroughfare in leafy Notting Hill that he spotted a shiny Aston Martin parked in front of a house.

> The car was neatly positioned four inches from the kerb, well within the designated

markings. Stuck to the windscreen was a resident's permit, which was valid for that borough and still had six months to run.

I walked on, but there was a nagging doubt at the back of my mind. Something wasn't right, but I just couldn't put my finger on it.

Then it hit me. The sticker was displayed on the nearside of the windscreen, not the offside as clearly specified in the council's terms and conditions. I reached for my pad and started writing out a fixed penalty notice FP34/B - for failure to correctly display a valid residential parking permit.

As I lifted the wiper and slipped the ticket underneath, I heard a man's voice. *"Excuse me. I've* got a permit,*"* he said. I turned to see the familiar figure of actor **HUGH GRANT**, star of *Four Weddings and a Funeral* and countless other films. I pointed out that the permit was stuck on the wrong side of his windscreen, and his face fell. It certainly didn't look like he loved actually the idea of being caught bang to rights in breach of the parking regulations.

current

Reaching into his chinos, he pulled out a huge wad of banknotes. *"Surely this ten grand says my permit is on the correct side..."* he said. Many other traffic control officers would have been tempted by the offer. But not me. I knew it would have been more than my job was worth to accept his bribe.

Grant's millions may be able to buy him anything he wants... big houses, fine wines, cheap blowjobs off prostitutes, anything. but there's one thing it will never be able to buy him. And that's my integrity as one of her majesty's traffic wardens. "

Parking crime is a 24-7 problem in Britain's cities. Such is Alan's dedication to the job that he often goes out on patrol at weekends, even though he isn't paid to. And he remembers one particular Sunday near St

Paul's Cathedral when he spotted a Morris Minor with the registration number ABC1 parked on a single yellow.

> It was a clear-cut case, so out came my ticket book. People often ask me if I enjoy giving out fixed penalty notices and I always tell them: It gives me no pleasure... *but it causes me no pain.*

As usually happens, the car's owner chose this moment to come scuttling up to plead for leniency. And who should it be but Archbishop of Canterbury **DR ROWAN WILLIAMS**, in his full clerical regalia complete with robes, crook and mitre!

He was confused and a little angry to be getting a ticket. He seemed to think that parking regulations didn't apply on Sundays and Bank Holidays. It's a common misconception, but ignorance is no defence in the eyes of the law.

For the avoidance of doubt, restrictions on stopping on an urban clearway are NOT suspended at weekends. Not for Archbishops. Not for anybody.

I'd seen Dr Williams on the telly, doing Royal weddings and pontificating about the Ten Commandments, so when he was caught red-handed, I expected him to confess and take his punishment like a man of the cloth. But there's something about getting a ticket that brings out the worst in people, and pretty soon the Archbishop showed his true colours.

extra-marital

He offered me a deal. If I tore up his ticket, he told me, he would have a word with *"the man upstairs"* and secure me a reserved place in the hereafter!

Continuing to write, I replied that it was more than my job was worth to accept any form of inducement ... and that included eternal life at God's right hand. This seemed to make him really cross. He'd tried the carrot approach and failed. Now he brought out the stick.

"Put that ticket on my windscreen and I'll make sure you

spend the rest of eternity in the infernal lake of fire," he raged.

"Is that what you want? Demons sticking red hot pitchforks up your arse and boiling you in a sea of burning excrement?" he added.

But I wasn't rising to the holy man's bait. I simply smiled and reminded him of the Eleventh Commandment: Thou shallt not park thine car on a single yellow line even on the Sabbath. 🙶

As a traffic warden, Alan could be deployed anywhere. One day he might be patrolling the pavements of Peckham, the next he could find himself stalking the streets of Stepney Green. So it came as no surprise when Alan's boss called him into his office one morning and told him he was booked on the next plane to Los Angeles, USA!

> A traffic warden in Beverly Hills had called in sick and I was needed to make sure no-one was parking in breach of the statutes on Sunset Strip, Laurel Canyon and Melrose Avenue.

A few hours later I was pounding the sidewalk along Hollywood Boulevard when I noticed

"Put that ticket on my windscreen and I'll make sure you spend the rest of eternity in the infernal lake of fire"
~Archbishop of Canterbury

a giant Hummer parked outside the MGM Studios lot. It was a big, heavy car and the driver had left one of the wheels touching the kerb, a clear breach of the LADOT regulations, which prohibit parking a vehicle in such a manner that it might obstruct free use of the street. I reached for my pad and started writing out a fixed penalty citation.

As I lifted the wiper and slipped the ticket underneath, I heard a familiar voice with a thick Austrian accent behind me: *"Excuse me. Is everything alright?"* I turned around to see the familiar muscle-bound figure of action movie star **ARNOLD SCHWARZENEGGER.** It seemed the Hummer was his, and he was none too happy to be facing a $40 fine for his careless parking. *"Is there a problem of some sort?"* he raved.

I'd come up against this sort of movie star arrogance before, back in the UK, so I tried to defuse the situation with a little good-natured humour.

"No problem for me, sunshine," I

smiled. "But I can't say the same for you."

I explained about his offence, and Arnie came over all innocent, apologising and offering to move the car so the wheel wasn't up on the pavement. But his weasel words cut no ice with me.

I pointed out that I had already filled his licence plate number in the box, and my dockets were sequentially numbered. I made it clear to Schwarzenegger that it would be more than my job was worth to screw that ticket up.

But the *Terminator 2* star seemed desperate to dodge the judgement day that was coming his way. *"Isn't there anything I can do to change your mind?"* he said. It was then that he tried to bribe me. There was nothing subtle about his approach; he just came right out with it and offered me the starring role in his next movie.

Mars

He outlined the plot; the film was set in the future and I was to play a renegade cop who was half-robot, sent to rescue a beautiful princess played by **Angelina Jolie**, who had been kidnapped and taken to Mars by mutant space pirates. The climactic scene was to be a huge battle where I would do lots of forward rolls and kill all the pirates with a special ray gun, before rescuing Jolie and blowing up Mars with a laser bomb.

I can't say part of me wasn't a little bit tempted. Who hasn't fantasised about being a hero on the silver screen? But, as I told him, I'm a traffic warden first and foremost, and as long as people continue to flout the rules, you'll find me out on the streets fighting the real baddies.

The look on Schwarzenegger's face when I said *Hasta la Vista* to his offer was a picture. In fact, I'd love to have taken a snap of it.

Pay & Dismay ~ car parks are easy pickings for Fistula with many drivers unaware of the minutiae of parking regulations.

But the camera I carry with me whilst on duty is for photographing badly-parked cars to provide evidence in the event of an owner disputing liability, and for that express purpose only. 🙶

Sadly, the traffic warden today has to be able to handle himself. Drivers can quickly turn nasty when they get a ticket they think they don't deserve. It's all too easy in the heat of the moment for tempers to flare and fists to fly. Alan remembers clearly one such occasion when he was putting a penalty notice on a Porsche parked near Wandsworth Common.

> There were still three minutes left on the meter, but I had a hunch no-one was going to turn up before the time ran out.

iron

After thirty years in the business, you get a gut feeling about these sorts of cases, a sixth sense. I made a start on filling in the ticket, and as it turned out, it was a good call; the car's owner came back just as the clock ticked into the red. As he hadn't actually touched his car at that moment, he was technically parked. The ticket stood. The job was a good 'un.

I recognised the owner immediately as cockney TV hard man **ROSS KEMP**, and he didn't look too impressed at my display of intuition.

True to his tough TV soap character, he didn't plead or attempt to bribe me. He just got straight down to it and offered me out there and then, mano a mano.

Pulling the ticket off his windscreen and holding it up in front of my face, he squared up to me, his bald head bristling with anger. *"You can take this and stick it up your effing arse,"* he screamed. Only he didn't say effing, he said fucking. I could read the signs; Kemp was looking for a dust-up.

No matter what the verbal provocation, I knew it would have been more than my job was worth to throw the first punch. However, the law does permit me to use reasonable force to defend myself.

Kemp drew back his fist. That was a big mistake; he may have joined the Paras for a frontline tour of duty in Afghanistan and come up against some of the World's most dangerous gangs, but the ex-*EastEnders* bruiser certainly met his match the day he picked a fight with the 1979 Hendon Parking Enforcement College boxing champ. He never knew what hit him.

I gave him the old one-two. After a jab to the solar plexus, a left hook to the jaw and good old-fashioned haymaker round the earhole, he was flat on his back on the pavement and out for the count. As I finished filling in his ticket, I was half-tempted to screw it into a ball and push it into his mouth, like in the films.

But that's not how it's done. Unless a ticket is placed under the driver's side windscreen wiper, it is not deemed to have been issued in accordance with the directives contained in the Civil Enforcement of Parking Contraventions (England) General Regulations 2007. 🙶

NEXT WEEK...

"How a Winnebago parked 9.8 metres from a junction (and not at least 10.0 metres as stated in the Highway code section 243(v)) nearly led to me having a six-up with **The Pussycat Dolls.***"*

...I CAN'T READ A BLOODY **THING** WITHOUT THEM... FULLY... SOMETHING OR OTHER...

WHERE ARE THEY?

HERE THEY ARE, ROGER

THANKS... OH, **NO**!.. THEY'RE MY **DRIVERS**... I NEED MY **READERS**...

I'VE HAD 'EM TODAY... WHERE THE **FUCK**..?

HERE THEY ARE

GREAT... RIGHT... THIS IS 'FULLY-LOADED CLIP' BY FIVE-NOUGHT CENT...

...NEVER HEARD OF THEM

YOU WANN' PROBLEM WIT ME? NO PROBLEM. IT'S ALL GOOD! I AIN'T FRESH OUT THE HOOD! I'M STILL IN THE HOOD!

THE CONTROLLER WOULD LIKE A WORD AFTER THE SHOW, ROGER

RIGHT-HO, TOM

SHORTLY...

ROGER!... NICE TO SEE YOU. COME IN... SIT DOWN

OKAY... LOOK, ROGER... I THINK WE BOTH KNOW IT'S TIME TO MAKE SOME CHANGES ON THE BREAKFAST SHOW...

YOU'RE TELLING **ME**!..

...THAT FUCKING POSSE IS NEXT TO **USELESS**! I TRIED TO GET THAT BIT GOING ABOUT THE COOKIE BEAR ON THE ANDY WILLIAMS SHOW AND THEY JUST LOOKED FUCKING **BLANK**!

NO, ROGER...

...IT'S **YOU**! YOU'RE SIMPLY NOT SPEAKING TO OUR TARGET DEMO-GRAPHIC OF 15-22 YEAR-OLDS

EH?

THEY DON'T KNOW WHAT YOU'RE TALKING ABOUT SOME OF THE TIME. WELL, **MOST** OF THE TIME, ACTUALLY. I'M BRINGING IN A NEW, YOUNGER PRESENTER FOR THE BREAKFAST SHOW...

I'VE ARRANGED A TRANSFER FOR YOU TO THE SUNDAY MORNING SLOT ON OUR SISTER STATION, **SENIOR F.M.**

SENIOR FUCKING F.M.? TELL ME YOU'RE JOKING

YOU'LL BE **GREAT**!

NO I **WON'T**! CHATTING ON TO A LOAD OF OLD FUCKING COFFIN DODGERS... **ME**?

WELL THE AUDIENCE **ARE** MORE MATURE, ROGER, BUT I THINK YOU'LL GO DOWN WELL

YOUR BLEND OF GENTLE REMINISCENCE AND NOSTALGIA FOR THE OLD DAYS IS JUST WHAT THE STATION NEEDS...

...AND YOU'LL BE IN **FULL CONTROL**

YOU'LL GET TO CHOSE THE RECORDS AND INVITE YOUR OWN GUESTS ON THE SHOW

NEXT SUNDAY...

WELL, THAT WAS 'I'LL REMEMBER YOU' BY FRANKIE IFIELD, AND I'M SURE WE ALL REMEMBER **HIM**! I RECALL SEEING HIM IN 1961 AT THE FULCHESTER PALAIS... SADLY NOW GONE TO MAKE WAY FOR A BRANCH OF **DALLAS CARPETS**...

...WHICH YOURS TRULY WILL BE OPENING TOMORROW...

...SO POP ALONG AT 2:00 AND SAY HELLO... PERHAPS BUY A COPY OF MY NEW BOOK...

...NOW A LITTLE SOMETHING FROM GLEN MILLER

HE'S DOING A **GREAT** JOB, ISN'T HE, TOM

YES. HE'S DONE WONDERS WITH THE FORMAT

AND HE HASN'T SWORN ONCE

WELL THAT WAS GLEN MILLER WITH 'STRING OF PEARLS'... A BEAUTIFUL TUNE...

...IT ALWAYS PUTS ME IN MIND OF THE FIRST PEARL NECKLACE I EVER GAVE TO MY WIFE...

...TONS OF THE STUFF, THERE WAS... WENT RIGHT UP HER CHIN AND EVERYTHING...

AH... HAPPY DAYS.

ANYWAY, IT'S TIME FOR "SUNDAY THOUGHT"... AND I'M PLEASED TO WELCOME A GOOD FRIEND OF MINE...

VICAR OF ST. BARDOLPHS, THE REV. PAUL WHICKER

THANK YOU, ROGER...

...NOW THESE DAYS PEOPLE OFTEN ASK ME MY POSITION ON WOMEN IN THE CHURCH...

...AND I ALWAYS ANSWER... REVERSE COWGIRL ACROSS THE ALTAR... WITH MY THUMB UP THEIR ARSE.

LETTERBOCKS

Viz Comic, PO Box 841, Whitley Bay, NE26 9EQ *letters@viz.co.uk*

ST★R LETTER

☐ **CAN I** just say, 'well done', to Prof. Stephen Hawking. It would be easy for him not bother his arse and just sponge, say, £250-a-week off the state. But instead, he has gone and found himself a job as a theoretical physicist. It makes me wonder if some of these other, so-called 'disableds', couldn't find jobs as professors if they tried a bit harder. Perhaps then we wouldn't find ourselves in the economical mess we're in.

C Lapperton, e-mail

☐ **DAVID** Bowie was born David Jones and only chose his zany name because he didn't want to get confused with the cheeky lead singer chap from The Monkees. Now that ex-Monkee Davey Jones is dead I, think its about time Mr. Bowie reverted to his original name. It's not as if it's going to affect his record sales at all. Also, someone else could then take the name David Bowie to avoid any further confusion.

Sparkley Mark, Adelaide

☐ **CAN** a zoologist please settle an argument for me? I maintain that anteaters who eat fire ants are doing the equivalent of us going out for a really hot curry, whilst my mate Growler claims that all ants taste the same, and none of them are any spicier than any others. Thanks in advance.

Orangeman, e-mail

* *Well, readers, are you a zoologist who has studied the dietary habits of anteaters?*

Perhaps you're an entomologist who has looked into the chemical composition of social insects. Or maybe you are someone whose elder brother made you eat ants. Write and let us know if any were spicier than others.

☐ **I UNDERSTAND** that the FIA is looking for ways of slowing down Formula 1 racing cars in order to improve safety. It strikes me that the best way would be for the drivers to leave their cars in the car park and walk around the track.

Alan Heath, e-mail

☐ **HOW** come prisoners always had to be hung or shot at dawn in the olden days? Would it have hurt to give them a bit of a lie in?

Terry Corrigan, e-mail

☐ **IN** response to his statement that anyone wearing a Pepsi T-shirt would not be allowed into an Olympic event, Lord Coe told the BBC that "Coca-Cola and other sponsors had spent huge sums on the London Games and their rights must be protected." Well done, Lord Coe. It's about time that members of our House of Lords stood up for these defenceless corporate giants.

Hector Rampton, Newcastle

☐ **AFTER** reading about the recent growth of erotic fiction for women, I decided to buy *Fifty Shades of Grey*. However, due to a mix-up at the check-out I inadvertently bought fifty copies of *Shades of Gray*, the ill-fated autobiography of Aston Villa striker-turned-misogynistic-pundit Andy Gray. I found it hard to get off to, but I got there in the end. Who says women can't enjoy a bit of titillation?

Janice Flagellant, e-mail

☐ **HOW** is it that the women of London can freely ride the tube reading badly-written pornography in the shape of 50 Shades of Grey, whilst I am roundly chastised and vilified on my trip to work for perusing the gentlemen's periodical Men Only? Fuck you, Germaine Greer. Not literally, of course.

Christopher Dickson, e-mail

Timmy Mallett's

IF YOU'RE in France and you need to knock a nail into a piece of wood, don't ask for a hammer. That's because the French word for hammer is "marteau".

HAMMER

IF YOU'RE in France and you're making a salad, don't ask for a tomato. That's because "trois marteaux" is French for three hammers.

IF YOU'RE in France and you want three hammers, don't ask for a tomato. That's because the French for tomato is "une tomate".

☐ **ON** my way to work I came across this bird poo that looks just like a bird. Have any other readers come across the waste product that looks like the animal that produced it? Not including snakes.

Jimmy Mallet, Sheffield

☐ **I MADE** an extra effort to celebrate the Queen's Jubilee earlier this month. My wife and I went into London on the Sunday and ended up on the Strand, standing 7-deep, shoulder to shoulder with thousands of people for about 2-hours waiting for her majesty to pass. It was pissing with rain, someone in front of us kept farting, you couldn't move for shit, and as I am fairly small I couldn't really see much anyway. However, when

the Queen's motorcade swept by us on the way back from St Pauls I stood on tip-toes and managed to catch a glimpse of what I think was her hat for about a millisecond. What a glorious day. I'll certainly be regaling my grandkids with this tale in the years to come. God Bless her!

Ben M, Rochester

☐ **IMAGINE** if Rod Hull's house was haunted. The horrific daily repetition of

It shouldn't happen to a VEST!

Singlet Bloopers from the Movies *with* Mark Commode

● **AT** the start of the climactic courtroom sequence in *Oliver Stone's* **JFK** (1991), *Kevin Costner's* character Jim Garrison can clearly be seen to be wearing a vest under his shirt. However, later in the same scene, he is seen from the back whilst wearing a jacket, and the vest isn't visible!

● **WHEN** *Bruce Willis* first takes his shirt off in the early scenes of **Die Hard** (1988), his character John McClane is wearing a clean white vest. However, by the end of the film, the same vest is clearly seen to be filthy.

● **IN Tarzan and the Leopard Woman** (1946), *Johnny Weissmuller* as Tarzan is clearly seen to be wearing a string vest during a fight with a crocodile. The actor habitually wore the garment to ward off chills between scenes, and apparently on this occasion forgot to take it off when the camera rolled. Nobody noticed the gaffe until the film's premiere, when it was too late to reshoot the sequence.

● **THROUGHOUT** the shooting of prehistoric blockbuster **1 Million Years BC** (1966), director *Don Chaffey* insisted on wearing a modern vest under his shirt ... despite the fact that the movie was set in caveman times, more than a million years before vests were invented!

THIS IS MASTERCHEF. COOKING DOESN'T GET ANY TOUGHER THAN THIS.

"COOKING DOESN'T GET TOUGHER THAN THIS." WHAT'S HE TALKING ABOUT? I'M ONLY MAKING A CANNELLONI.

RELEASE THE TIGERS!

FUCKING HELL!

TOP

GIRLS. Save spending money on expensive hair extensions by growing your hair longer.
Paul Tyler, e-mail

PREVENT your biscuits getting wet when dunking them in your tea by wrapping them individually in clingfilm.
Will West, e-mail

MOTORISTS. When stuck in a traffic jam on an uphill road, simply release you handbrake. This will allow your car to roll backwards, thus giving the impression that the car in front is moving forward. Hey presto! It'll feel like you're on your way!
Dan, Lincoln

DOLE cheats. Add credibility to your disability by popping an NHS aluminium walking stick in your golf bag.
Terence Blackfly, e-mail

AUTOMATIC drivers. Fool the driver behind into thinking you drive a manual by sitting forward and wiggling your left arm as traffic lights change to green.
Chris Sheehan, e-mail

SAVE money on expensive belts. Simply put on weight until your jeans stay up.
Fat John, e-mail

CREATE your very own *One Show* experience by selecting the 'Random Article' button on *Wikipedia*, then imagining someone who used to be on *Eastenders* reading it.
David Milner, e-mail

VICARS. Never attempt to do any odd jobs around the house whilst naked under a loose-fitting dressing gown, as you will invariably slip, something will go up your arse and they won't believe your explanation at A&E.
JF, Truro

BIG Issue sellers. Cross to the other side of the road so that when unsuspecting members of the public cross over to avoid you, you are already there.
Terry Corrigan, e-mail

GENTLEMEN. Take an old 12 inch ruler and cut a few inches off the end. Just before having sex with your wife, hold it against your cock and say "look at this". She will be impressed as your cock will appear to be larger by the number of inches you have cut off.
Darryl Darkly, e-mail

DR WHO fans. Want to know what the cost of shopping in the UK will be in 50 years time? Simply visit the supermarket at *Centre Parcs* for your very own Timelord consumer experience.
David Milner, e-mail

GENTLEMEN. Gain a little extra purchase when making love to your wife by applying gymnast's resin all over her.
Edmund Staveley, e-mail

VICARS. Fit your church out with digital bells, Mpeg organ music, a karaoke machine, bible apps and chip & pin instead of collections. Also get the Bible updated with some car chases and proper sex scenes. You have to upgrade to keep up with the times. Keep Christmas though, I love Santa and getting prezzies.
N Moist-Trousers, e-mail

PAINT pupils on your eyelids so you can have a kip at funerals without appearing inconsiderate to fellow mourners.
Tomb Bomb, e-mail

GIVE ants an alien abduction experience by shining a torch at them and sucking them up with a hoover.
Cal Brighton, e-mail

toptips@viz.co.uk

WITH not being allowed to enjoy a pint, a bacon butty or a flutter on the horses, it's easy to see why radical Islamists want to blow themselves up. However, why can't they go somewhere like the middle of Dartmoor to do it? They are very selfish and inconsiderate, exploding in public where other people are going about their daily business.
W Eckerslyke, e-mail

Rod's spirit trudging up onto his roof and then tumbling off again would drive the new occupants to distraction. I wonder if his ghost would have Emu and a rubber arm, or would his macabre apparition simply be stood there, miming holding the mischievous bird? The former would be hilarious; the latter, deeply pathetic. Perhaps other *Viz* readers could shed some light on this.
Ross Urmston, e-mail

* *Have YOU seen the ghost of Rod Hull? If so, did it have its head under its arm like normal ghosts, or was it holding an emu? Write to us at the usual address and let us know. Mark your envelope 'I've seen the ghost of Rod Hull.'*

HATS off to Johnny Rotten for not selling out to the establishment. I'm sure the people who made the Country Life television advert were appalled by the way he wore his cap at a jaunty angle and wouldn't wear it otherwise, refusing to bend to their capitalist will.
Terry Corrigan, e-mail

MAY I take this opportunity to commend Buckingham Palace for putting the Queen's diamonds on display to cheer us up during this bleak recession. It's great to see that during these times of increasing class divide, the royals are still in touch with the man on the street.
Ste Porter, Merseyside

ONE way to tackle rising sea levels would be to dig more canals and fill them with the excess water. The canals could be used to take the pressure off our busy roads, by people with less urgent journeys to make.
T O'Neil, e-mail

AFTER weeks of watching luscious, long-haired European beauties cheering on their husbands at Wimbledon, it's about time the world's top dart players did something about their wives. Until their heavy set, sovereigned-up companions are replaced by more glamorous young starlets, I for one, will not take this so-called sport seriously.
James Brown, Edinburgh

I BET the water companies regret imposing a hosepipe ban on us this spring. If all the water had of been wasted on our flowers then, come the rains, it would merely have all been replaced and there would be no flooding. Once again it takes Joe Public to state the bleeding obvious to the fat cats.
Howitt, e-mail

SO much for June 21st being the 'Longest Day'. I woke up on the couch at 3pm, had another couple of tins of Special Brew, and was passed out again before tea-time. These so-called experts don't know what they're talking about.
Craig Scott, e-mail

JOKE: GRADE-E

YOU'RE RUBBISH IN BED.

Depp Announces Separation from Paradis

Depp: Good looking, yesterday

JOHNNY DEPP has spoken for the first time about his separation from his partner of 14 years, French singer and actress *Vanessa Paradis*.

At a press conference yesterday the Tim Burton film actor gave his reasons for their split.

"When I met Vanessa she was still in her twenties and extremely fit-looking. However from about thirty onwards I noticed she was losing some of the sparkle in her eyes and generally looking rougher, especially in the mornings," he said.

"Now she's hitting forty and losing it fast. Her lips seem much less full and she's also getting crow's feet. If I wasn't married to her I doubt I'd give her a second glance."

"The other thing is that I'm still good looking as well as famous and I'd really like to take advantage of that and fuck some fit birds while I can."

Depp said he'd received criticism from some friends over his reasons for the break-up, with one even calling him 'superficial.' But he explained it wasn't only about the way she's starting to look.

"It's also a sexual thing. She hardly ever gives blow jobs and when she does she tends to go too fast with her mouth and she doesn't use her hands at all. It's a shame really because on a personal level I still quite like her."

Before meeting Paradis, Depp was with the supermodel Kate Moss but decided to end the relationship when he realised her tits were too small.

Depp said that he had explained the reasons for the break up to their children Jack (9) and Lily-Rose (12) and told them that they shouldn't blame their mother as it wasn't really her fault.

Depp's publicist has asked the public to respect his and Paradis' privacy and that of their children.

UNCOMFORTABLE HOLIDAYS

See the Wonders of Europe from a Cement Mixer!

ReadyMix Tours

14 Days ~ 14 Countries ~ from £499 per person!*

'Mix' with fellow tourists on a whistlestop journey around the sights of the continent in the revolving drum of a 15-ton cement lorry. See • The Eiffel Tower • The Leaning Tower of Pisa • The Parthenon • The Brandeburg Gate and many more, all while being revolved at 12-15rpm!

*Price does not include holiday medical insurance.

"I joined the tour at London Victoria and had broken my back by the time we reached the Blackwall Tunnel. I shall certainly be re-booking next year!"
Mrs F, Redditch

"Until you've glimpsed the Colosseum whilst being tumbled in the drum of a cement mixer along with 50 other sightseers, you simply can't appreciate its grandeur."
Mrs D, Wensleydale

"A holiday I shall never forget. I spent two weeks vomiting and the constant nausea has stayed with me for over 6 months now."
Mr T, Basildon

For further details see our website: www. readymixsightseeingtours.co.uk

ANKLE BREAK HIKES

This year why not hike the Canadian Rocky Mountains in completely unsuitable footwear

THE Canadian Rockies are the last great wilderness on earth. And what better way to see them than on foot in the wrong shoes. A two week trek stumbling about costs from as little as £599.

Choose from – Ice skates • Flip-flops • Heelies Fetish boots • Ballet points • Clown shoes

Prices include flights, transfers, tented accommodation, camp meals, plaster casts and crutches.

Guaranteed break or sprain or your MONEY BACK!

"We were driven to the trailhead where I put on a pair of Garry Glitter boots. I hadn't walked 100 yards when I went over and my ankle snapped like a twig" Mrs B, Essex

www.owmefuckingankle.co.uk

AFRICAN SACK DRAG SAFARIS

Spend a week getting dragged in a sack around the Masai Mara Game Reserve

Getting dragged around in a sack has never been so affordable. Prices from just £1296 for 7 days (including flights to Kenya, airport taxes, all transfers, sack behind Land Rover and 5 star accommodation).

There were elephants, lions, hippos, zebras and giraffes, all in their natural habitat. I saw none of them from inside my sack. The friction burns were excruciating. All-in-all, a magical experience I shall remember forever.
Mrs B, Essex

www.africansackdragsafaris.com

Bucking Bronco Treks

Enjoy the breathtaking landscape of Wales's Gower Peninsula whilst clinging desperately to the back of an angry horse. The holiday doesn't end until you fall off. We provide everything, from hats and chaps to distracting clowns hiding behind barrels.

7 nights on an unbroken Mustang from just £299.

"Yee-ha!" Mrs B, Essex

www.welshbroncotours.tv

Up until now, you have only dreamed of floating above the clouds locked in a fridge...

FRIDGE BALLOON TOURS

Hot Air Fridge Ballooning Tours make that dream come TRUE!

Soaring uncontrolably 9,000ft above hill and dale locked in a fridge at 5°c with some out-of-date meat products and lettuces on the turn is cheaper than you think. Call us today and ask for a brochure

"I was so terrified that I soiled myself. I have booked to go again next year."
Mrs Anus, Hull

"It's a balloon"
Mrs B, Essex

www.hotairfridgeballoons.org

MEDDLESOME RATBAG

JOHN the BAPTIST the JOHN

Palace on Jubilee Red Alert

BUCKINGHAM PALACE was put on high alert last night as fears grew that the Queen could come under attack during the run up to this year's Diamond Jubilee celebrations. But the sinister threat doesn't come from Al Qaida, the Taliban or foreign anarchists, but a source much closer to home ... *NITS!*

According to Home Office sources, intelligence services fear the hair-dwelling lice could be planning to infect her majesty's head within the next few weeks, potentially derailing the high profile royal celebrations marking the Queen's 60 years on the throne.

infestation

"There has been a lot of nit activity around central London in the past few weeks," said an MI5 spokesman. "Intelligence suggests that an attempted infestation within the palace could be imminent," he added.

And a royal louse invasion could spell disaster for Diamond Jubilee bosses, who privately fear foreign visitors could avoid the UK in their droves for fear of catching nits off the monarch during walkabouts or garden parties, costing the country untold billions in tourist revenue.

ruined

The pomp and ceremony of the patriotic landmark occasion could

"Real and present danger to Head of State" ~ MI5

Head Alert : Potentially nit-ridden common people outside Buckingahm Palace

also be ruined if members of the public spot the Queen...

- *SCRATCHING* her itchy scalp constantly on state occasions
- *GIVING* off the smell of Hedrin at banquets
- *TROOPING* the colour with all purple nit paint on her head

Louse of Windsor: Queen's barnet could be lifting with cooties for Coronation celebrations, fear big-wigs.

"I've waited sixty years for this party," Chelsea Pensioner William Buttons, 118, told us. "I purposely haven't died yet just so that I could attend my local Diamond Jubilee street party, and I don't want all my efforts to come to nothing simply because of a load of blooming dickies."

broke

Royal spokesman Sir Humphrey Cushion insisted that everything that could be done to prevent an attack was being done. "We have

the situation in hand," he told reporters. "All foreign ambassadors, heads of state and dignitaries are being checked for hair lice by a nit nurse at the Buckingham Palace gatehouse."

"Anyone found to be infected will be denied access and sent back to their embassies with a yellow note."

"In addition, all staff have had their heads shaved as a precaution and will remain hairless until the Jubilee celebrations are over," Sir Humphrey added.

skint

Meanwhile security around the Queen's London home was last night even tighter than usual. Anyone suspected of coming from a council estate was being prevented from approaching any closer to the palace than The Mall, and police marksmen had been authorised to use lethal force against anyone whose head they suspected of harbouring the tiny parasitic arthropods.

"Our instructions are to shoot first and check for nits later," a Scotland Yard spokesman told us.

'It' Girl... or 'Nit' Girl?

HEAD LICE are so small that they can barely be seen with the naked eye. Indeed, without going up to someone and sort of pulling their hair apart and looking at the roots, it can be hard to tell whether they've got them or not. So just for fun, using your skill and judgement, can **YOU** identify which of these female celebrities have got hair infested with scalp-dwelling ectoparasites?

Answers:
It Girls: A, B, D.
Nit Girls: C, E, F.
Nit girl F also has crabs.

A *Paris Hilton*

B *Nicola Ritchie*

C *Tarara Piranha Tompkinson*

D *Pyjama Beckwith*

E *Kin Kardaspitan*

F *Lindy Loham*

UNLUCKY FRANK

Daily News
PICKING 4-LEAF CLOVERS LINKED TO CANCER

THAT WAS A NICE HOT SHOWER!

NOW TO OPEN THE BATHROOM WINDOW AND LET THE STEAM OUT.

LOOK A THAT! A FREAK GUST OF WIND JUST BLEW A ROLLER SKATE AND A GIANT DILDO IN THROUGH THAT OPEN BATHROOM WINDOW!

SUDDEN GUST

DILDO AND ROLLER SKATE DELIVERIES

COULD CAUSE A NASTY ACCIDENT, COULD THAT.

GAH! I'VE JUST SKIDDED ON A ROLLER SKATE AND LANDED ON A GIANT DILDO!

SLIP
IMPALE!

HOW UNLUCKY IS THAT?

AT HOSPITAL ...HONESTLY, DOCTOR! I'D JUST GOT OUT OF THE SHOWER, AND FROM NOWHERE THIS ROLLER SKATE...

YES, YES, WE UNDERSTAND.

NOW, JUST ONE MORE TWIST AND WE SHOULD BE ABLE TO REMOVE THIS THING FROM YOUR BOTTOM.

SHORTLY OH GOD, THAT WAS SO HUMILIATING!

HOSPITAL

THEY DIDN'T BELIEVE THAT THE WHOLE THING WAS MERELY AN UNFORTUNATE MISHAP!

YONK! A LORRY HAS SHED ITS LOAD OF DILDOS AND ROLLER SKATES ALL OVER THE STREET!

I'M NOT GOING TO RISK WALKING THROUGH THAT LOT!

I'LL GO HOME ROUND THE BACK WAY, INSTEAD

ACME VACUUM CLEAN

FACTORY REAR ENTRANCE

NOW TO TEST THE SUCTION ON OUR NEW POWERFUL VACUUM CLEANER.

VROOM!
YOWP!
SHLOOP!

BACK AT THE HOSPITAL ...HONEST DOCTOR, I WAS JUST RUNNING PAST THE DOOR OF A VACUUM CLEANER FACTORY, WHEN...

OK NURSE, I'M GOING TO NEED A HACKSAW AND SOME VASELINE...

Finbarr Saunders & his DOUBLE ENTENDRES

SERGEI - THE TAX INSPECTOR'S HERE TO SEE YOU.

GOOD AFTERNOON, MR DURAKOV. IT'S JUST A ROUTINE VISIT.

DA. YOU ARE HERE FOR ANAL POKE..?

!
SPAG! SPAG!
BOL! BOL!
F-NOOT! F-NOOT!

I BEG YOUR PARDON...!?

ERM... HE MEANS DO YOU WANT TO TAKE YOUR "ANNUAL PEEK" AT HIS ACCOUNTS?

DA. SERGEI'S ENGLISH IS NOT TOO GOOD.

I SEE, WELL PERHAPS I COULD START WITH A LOOK AT YOUR RECIEPTS, INVOICES AND PETTY CASH..?

DA...

I HAVE BEEN SHAVING MY PENIS AND BALLS IN THE SPARE ROOM.

GROOB! GROOB!
FNARR! FNARR!
WOFF! WOFF!

HE'S BEEN "SHOVING HIS PENNIES AND BILLS" IN THE SPARE ROOM. THAT'S WHERE HE KEEPS ALL HIS FINANCIAL RECORDS, YOU SEE...

?

OKAY. WELL CAN WE TAKE A LOOK AT THOSE, THEN, MR DURAKOV..?

DA. FOLLOW ME.

...NOW IT IS TIME FOR SERGEI TO GIVE YOU YOUR ANNUAL PEEK...

...RIGHT UP THE SHUTTER.

111

BUYING A NEWSPAPER (AT THE) RAILWAY STATION

BLIDDIP!

Magazines

Please Pay Here

JUST THE PAPER, PLEASE. I'M IN A BIT OF A HURRY TO CATCH MY...

DO YOU WANT A BIG BAR OF CHOCOLATE FOR A POUND?

ERM... NO THANKS.

I'M DIABETIC.

THEY'RE USUALLY TWO NINETY-NINE.

ERM... ALRIGHT THEN. I'LL TAKE ONE.

WE'VE GOT THEM ON SPECIAL OFFER. BUY ONE GET ONE FREE.

OH... RIGHT.

...AND IF YOU BUY TWO BARS OF CHOCOLATE, YOU CAN HAVE A BOTTLE OF SPRING WATER FOR A POUND...

NO. I DON'T REALLY...

OR IT'S THREE FOR FIFTY PEE.

THREE FOR FIFTY PEE? WELL, THAT DOES SOUND LIKE A GOOD DEAL, I MUST SAY.

FILL IN THIS VOUCHER AND YOU CAN CLAIM ANOTHER THREE BOTTLES FOR FREE!

WHAT'S TODAY'S DATE AGAIN..?

SIXTEENTH.

THERE YOU GO. LOOK... I'M IN A BIT OF A RUSH, ONLY MY TRAIN...

YOU'VE NOT PUT YOUR MOBILE NUMBER ON HERE...

JUST HERE, LOOK... IT'S IN RED, SEE..?

OH RIGHT...

ERM... HANG ON...

NOW... HOW DO YOU FIND OUT YOUR OWN NUMBER..?

AH, HERE WE ARE.

RIGHT-THAT'LL BE TWO POUND TWENTY...

HERE YOU ARE.

DO YOU HAVE A LOYALTY CARD?

NO.

DO YOU WANT ONE?

NOT REALLY...

YOU GET A FREE GIFT... WORTH £34.99 JUST FOR APPLYING.

£34.99?

NO, NO. I CAN'T. IF I DON'T GO NOW I'LL MISS MY...

IT ONLY TAKES A MINUTE TO APPLY.

YOU CAN FILL IN THE FORM WHILE I GET YOUR FREE GIFT...

SIXTEENTH.

TA.

RIGHT, THIS IS YOUR LOYALTY CARD. I'LL JUST SWIPE IT TO ACTIVATE IT FOR YOU.

BLOOP!

NO. IT DOESN'T WANT IT.

BLOOP! BLOOP!

BLOOP! BLOOP! BLOOP!

TCH

I'LL JUST TRY IT IN THE OTHER TILL...

NO.! LOOK, IT REALLY DOESN'T MATTER. I'M GOING TO MISS MY TRAIN.

DON'T FORGET YOUR FREE GIFT.

HEE-HAW!

TERRY FUCKWITT

THE UNINTELLIGENT CARTOON CHARACTER

OOH! I MUST PUT BBC2 ON — IT'S TIME FOR UNIVERSITY CHALLENGE WITH JEREMY PAXMAN!

IT'S MY ABSOLUTE FAVOURITE PROGRAMME

I NEVER MISS UNIVERSITY CHALLENGE — IT BRINGS BACK SUCH MEMORIES OF MY DAYS AS AN UNDERGRADUATE AT OXFORD. OH, OXFORD...

CLICK!

.. THE DREAMING SPIRES... THOSE CAREFREE AFTERNOONS IN A PUNT READING A BOOK OF POETRY STAINED WITH THE BUTTERDRIPS FROM CRUMPETS...

YOU WON'T GET BBC2 ON THERE TERRY. THAT'S THE MICROWAVE OVEN.

FUCK ME, SO IT IS!

HMMMMM

AND WHAT'S ALL THIS ARSEWASH ABOUT YOU HAVING BEEN TO OXFORD UNIVERSITY?

YOU NEVER WENT TO ANY UNIVERSITY, SON. YOU WERE EXPELLED FROM SCHOOL AT THE AGE OF SIX FOR BEING A HOPELESS CASE. REMEMBER?

THIS IS TO CERTIFY TERRY FUCKWITT has achieved the level of COMPLETE WASTE OF FUCKING SPACE

OH.. THAT'S RIGHT

HERE'S THE CERTIFICATE THE HEADMASTER PRESENTED TO YOU ON YOUR FINAL DAY.

YOU HAVE NO ACADEMIC QUALIFICATIONS, AND ZERO PROSPECTS OF EVER GETTING A JOB.

WHICH REMINDS ME. IT'S TIME FOR YOU TO GO TO THE JOB CENTRE AND SIGN ON FOR YOUR DOLE.

BUT CHEER UP, TERRY! YOU'RE TWENTY YEARS OLD!

ASSUMING YOU LIVE TO BE SEVENTY, YOU'LL ONLY HAVE TO GO AND SIGN ON ANOTHER 1,300 TIMES BEFORE YOU DIE!

BUGGER ME! I HATE GOING TO THE JOB CENTRE.

FULCHESTER JOB CENTRE

THEY ALWAYS TREAT ME LIKE I'M A COMPLETELY USELESS SHIT-FOR-BRAINS.

GOOD NEWS, MR FUCKWITT! WE HAVE REVIEWED YOUR BENEFIT CLAIM, AND FROM NOW ON YOU WILL BE RECEIVING THE REDUCED RATE OF ONE PENCE PER WEEK!

RIGHT! ERM...THAT'S GOOD, IS IT?

OF COURSE IT IS! YOU SEE, YOU'RE SUCH A DENSE CUNT THAT US GIVING YOU ONE PENCE A WEEK WILL **STILL** MEAN THAT YOU'LL HAVE MORE MONEY THAN SENSE!

SOUNDS GOOD TO ME!

I'D BETTER PUT MY PENNY IN THE BANK FOR SAFEKEEPING.

FULCHWEST BANK

I WOULDN'T WANT TO FRITTER IT AWAY FOOLISHLY!

I'D LIKE TO DEPOSIT THIS ONE PEE IN MY ACCOUNT, PLEASE

CASHIER CASHIER

CERTAINLY TERRY! ACTUALLY, WHILE YOU'RE HERE, PERHAPS YOU COULD DO ME A SMALL FAVOUR..?

I JUST NEED TO NIP OFF TO THE TOILET AND HAVE A WEE.

CASHIER CASHIER

I WONDER IF YOU COULD SIT HERE IN MY SEAT AND KEEP AN EYE ON THINGS IN THE BANK WHILE I'M GONE?

THAT'S RIGHT. JUST STAY THERE AND **DON'T TOUCH ANYTHING.**

I'LL BE BACK IN A COUPLE OF MINUTES.

EEH! FANCY ME BEING LEFT IN CHARGE OF A BANK!

IT'S A BIG RESPONSIBILITY FOR A THICK TWAT LIKE ME

HM! I WONDER WHAT WOULD HAPPEN IF I PRESSED **THIS** BUTTON ON THE COMPUTER KEYBOARD...

INVESTMENTS

MOMENTS LATER

WHAT FUCKWITT IS RESPONSIBLE FOR PLUNGING THIS BANK INTO FINANCIAL RUIN AND SENDING THE COUNTRY INTO ANOTHER DOUBLE-DIP RECESSION?

BANK MANAGER

FULCHWEST BANK

OOPS! HEY, WHAT AM I LIKE?

YOU'RE A HOPELESSLY INCOMPETANT IGNORAMUS! TAKE THIS TEN MILLION POUND BONUS AND GET OUT OF MY SIGHT!

£10 MILLION

BUGGER MY BOOTS! I'M RICH!

LATER

WELL, I FINALLY GOT TO REALISE MY DREAM READERS.

I USED THAT MONEY TO SET UP AND FUND MY OWN PRIVATE UNIVERSITY COLLEGE IN OXFORD!

YOUR STARTER FOR TEN! WHICH PART OF THE HUMAN BODY HAS TWO FAT HAIRY CHEEKS AND A HOLE IN THE MIDDLE WHERE ALL FARTS AND TURDS COME OUT?

UNIVERSITY CHALLENGE

FUCKWITT DIMBULB ARSEBRAIN DULLARD

PIGSHIT COLLEGE OXFORD

BZZZZZZZT!

PIGSHIT COLLEGE, FUCKWITT

ERM...ERM... IS IT THE ELBOW?

WHILST TRAVELLING TO A SYNOD IN THE CONGO, ARCHBISHOP OF CANTERBURY ROWAN WILLIAMS'S SINGLE-SEATER CESSNA PLANE CRASHES INTO DENSE JUNGLE. RESCUED FROM THE WRECKAGE AND NURSED BACK TO HEALTH BY A FLANGE OF KINDLY MOUNTAIN GORILLAS, HIS WISDOM, HIS PIOUSNESS AND THEOLOGICAL KNOWLEDGE SEE HIM RISE TO BECOME LEADER OF THE TROOP. NOW, ESCHEWING CIVILIZATION AND TENDING TO THE SPIRITUAL NEEDS OF THE BEASTS OF THE EQUATORIAL RAIN FOREST, HE IS PRIMATE OF THE PRIMATES. DR ROWAN WILLIAMS IS...

ARCHBISHOP OF THE APES

IT WAS SUNDAY MORNING, AND DR ROWAN WILLIAMS WAS ON HIS WAY TO HIS JUNGLE CATHEDRAL TO CONDUCT A SERVICE OF THANKSGIVING FOR ALL SAINTS' DAY.

HAAAA-EE-AA-EE-AA-EE-AA

...OOO LE-LU-EE-UU-EE-UU-YAAAH!

RIGHT ON TIME, THE ARCHBISHOP MADE HIS WAY TO THE PULPIT, READY TO BEGIN HIS SERMON.

I'D LIKE TO WELCOME YOU ALL TO ST MARTIN'S-IN-THE-JUNGLE. HOW LOVELY TO SEE SUCH A FULL CONGREGATION JOINING US HERE THIS FINE NOVEMBER MORNING FOR THIS VERY SPECIAL SERVICE OF THANKSGIVING.

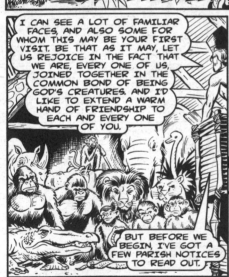

I CAN SEE A LOT OF FAMILIAR FACES, AND ALSO SOME FOR WHOM THIS MAY BE YOUR FIRST VISIT. BE THAT AS IT MAY, LET US REJOICE IN THE FACT THAT WE ARE, EVERY ONE OF US, JOINED TOGETHER IN THE COMMON BOND OF BEING GOD'S CREATURES. AND I'D LIKE TO EXTEND A WARM HAND OF FRIENDSHIP TO EACH AND EVERY ONE OF YOU.

BUT BEFORE WE BEGIN, I'VE GOT A FEW PARISH NOTICES TO READ OUT.

THE YOUNG BABOON MOTHERS' COFFEE MORNING ON TUESDAY HAS BEEN MOVED TO THE LARGE IROKO TREE BY THE WATER HOLE, AS THE USUAL VENUE OF THE ESCARPMENT MAHOGANY TREE HAS BEEN DOUBLE BOOKED.

THERE WILL BE A JUMBLE SALE - OR SHOULD I SAY "JUNGLE SALE" - IN AID OF THE OLD RHINOCEROSES' HOME ON THURSDAY AFTERNOON IN THE CLEARING. AND FINALLY, IF ANYONE IS ABLE TO SPARE JUST A COUPLE OF HOURS A WEEK, I'M LOOKING FOR VOLUNTEERS TO CUT THE GRASS IN THE ELEPHANT'S GRAVEYARD.

AND NOW WE SHALL JOIN TOGETHER IN A PRAYER OF THANKS. OH LORD, WE THANK YOU FOR YOUR PRECIOUS GIFTS OF COCONUTS, MANGO AND BANANAS. WE THANK YOU FOR THE BOUNTEOUS JUNGLE AND THE MYSTERY OF YOUR CREATION. WE THANK YOU FOR THE LOVE THAT YOU HAVE FORSAKEN UNTO US. WE THANK YOU FOR...

SUDDENLY.

OOH-OOH-OOH-AAH! OOH-OOH-OOH-AAH!

BLIMBO - CHIEF OF THE GORILLAS! WHAT'S THE MATTER?

DURING HIS YEARS IN THE JUNGLE, DR WILLIAMS HAD LEARNED THE LANGUAGES OF ALL THE ANIMALS AND COULD CONVERSE WITH THEM FLUENTLY.

OOH-OOH-OOH-AAH! OOH-OOH-OOH-AAH!

WHAT'S THAT YOU SAY? BAD MEN WITH MACHINES? BAD MEN COME TO DESTROY JUNGLE?

OOH-OOH-OOH-AAH! OOH-OOH-OOH-AAH!

SHOW ME! UNGAWA! UNGAWA!

ARCHBISHOP OF THE APES DR ROWAN WILLIAMS FOLLOWED THE AGITATED GORILLA TO THE EDGE OF THE RAVINE.

OH NO, BLIMBO! LOGGERS!

I HAVE SEEN THIS BEFORE.

RUMBLE!

BUZZZZ

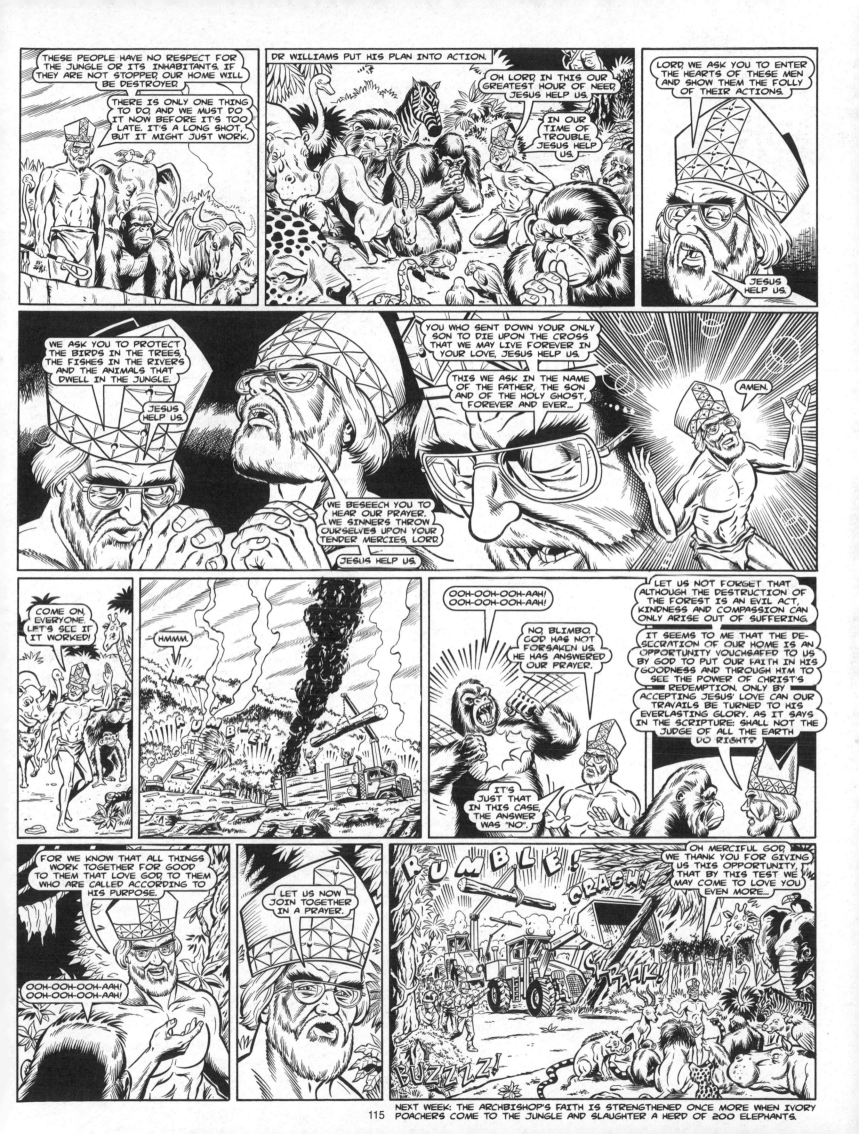

NEXT WEEK: THE ARCHBISHOP'S FAITH IS STRENGTHENED ONCE MORE WHEN IVORY POACHERS COME TO THE JUNGLE AND SLAUGHTER A HERD OF 200 ELEPHANTS.

It's Britain's LIVELIEST duck forum EVER!

Gaw! Love a DUCK!

with duck lover *Courtney Love*

" *Hi readers, Courtney Love here. You may know me best from being married to Kurt Cobain off Nirvana and being out of the pop group Hole. But whilst I've still got a 'Hole' lot of love for my late husband who shot himself, what I'm really crazy about is Ducks! I'm absolutely 'quackers' about these webbed-footed, yellow-beaked aquatic birds. And 'waddle' you know - it looks like Viz readers are mad about them as well, if the size of my postbag is anything to go by. So let's 'quack on' with a selection of the best letters I've received this 'beak' (week)!"* **"** *Courtney*

ACCORDING to zoologists, it's a scientific fact that the quack of a duck doesn't echo. Well I may not be a scientist, but I beg to differ, because I heard a duck quack in a flooded quarry the other day and there was definitely an echo. Actually, come to think of it, there was two ducks on the water at the time, so the echo I heard might have merely been the other duck responding to the first one's quack. The scientists may have been right all along, so I would like to take this opportunity to apologise for my ill-informed comments earlier in this letter.

Urquhart Farquhar, Cornwall

WHEN I was a girl, my grandad told me a joke about a duck knocking on a door, and when the man answered he said he was called Bill or something. He had a hat on, the duck not the man, I think. Anyway, I can't really remember it but it was really very funny. But I doubt I'll ever know how it went now because my grandad died of septicaemia after El Alamein and I'm in the tertiary stages of senile dementia. It might have been a knock-knock joke, possibly.

Edna Tremble, Vinyl-on-Sea

MY HUSBAND is called Donald and my maiden name was Duck. So to save his blushes, before we got married I changed my surname by deedpoll to Marsden. Wait a minute, it's just dawned on me that I didn't need to do that, did I? Just wait till he gets back from work. That'll tickle him, that will.

Mrs Ada Fartchops, Liverpool

WHY baby ducks are called ducklings whilst baby pigs are called piglets is anybody's guess. Come on British farmers, it's about time you got your act together and decided a standard suffix to use when naming baby animals. Ducklets and piglets or piglings and ducklings, I really don't care. I just want some consistency on the matter.

Rafe Cumberbund, Uttoxeter

EVERYONE knows that a swan can break a man's arm, so I think that dwarves, such as TV's Warwick Davies and that one who was in R2D2, should take extra care when they are near ducks.

Edna Gallstones, Wince

MY WIFE and I recently bought a pair of Khaki Campbell ducks to keep as pets, but we have been extremely dismayed by the mess they have made of our garden with their runny droppings. The vet assures us that watery feeshus is the norm in the duck kingdom and there is nothing we can do about it. Next time we go out to buy a pet, we will try to ensure we get one that does nice firm stools, such as a mouse or dog.

Fenton Parslow, Mablethorpe

I CAN sympathise with Mr Parslow *(above)*. After putting up with ducks ruining my garden for many years, I eventually decided to firm up their excreta by force-feeding them with a mixture of arrowroot and cornflour. It worked a treat for three days, during which their motions were like small, hard pebbles, and then on the fourth day they all died.

Lettuce Coleridge, Jismbridge

WHOEVER thought of the term "duck-billed platypus" ought to have their head examined. The fossil record clearly shows that these primitive monotremes were roaming the planet long before ducks evolved. If anything, ducks should be called "platypus-faced water-birds".

Prof. Chumley Featherstonehaugh Tasmania

IT ALWAYS makes me laugh when people say that ducks swim in the water. They do no such thing. If I went to the baths and stopped swimming half way through a length, I'd sink to the bottom of the pool. If a duck stopped wafting its feet about in the water, it would just stay floating about happily on the surface. Well that's not swimming in my eyes. It's about time we woke up and smelled the coffee.

Geraldine Scrotumseame, Lincoln

I COULDN'T agree more with Mrs Scrotumseame *(above)*. When my pet duck Toby died, I tried to flush him down the toilet but he just kept bobbing round on the top of the water. He could swim just as well when he was dead as in his heyday. In the end I had to push him round the bend with a plunger, and I'm not convinced he even went then because the bowl keeps backing up and there's always feathers in the bottom of the pan. I think I'll have to get Dyno-Rod round.

Dr M Candlestickmaker, Haltwhistle

WHILST at my local farm shop the other day, I was surprised to see how

♥ Ducklover Dating

Discreet Introduction service for people who like ducks

LONDON-based duck lover, 48, ex-military, divorced, non-smoker wltm lady, 35-40, to talk about life, love and ducks. **Box 7804.**

BUBBLY woman, gsoh, early-to-mid 30s, slim attractive, into all aquatic birds, looking for romantic gent for romantic moonlit strolls near ponds. Hampshire/Welsh borders. **Box 3874.**

MARRIED duck-loving gent, 50s. Wife has no interest in ducks. Wltm duck-loving lady to talk about ducks, maybe more. Send picture of ducks to **Box 3098.**

MAN, 35, into cinema, theatre, music and ducks seeks similar woman, W Midlands area for nights out, country walks, chats about ducks and unprotected anal. **Box 5636.**

FORENSIC SCIENCE JOKE

MORE WINE DARLING?

DATING HUMAN REMAINS

much bigger duck eggs were than chicken eggs, especially since I've always thought that chickens were quite a bit bigger than ducks. If you ask me, it'll be the egg farmers trying to pull a fast one as usual.

Yootha Feltch, Oswestry

WHOEVER invented the the phrase 'as tight as a duck's arse' needs their head examined. Ducks' eggs are quite large and I would imagine their sphincters are quite slack as a result. The lady ducks at any rate. Perhaps the term

should correctly be 'as tight as a drake's arse'.

Ada Trowbridge, Hull

MRS Trowbridge *(above letter)* is staggering in her ignorance. Eggs do not come out of ducks' arses, or the arses of any birds. They come out of their vaginae. The term 'as tight as a duck's vagina' would be ludicrous. 'As tight as a duck's arse' is perfectly rational.

Hector Dayglow, Luton

I'M A professor of zoology at Cambridge and I have rarely encountered such ignorance as that from your two previous correspondents. Ducks, and indeed all birds, have neither arses nor vaginae. They have a combined urinogenital opening called a cloaca through which urine, eggs and turds all pass. The term 'as tight as a duck's cloaca' is the only one which has any merit. ·

Prof. Norman Chuff, Jesus College

BOB Hope always reminded me of a duck. I don't know why, because he didn't have a beak or webbed feet.

Iris Soupspoon, Kenilworth

ICOULDN'T agree less with Mrs Soupspoon *(above)*. Bob Hope looked nothing like a duck. He always reminded me very strongly of a swan. And Kelsey Grammer out of *Frasier* is a goose.

Ada Leadbelly, Hull

---

duckology

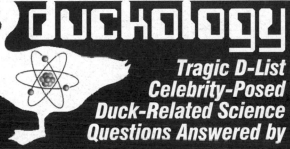

Tragic D-List Celebrity-Posed Duck-Related Science Questions Answered by

Senior Reader in ducks, L'Institut Français des Canards, Paris, **Prof. Giscard de Putain**

• **I'D LOVE** to know how much my duck weighs, but I can't get it to stand still on the bathroom scales long enough to get a reading. Is there any way to accurately measure the weight of a duck?

H out of Steps, Steps

Weighing a duck couldn't be simpler. Simply take a small bowl and place it inside a larger bowl. Then, fill the smaller bowl brim-full with water, taking care not to allow any to get into the larger bowl. Now place your duck on the surface of the water, making sure he doesn't move or splash about as this could lead to an inaccurate result. You will notice that the duck will displace an amount of water into the larger bowl. Archimedes' Principle dictates that the weight of this displaced water will equal the weight of the duck. Remove the smaller bowl from the larger bowl and carefully pour the displaced water into a perfectly cylindrical glass container. In metres, measure the height of the water in the container (h) and the internal diameter of the container (d). Now divide d by 2 to obtain the radius (r). Now work out the volume (v) of water by substituting the figures you have obtained into the following formula: $v = \pi r^2 h$. Since the density of water is 1000.00kgm^{-3} and 1 ounce=28.3495 grams, simply take your answer and divide it by 10^{-6} and multiply it by $^1/_{453}$ to get the weight of your duck in pounds.

• **A SPARROW** flew into my kitchen window the other day and splattered on the glass. I was wondering, if a duck flew into the window would it similarly splatter, or would it break the window?

Joe Swash, EastEnders

This is a very complicated problem. You would first have to weigh the duck in the same manner as I described to H out of Steps and then divide by the force of gravity, 9.81 ms^{-2} to determine its mass. You would then have to measure the speed at which it was flying at the time that it hit the window and multiply this by the mass to give the duck's momentum on impact. The force on the glass would then be equal to the rate of change of momentum, but whether this would be enough to break the glass would depend on many factors, including the type, thickness and temperature of the glass. It is extremely difficult to calulate, so it would probably be easier to determine what would happen by experiment. Simply get a number of ducks of equal mass and throw them at your window with increasing speed and record at what point the glass shatters.

Are YOU a D-list Celebrity such as Kerry Katona or that bloke off that thing? Do you have a scientific question about ducks? Write to 'Duckology, Viz Comic, PO Box 841, Whitley Bay, NE26 9EQ.

Miriam's True-Life Duck Photoproblems

Kirsty's Duck Dilemma ~ Day 32

Kirsty and Dave had been going out for nearly a year and everything was going well. But when she finds a secret stash of duck magazines hidden on top of his wardrobe, she confronts him...

Oh Dave. I thought I knew you, and then I find *these*!

Eh!?! *Loads* of blokes read duck magazines...

...What's the big deal?

Kirsty mentioned it to her friend, Trish...

Dave says there's nothing wrong with looking at duck magazines, Trish.

I wouldn't be too sure.

He might not think it's a problem, but reading magazines about ducks can lead to other things....

Before he knows it, ducks won't be enough.

I hope you're wrong, Trish.

But that night ...

I'll just change Dave's pillowcase.

GASP!

Oh no!

CONTINUES TOMORROW...

Dr Miriam's Duck Helplines

Duck's quack won't echo
0181 18055

Floating duck won't displace own weight in water
01 811 8055

Worried about weight of duck on moon
018 118 055

Unable to convert weight of duck from kgs to lbs
01811 80 55

Can't calculate angular momentum of duck swimming round a pond
0181 1 80 55

Vaginal dryness
01811 80 55

Calls cost from £3.50 and terminate at Slimbridge Wildfowl Trust, Gloucestershire.

THE YEOMAN OF THE QUEEN'S BODYGUARD IN "It's a Royal Knockers-out"

BUCKINGHAM PALACE

TCHOH! JUST LOOK AT THAT GOOD-FOR-NOTHING YEOMAN OF THE GUARD!

ALL HE DOES IS LOLL AROUND IN FRONT OF THE FIRE SCOFFING ROAST BEEF FLAVOUR CRISPS

GET UP YOU LAZY LUMP!

YOW!

JAB!

IT'S ABOUT TIME YOU STARTED EARNING YOUR KEEP AROUND HERE.

ANOTHER UNEMPLOYED IRISH LABOURER BROKE INTO MY ROYAL BEDCHAMBER AND HAD A FEEL OF MY TITS LAST NIGHT.

THAT'S THE THIRD TIME IT'S HAPPENED THIS WEEK.

YOU'RE SUPPOSED TO BE THE ROYAL BODYGUARD — WELL START GUARDING MY ROYAL HOOTERS!

OTHERWISE I'M GOING TO THROW YOU OUTSIDE IN THE SNOW!

RIGHT, I'M GOING TO HAVE MY AFTERNOON NAP ON THE CHAISE LONGUE. AND REMEMBER...

..IF ONE MORE UNEMPLOYED IRISH LABOURER BREAKS IN AND FEELS MY KNOCKERS WHEN I'M ASLEEP, IT'S THE DOGHOUSE FOR YOU!

HUP, TWO THREE FOUR

=SNORE= PLAP PLAP

NO TIT-GRABBING INTRUDERS WILL GET PAST ME

OHO! AN UNEMPLOYED IRISH LABOURER SCUTTLING FROM BEHIND THAT CURTAIN

ZZZ

AND HE'S MAKING A BEELINE FOR BETTY'S BAZOOMAS!

CROWN JEWELS

CRACK!

TRY FIDDLING WITH THIS ROYAL ORB, YOU PEST!

BEJASUS!

CROWN JEWELS

AND STAY OUT!

BOOT!

YOU PESKY FENIAN FUNBAG-FONDLER!

BUCK PALACE REAR ENTRANCE

A LITTLE MORE SECURITY IS CALLED FOR HERE

ZNORK.. ZZZ

I'VE SURROUNDED MA'AM'S MAMMS WITH BARBED WIRE — THAT'LL KEEP THEM SAFE.

SAW SAW SAW

EH? WHASSAT?

ZZZ

YIPES! ANOTHER UNEMPLOYED IRISH LABOURER

ZZZ

AND HE'S MAKING A SNEAKY ATTEMPT TO RUB THE REGAL RIB-CUSHIONS

LET'S SEE HOW HE LIKES A GIANT KOH-I-NOOR DIAMOND RIGHT ON THE BUTTON

CROWN JEWELS

SPANG

BULLSEYE!

BEJABBERS!

I GOTTIM!

OUT WITH YOU, YOU GAELIC GARBONZA-GROPER!

SWEEP!

GLUMPH!

HM — THAT DRESSMAKER'S DUMMY GIVES ME AN IDEA

I'LL CONSTRUCT A DECOY QUEEN WHICH I'LL USE TO ENTRAP THOSE UNEMPLOYED IRISH LABOURERS

AND I'VE CUT THE FACE OUT OF ROLF HARRIS'S ROYAL PORTRAIT AND STUCK IT ON THE DUMMY

AND A COUPLE OF THE QUEEN'S SPARE CROWNS MAKE AN IRRESISTIBLE PAIR OF TITS.

NOW FOR THE MASTERSTROKE — I'LL WIRE THE "CROWN KNOCKERS" UP TO THE MAINS

ANY UNEMPLOYED IRISH LABOURER WHO GIVES 'EM A SQUEEZE WILL FIND IT A SHOCKING EXPERIENCE!

HEH HEH! HERE COMES ONE NOW!

TIP-TOE

HE CAN'T RESIST HAVING A KNEAD OF THOSE NOBLE NORKS

Why not come INDOOR SKYDIVING!

GERONIMO!

1000...2000...3000...BANG!

Feel the wind in your face as you free-fall between 4 and 50 metres straight into the ground!

All the thrills and danger of parachuting, but with no fiddly parachute controls to worry about. The sense of speed as you plummet through the stairwell towards the hard floor has to be experienced to be believed.

Ideal for...
• Birthdays
• Anniversaries
• Corporate Bonding
• Stag Parties

email info@indoorskydivers.co.uk for booking details.

2m novice jumps

formation jumps

What are you waiting for!

"My husband bought me an indoor skydiving experience as a 50th birthday surprise. I'll never forget the thrill of jumping 10 metres onto the marble floor of the town hall reception area. The doctors said I'd never walk again, but I'm determined to prove them wrong!"
Mrs B., Essex

Prices start from just £10/metre for a solo free-fall. Or why not try a tandem jump harnessed to one of our experienced indoor skydiving instructors? The choice is yours!

LETTERBOCKS

Viz Comic, PO Box 841
Whitley Bay NE26 9EQ
e-mail: letters@viz.co.uk

ST★R LETTER

I WAS watching a BBC police drama the other day in which a man was murdered. But when the police were inspecting the scene of the crime, I distinctly saw the chest of the 'corpse' moving up and down slowly. The murder victim was being played by a live actor! Come on, BBC, there are plenty of dead actors who could have played this part more convincingly. John Thaw, for instance, or Victor Spinetti.

Frederick Treves, Luton

I USED to love George Michael's 1990 album *Listen Without Prejudice*. However, when I read that he had been arrested for cottaging in a public lavatory, I threw the ruddy thing straight in the bin.

Craig Scott, e-mail

IN the porn film *Patricia Diamond - Testing The Tools*, we see a rather nice lady get triple penetrated by 3 or 4 gentlemen in what appears to be a fish factory. She puts in a good session, but I don't understand why she is actually visiting the fish factory in the first place and why there aren't any other visitors there. I like to see a bit of red hot action as much as the next man but I also need a believable storyline so I can connect with the characters.

Boss Hogg, e-mail

WHY is it that people complain every time it rains, then bang on about saving the rain forest? Surely they can't have it both ways?

Alan Heath, e-mail

I SIMPLY ignore the warnings on fag packets which say that smoking reduces your life expectancy. They have always tested fag smoking on beagles, so if you're over sixty, you're actually about ninety-five in dog years. Do you want to live forever?

Terry Corrigan, e-mail

FOLLOWING George Formby's advice, I went to the seaside yesterday for a little stick of Blackpool rock. Imagine my disappointment when the lady behind the counter said they didn't sell it. That's the last time I go to Great Yarmouth.

Bobby Bowels, e-mail

I RECENTLY purchased a new car and paid an additional £200 for electric windows. Imagine my horror on delivery to discover the windows were in fact made of glass! No refund, no apology. No wonder they call it rip-off Britain.

Richard Linley, e-mail

HOW can Christian men be against homosexuality but claim to love Jesus who was a man? Answer that one, so-called Archbishop of Canterbury.

Ross Kennett, e-mail

WHY is it that in modern society it's socially acceptable to have a collection of vibrators with veins, lumps and nobbles all over them, but mention that you have an electric vibrating vagina at home and the conversation dies?

Gilbert Nadpants, e-mail

THE other day I found myself slightly drunk attempting to put a king size duvet into a new cover, whilst a Michael Bolton song was playing on the radio. To make things worse, I could also make out the theme tune to *What's the Story in Balamory?* coming from the next room. Can any other readers beat this for a 'hell on earth' experience?

Gary Sprake, e-mail

THE LONDON 2012 OLYMPIC GAMES have been called the greatest ever seen, not just in terms of the spectacular medal haul by the host nation, but in terms of the sporting spirit of the competitors and good humour of the volunteers and spectators. Everyone except Morrissey enjoyed 17 days of spectacular sport, and now that it's come to an end, your letters have been flooding in telling us of your thoughts about the greatest Olympic Games ever held...

OLYMPIC GAMES ROUND-UP 2012

I HAVE enjoyed every minute of the recent 2012 London Olympics. The only thing that spoilt it was the ladies beach volleybal. It was such lovely weather, and the competitors looked uncomfortably hot in their costumes. And it's going to be even hotter in Brazil in four years time. Perhaps at Rio 2016 they could keep cool by wearing something a little skimpier, or perhaps play in the buff.

H Doubleday, Lambton

I AGREE with Mr Doubleday *(above letter)*. I felt very sorry for the lady beach volleyball players who were constantly having to tug at the legs of their bikini bottoms to release sand. It must become very tiring. In Rio 2016, why don't they have someone who could do that for them, and perhaps brush the sand from their cleavages so as the players could concentrate on the game. I would happily do it. I wouldn't need to be paid, I would do it for the love of the sport.

Len Chilselhurst, Acton

THE BBC athletics commentator at London 2012 said that "You'll always remember where you were when you saw Mo Farah take gold in the 10,000 metres." And he was right, I certainly remember where I was. I was lying on my sofa in my underpants eating steak pie and chips.

Arthur Dury, Whitley Bay

I'VE JUST watched the Olympic closing ceremony and I'm disgusted at Freddie Mercury. His band were playing in front of the entire world and he couldn't even be bothered to turn up. Boo! Bad show, sir!

Nathanial, e-mail

WHY CAN'T medal winners at the Olympics find the time to get changed into a shirt and tie or nice dress before their presentations? Wearing tracksuits makes them all look scruffy and gives the wrong impression to the kids they should be inspiring!

Wonderman, e-mail

LIKE 99% of Britons, I didn't have the foggiest idea who Bradley Wiggins was until last week. Now I think he is without doubt the greatest man ever to come from these shores, so much so that I have decided to name my son after him. Which is easier said than done as he's been called Brian for the last 42 years.

Ian Hunter, Newcastle

SYNCHRONISED swimming would be a lot more interesting if the beaming contestants performed their sport naked. And got out of the pool. And performed sex acts on each other. International Olympic Committee please take note.

Jim Alsopp's chum, e-mail

I NOTICED that Mo Farah ran his races wearing a gold chain. If my old games teacher Mr Fenton had been in the crowd, he would have stepped out and insisted Mo removed the chain. Then he would have given him a couple of whacks across the buttocks with a plimsoll. And had he forgotten his kit, he would have been forced to run his medal-winning race in the biggest pair of shorts from the lost property box. That would have taken the shine off his victory somewhat.

R Marmalade, Nottingham

I WAS looking forward to the Olympic Taekwondo fights. The thought of seeing competitors leaping several feet into the air screaming oriental threats and oaths at one another, the staves and rice flails being wielded, the wounds and bruises inflicted by those masters of the martial arts was all very exciting. Imagine my disappointment when it turned out to be nothing more than glorified arse kicking contests.

Mike Chase, Lowestoft

T★P

FOOL your next door neighbour int thinking it's green bin week by put ting your green bin out before the get back from work.

Borris Hoddinot, e-ma

STRUGGLING with increasing pet rol prices? Save pounds by simpl half filling your tank with stone before you next fuel up!

Desulph Daz, e-ma

STOP your cat from scatching eve rything in the house and crappin in your garden by making it live in cage with your budgie. If you hav two cats, use a parrot cage.

P McIntyre, e-ma

SCHOOL bullies. Ensure maximun tear production from your victims t punching them with a halved onion your clenched fist.

Tam Dale, e-ma

ICE CREAM sellers. Play a practic joke by cooking a vat of mashe

Big Twat Strikes Again!

Have Your Say

Smiths Frontman Slams 'Nazi' Brits

ON HIS OWN FAN WEBSITE, outspoken pop twat Morrissey recently sparked outrage when he launched a blistering attack on the London Olympics. The former Smiths front-bellend claimed that the country was now "foul with jingoism", adding that "the spirit of 1939 Germany now pervades throughout Britain". His words were angrily denounced, but does he have a point? Did the population's wholesale embrace of the 2012 games spill over from innocent enjoyment into genocidal nazism? Or was Morrissey talking out his arse as usual? We went out on the street to find out what the Great British public had to say on the matter...

"...I'M A SPORTS fan, but I must admit that I think Morrissey has a point. I got tickets to see Canada versus Switzerland in the qualifying rounds of the ladies' football competition at St James' Park, and I'm pretty sure I saw one of the stewards trying to round some Jews up at half time."

Hugh Laidlaw, plumber's mate

"...MORRISSEY was 100% right in what he said. At the opening ceremony, I was disgusted to see athletes from Grenada and Tuvalu being forced to walk behind flags bearing yellow stars. The sickening spectacle brought to my mind the horror of Hitler's Final Solution, and I had to leave the room until Paul McCartney came on. Then I had to leave the room again when he started singing."

Yolande Chertsey, apprentice tree surgeon

"...MORRISSEY should be given a knighthood for speaking up. Whilst the rest of the country sat back like sheep and allowed itself to enjoy a fortnight of spectacular sport, only he managed to see the bigger picture, recognising that London 2012 was nothing more than a re-run of the Holocaust."

C Piles, optometrist's labourer

"...WELL SAID Morrissey. I lost my parents, grandparents and many other relatives in the death camps at Auschwitz and Treblinka. It was only when I saw Team GB taking gold in the Team Dressage event that the full enormity of the atrocities perpetrated against my family by the Third Reich was brought home to me."

Transom Hirschfeld, rostrum cameraman

"...MORRISSEY was quite correct. I grew up in Germany during the 1930s and witnessed at first hand the vile acts of the Hitler Youth. After the war, I thought times had changed and we had learned the hard lessons that the mistakes of the past had taught us. I was looking forward to a brighter future, but when I saw my grandson leaping up and down with delight as Mo Farah crossed the line to take his second gold, I realised we had learned nothing at all, and history is just going to go on repeating itself."

Eva McTavish, Lady Mayoress

"...I COULDN'T agree more with Morrissey. At the opening ceremony, the smiles on the faces of the athletes brought to mind the smile on the face of Hitler's deputy Josef Goebbels in that picture of him when he's smiling. It chilled my blood and I was unable to watch any of the games after

that. Except the women's beach volleyball."

Pete Glans, Unemployed headhunter

"...I COULDN'T agree more with Morrissey's statement. Everyone who took part in the Olympics should be brought to justice for their part in the games in a series of Nuremberg-style trials. Whilst the gamesmakers, volunteers, athletes and spectators will all doubtless claim they were merely 'following orders', anyone found guilty should be hanged or at the very least imprisoned in Spandau jail for the rest of their life."

Una Toes, Anal hygienist

WHAT DO YOU THINK?

Morrissey says that the British people behaved like Nazis during the Olympics, but what do *you* think? Is he a bellend or a twat?

Text **BELLEND** or **TWAT** to 018118055.

Last week's Morrissey text-in results:
Arsehole; 100%
Wanker; 100%.

WHY should I have to stand up on the train on the way home, so that unemployed people can sit down? It really makes me mad.

J Jensen, e-mail

'GOOD fences make good neighbours' as the old saying goes, and I couldn't agree more. Last week I got an iPad, a 48-inch plasma TV and six bottles of scotch for a hundred quid.

T Harwood, Doncaster

I WORK from home. I wonder what people who believe 'a woman's place is in the home' make of that.

Christina Martin, e-mail

...potato and serving it to anyone who orders vanilla flavour. Burned cocktail sausages can be used as a substitute for flakes.

H Sherwood, e-mail

...OBSEEKERS. Feel like a famous celebrity the next time you sign on by signing a large, extravagant autograph in marker pen and adding 'All the best xx'.

Ross Hendrick, e-mail

...KIDS. Why not make a trip to the supermarket more interesting by using the nutritional information on packets to play Top Trumps? If the product on the shelf beats the one in your mum's trolley, swap them over.

S Stacker, e-mail

...ON'T waste money on expensive moist toilet tissue. Simply take a standard sheet of toilet paper and run under a tap.

Lee Healy, e-mail

...OOL your friend into thinking that e is a Formula 1 driver, by commentating on everything he does in a Murray Walker voice.

Robin Shaw, e-mail

WANNABE Spies. Communicate with your neighbours using Morse Code messages by switching your lights on and off

Mark Walton, e-mail

RECREATE the excitement of Alfred Hitchcock's *The Birds* by walking down Llandudno seafront with an open tray of chips.

C Dodgson, Oxford

SUPERMARKETS. Help reduce childhood obesity by putting parent and child parking spaces as far from the door as possible to make the lazy bastards walk.

Gingergav, e-mail

FOOL your neighbours into thinking you have an expensive wind chime by simply playing a few odd notes on a glockenspiel in your garden when it's windy.

Matt haines, e-mail

toptips@viz.co.uk

I VISITED New York in 1997 and I went to see the Statue of Liberty. So I was delighted to see a photograph of it on page 48 of issue 218. I couldn't believe my eyes when I looked at three tiny figures at the bottom left of the statue as I'm pretty sure that the one in the middle is me! I'm not sure who the other two people either side of me are, however, as I thought I was on my own at the time. Perhaps I went with two friends, I can't remember.

Jason Wristwhiskers, Surrey

IF chimney sweeps are considered to be so lucky, how come most of them went bankrupt in the 70s with the advent of gas and electric fires?

T Corrigan, e-mail

WHILST pinching one out at work today, a colleague entered the cubicle next to me and inadvertently triggered the Siri voice command on his phone. At precisely the same time I emitted a very long, baritone teeth-rattler, a bit like a castle door opening in a Hammer horror film. Anyway, Siri told my colleague that he didn't recognise the command. I mean, come on Apple, keep up with the demand of the consumer market will you?

Ross Urmston, e-mail

MY girlfriend has just left me, saying I was a 'useless tosser'. If you're reading this Moira, check out some of my eBay feedback. *'Welcome back anytime, 5 stars', 'Great eBayer, perfect', 'A credit to eBay'.* Useless tosser? I don't fucking think so.

Terry, e-mail

Kim for a Day

WE'VE all wondered what it would be like if we were *Kim for a Day*. But which Kim would you be, and how would you spend your 24 hours as Kim? We asked a random selection of stars of stage and screen and asked them who would they be and what would they do if they were *Kim for a day...*

Eddie Izzard
Bilingual comedian

"I love dressing up in womens' clothes and I've got a wardrobe full of bras and dresses. However, when I put them on, I never fill them because I haven't got women's tits. So if I could be a Kim for a day, I'd be *Kim Kardashian* because she's got massive knockers. I'd spend the day trying on all my frocks and looking at myself with a heaving cleavage in the bedroom mirror."

Bono
Pop bellend

"The people of North Korea live under a brutal dictatorship who ban the use of the internet to deny them information. It breaks my heart because these oppressed people have probably never heard of me. I'd love to be North Korean ruler *Kim Jong-Un* for a day. I'd announce that everyone could use the internet to read all about me on Wikipaedia, look at some U2 vidos on YouTube, or download some of my songs on iTunes. That means that by the end of the day, everyone on the planet would know of me."

The Chuckle Brothers
Comedy twosome

"If we were Kim for a day, both Barry and I would be Swedish International midfielder *Kim Källström*. We've long admired the *FC Spartac Moscow* goal machine for his pace and his mastery of the long shot. If me and my Chuckle brother were Kim for a day, we'd go to somebody's house to do some decorating, and Barry would push the step ladder through a glass window. Then I'd spill a bucket of wallpaper paste on his head before painting someone's face blue with a paint roller as they stood in a doorway."

THE INCREDI-BILL HULK!

MILD-MANNERED *BBC Breakfast* host **BILL TURNBULL** is hiding a secret. For the 55-year-old presenter has started turning into an **INCREDIBLE HULK**... often during live broadcasts!

EXCLUSIVE

Programme staff first feared all was not well when Turnbull was presenting an item about a pensioner being mugged for 20p. A show insider told us: "It was a horrifying story. A 90-year-old lady had been pushed over in the street by a gang of hoodies. You could see that Bill and his co-host Sian Williams were really angry as they read the report off the autocue."

"Half way through, the producer noticed that Bill's face was starting to look a little green, and she called through to the vision mixer to adjust the colour balance. To her surprise, the message came back that there was nothing wrong with the settings. Bill really was turning green," the insider continued.

"The next thing we knew, he had got to his feet. He had grown huge muscles and was roaring and flexing his arms. His jacket and shirt were ripping at the seams. The director quickly cut to Carol Kirkwood doing the weather in the *Blue Peter* garden, whilst Bill went on the rampage in the studio."

KNEES

"By now he was just wearing his suit trousers, which were hanging in tatters from the knees downwards. Even his shoes and socks had popped off during his metamorphosis into an incredible hulk," the source added. "Everyone dived for cover."

Production staff could only look on in horror as the now 8-foot-tall bright green man-monster went berserk and began trashing the set, picking up sofas and cameras and hurling them round whilst bellowing and baring his teeth. Within seconds, the BBC Breakfast studio had been reduced to matchwood.

As his rage over the news story subsided, Turnbull returned to his normal size and colour, before falling asleep in a corner, wearing just his now-ragged trousers. "His rampage had really taken it out of him," the insider told us. "There was no way he could present the rest of the programme after that."

WAX

"Somehow we got through the remainder of the show. An emergency sofa was brought down from the *Autumnwatch* studio so Sian could conduct an important interview about *Strictly Come Dancing*," he continued. "Thanks to her consummate professionalism, the viewers probably didn't suspect anything was amiss."

"When he finally came round, Bill apologised to everyone," continued the source. "He explained that he had got stang off one of his bees, and it must have eaten some radio-active pollen."

"This had caused a mutation in his cells at the metabolic level, causing him to go green, muscly and 8-foot tall when he lost his temper," he added. "He promised that it wouldn't happen again."

However, during the very next day's broadcast Turnbull became enraged once more. Whilst reading news items about a woman who urinated on a war memorial, a council that had banned children from playing conkers on health & safety grounds, and some kittens that had been abandoned in a skip, he turned into an incredible hulk and wrecked the studio no fewer than three times.

And the attacks continue to occur with alarming frequency. The veteran host now transmogrifies into an incredible hulk nearly every morning, and many production staff on the programme say they are fearful for their own safety on set.

A close friend who didn't wish to be identified told us: "It's terrifying. On a bad day, Bill can get through half a dozen suits during a programme."

Don't make Turnbull angry. You wouldn't like him when he's angry, Beeb bosses warned

GREEN AROUND THE BILLS: *Turnbull (above) turns into terrifying incredible hulk, say Beeb insiders.*

"The producers try to give him only happy stories to read out, but sometimes a rogue item slips through during a live broadcast. When that happens, we know we've got just seconds before he goes green, rips his shirt across his shoulders and runs amock."

"All credit to the directors for keeping the cameras off him during the metamorphic process, so the viewers at home remain none the wiser," Williams added.

BBC Breakfast GP Dr Rosemary Leonard says that anger manifests itself in many different ways. She told us: "Some people bottle it up whilst others go sulky. In a minority of cases, however, people turn green and double in size whilst roaring."

TUESDAY

"If you find yourself turning into an incredible hulk unexpectedly, it may be a sign that you are allowing work stresses to affect your life," Dr Leonard continued.

"Take deep breaths to calm down, do more exercise and eat plenty of fresh vegetables. If the symptoms persist, go and see a pharmacist, as your GP's probably on the telly mouthing off about flu jabs, prostate exams and shit," she said.

A BBC spokesman told us: "The BBC is an equal opportunities employer, and we will not sack one of our most popular and experienced presenters simply because he is suffering from a condition that turns him into an incredible hulk. However, we are taking steps to minimise the risk of him becoming angry during live broadcasts."

"This means that he will only be given light-hearted news stories to read until he can find a way to control the raging spirit that dwells within him," the spokesman added.

THERE'S A BIG LEEK UNDER YOUR CAR.

THRILLING NEWS, MR SNODWORTHY!

THE EDUCATION SECRETARY IS HOLDING A COMPETITION FOR THE MOST TECHNOLOGICALLY ADVANCED SCHOOL IN THE COUNTRY!

THIS SCHOOL IS GOING TO REQUIRE SOME SERIOUS MODERNISATION IF WE'RE GOING TO WIN THAT CONTEST!

WE NEED TO CREATE A STATE-OF-THE-ART EDUCATIONAL ENVIRONMENT WHERE OUR STUDENTS ARE MOTIVATIONISED TO MAKE USE OF INTERACTIVE LEARNIVATION FACILITIES!

MICHAEL GOVE'S MOST UP-TO-DATE-EST SCHOOL CONTEST grand prizes

THE OLD-FASHIONED BLACKBOARDS AND CHALK WILL HAVE TO GO, FOR A START

THESE NEW-FANGLED "OVERHEAD PROJECTORS" ARE FAR MORE TECHNOLOGICALLY ADVANCED!

GOOD GRACIOUS! WE CAN'T AFFORD THESE PRICES!

MY ROBOT CHUM WILL PROVIDE YOU WITH AN OVERHEAD PROJECTOR, HEADMASTER.

FIRST WE LAY MR SNODWORTHY DOWN IN FRONT OF THE BLACKBOARD AND FORCE HIM TO DRINK A DOZEN BOTTLES OF SCHOOL MILK

GLUG! GURGLE!

NOW HEADMASTER, HOLD THAT CARDBOARD CUT-OUT STENCIL OF A MATHS PROBLEM IN FRONT OF THE BOARD...

$1+1=$

GAG! ACK!

...AND I'LL STICK TINRIBS'S FINGERS DOWN MR SNODWORTHY'S THROAT.

BLORRGH!

UP COMES THE MILK!

AND HEY PRESTO! THE MATHS PROBLEM HAS BEEN "PROJECTED" ONTO THE BLACKBOARD!

$1+1=$

SUPER!

GROAN!

WELL DONE TAYLOR! YOUR COMPUTERISED COHORT IS A MARVEL!

PERHAPS I CAN GET ON WITH THE CHILDREN'S MATHS LESSON NOW?

NOW, ON PAGE 14 OF YOUR TEXTBOOKS I WANT YOU TO MEASURE THE DIAMETERS OF THE DIFFERENT SIZED CIRCLES...

NO, NO, NO MR SNODWORTHY!

WE'LL NEVER WIN THE MOST UP-TO-DATE SCHOOL CONTEST BY USING OLD-FASHIONED 'BOOKS' AND 'PAPER'!

RI-I-P!

THE STUDENTS SHOULD BE MEASURING DIFFERENT SIZED CIRCLES ON A **MODERN COMPUTER SCREEN!**

HM. UNFORTUNATELY, I SMASHED THE SCHOOL COMPUTER IN A FIT OF SELF-DISGUST AFTER LOOKING AT SOME NUDE LADY PICTURES..

MY MECHANICAL PAL CAN HELP, HEADMASTER!

I'LL JUST REMOVE THE BASE FROM TINRIBS'S CARDBOARD BOX...

CLONK!

HI. I'M BARBIE.. I LOVE YOU VERY MUCH.

NOW I PUSH THE FRAME UNDER MR SNODWORTHY'S EYELID - LIKE SO!

YOW!

WHY, IT'S JUST LIKE A COMPUTER SCREEN...WITH AN EYE IN THE MIDDLE!

NOW WATCH WHAT HAPPENS WHEN WE USE MR SNODWORTHY'S GENITALS AS A "MOUSE"...

UNZIP

WHENEVER I FIRMLY "RIGHT CLICK" ON MR SNODWORTHY'S TESTICLE, IT MAKES HIS PUPIL CONTRACT...

SEE, NOW IT'S A BIG CIRCLE...

...NOW IT'S A SMALL CIRCLE!

CLICK!

EEK!

...THE DIAMETER OF THE SMALL CIRCLE IS 1 MILLIMETRE..

OW OUCH YEEK!

GOOD WORK TAYLOR! YOUR HIGH-TECH FRIEND HAS SAVED THE DAY AGAIN!

CLICK! CLICK!

SUBSEQUENTLY

GURR!

BASEBALL BATS

I'LL SHOW YOU WHAT I THINK OF MODERN TECHNOLOGY...

...BY SMASHING THAT STUPID ROBOT INTO TECHNOLOGICALLY ADVANCED SMITHEREENS!

WOW! I'VE SLIPPED ON A PUDDLE OF MILK I VOMITED UP EARLIER!

OOF!

SKID!

CAREFUL, MR SNODWORTHY! YOU'VE LANDED RIGHT ON TOP OF TINRIBS!

CRASH!

HELLO! IT'S THE EDUCATION SECRETARY MICHEAL GOVE ON A SURPRISE VISIT!

HI. I'M BARBIE. I LOVE YOU VERY MUCH.

I SAY! A ROBOT TEACHER!

THAT'S THE MOST TECHNOLOGICALLY ADVANCED INTERACTIVE EDUCATIONALISATION FACILITY I'VE EVER SEEN!

THIS SCHOOL IS THE CLEAR WINNER OF OUR COMPETITION!

1ST PRIZE

HOORAY!

BY GOVE!

'Yacht' a Good Idea!

POB-faced politician **MICHAEL GOVE** recently sparked a public debate with his suggestion that we should buy **THE QUEEN** a new £60 million Royal Yacht to celebrate her Diamond Jubilee. But has the weedy, wet-lipped twat badly misjudged the mood of a cash-strapped nation? Or would a spectacular grand gesture of this sort be just the thing to restore some much-needed national pride, as the cunt-witted Education Secretary believes? We went out on what's left of Britain's streets to find out what the public had to say on the matter.

IT'S ALL very well spending £60 million on a big, fancy yacht. But if the Queen's anything like my niece, she'll get bored of it after a day and just end up playing with the box.

Frank Rossington, Doncaster

TO THE ordinary man on the street, £60 million might be a lot of money, but it is a trifling amount to the Queen, who has a personal fortune of £17 billion. Buying her such a cheap yacht would be the equivalent of giving a £60 gift, such as a middle of the range coffee machine or DVD player, to someone on the average wage. That's not much of a thank-you from a grateful nation for 60 years of faithful service. Michael Gove should hang his head in shame for this insulting suggestion.

Darren Beltoft, Owersby

I'VE BEEN unemployed since 1988, and it's only the thought that the Queen would one day receive such a splendid gift that has kept me getting up in the afternoons for the last twenty-four years.

Adrian Butterwick, Stowe

I'M WORRIED that if we buy her majesty a yacht, it might be at the menders or being cleaned when she fancies a trip to the Bahamas. I reckon we should get her two yachts, so she's always got one that's ready to go. In fact, best get her three, just to be on the safe side.

Glenda Bigby, Dogbreath-on-Clyde

WE ALREADY got her one yacht before and she didn't look after that one properly and let it go rusty. Now it's just floating about under some bridge in Scotland. We shouldn't buy her anything else until she learns to look after it properly.

Mrs Gashforth, Hatcliffe

THEY ought to fill it with fruit machines and casinos like a normal cruise liner. That way we might get a few quid of our money back off the old cow.

Rev J Foucault, Truro

ACCORDING to an article I was reading, these super-yachts cost about a million pounds per foot, so £60 million will only buy one that's about the length of a small trawler. To make this tiny vessel look more impressive than it actually is, they should never bring it in to port, and they should hire dwarves to crew it, with TV's Warwick Davis as the captain. As long as her majesty doesn't fancy a cruise during panto season, she should get away with it.

George Castor, Pollux

THERE'S no way the Queen is going to write sixty million thank-you notes to her subjects for her yacht, unless her mam's there nagging her to do it, and the Queen mum's been dead ten years.

Lee Binbrook, Tetney Lock

THE LOOK on her little face when she opens her present will be worth £60 million in itself.

Ada Shitbag, Cookswold

ALL THIS publicity about the funding of her yacht means that the Queen will know how much we have spent on her present. It will be like leaving the price label on. We may as well put the receipt in with it so that she can take it back and change it for a bigger one, if she wants.

Auntie Pat, Hull

WHY don't we buy her a £60 million box of Thornton's Continental chocolates instead? That way, we could all share in the gift. The Queen could have first choice, possibly even helping herself to two because it's her jubilee, and then pass the box round the rest of Britain.

Noreen Whore, Bishop Norton

I AGREE with Mrs Whore (above). We should pass the Queen's box of chocs round Britain anti-clockwise so that the people in Cornwall would end up with all the coffee ones, nut ones and Montelimars.

Mrs Freda Clayworth, Bristol

AS A Cornish nationalist, I couldn't disagree more with Mrs Clayworth (above). Situated as it is at the tip of Britain's most historic peninsula, Land's End is clearly the natural starting point for the box of chocolates's tour of Britain. It could end in John O'Groats, leaving all the shit chocolates for the Scotch.

Trelawney Penhooligan, St Just

FURTHER to Mr Penhooligan's letter (above), that is all well and good, but how could we ensure that the Scousers and Mancs didn't start dibbing into the second layer whilst there was still chocolates in the top layer? The only way forward I can see is to have a single layer box of chocolates, or else to make all the chocolates the same, such as my own favourite, Viennese Truffles. Or a box of After Eights 250-miles long.

Dr Walter Bealsby, Anderby Creek

IT'S NOT dibbing into the second layer that's the problem with the Scousers and Mancs, it's the likelihood that they'll pinch more than their fair share. Let's face it, it's just putting temptation in their way and a leopard can't change its spots. The courts will need to be granted special powers to hand out exemplary, harsh sentences like they were after the riots.

Widdecombe Milpmop, Belleau

ACCUSING the inhabitants of Liverpool and Manchester of being thieves is tantamount to regional racism. And in any case, it's those light-fingered bastards from Birmingham who are most likely to turk her majesty out of her chocolates.

Illluwayn Llllwywllll, Borth

THE ARMY should be brought in to maintain order whilst the box is being passed round. The prospect of being water-cannoned or shot with a plastic bullet will soon make these northerners think twice before helping themselves to more than one chocolate.

Audrey Epworth-Keadby, Cheltenham

IN MY experience plastic bullets just cause bruising, and these people will wear their bruises as a badge of honour. No, there's only one type of bullet these anarchists understand. I for one am already stock-piling ammunition, and when the shit hits the fan I intend to shoot first and ask how many chocolates they've taken later.

PC Jared Burwell, Chapel St Leonards

Bum Deal!

Pippa's arse nets £1/2million book advance

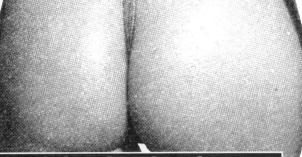

WRITE CHEEK: *Pippa's pert buttocks are set to pen bestseller.*

PIPPA MIDDLETON's backside was celebrating last night after securing a six-figure publishing advance. The pert arse, 28, shot to fame at this summer's royal wedding when it stole the show in a figure-hugging Sarah Burton frock.

And now the bootylicious derriere looks poised to take the publishing world by storm too, after signing a half-million pound deal to write a cookery book.

The book, *Pippa's Perfect Buns' Perfect Buns*, will contain over 100 recipes for rock buns, scones and fairy cakes, as well as handy baking tips to ensure perfect results each time.

A spokesman for publishers Pan Macmillan told us: "We're really excited to welcome Her Royal Hotness Pippa Middleton's bottom to our roster of top authors, and we're sure its book will be the publishing sensation of 2012."

"You can be certain the recipes inside will be every bit as mouth-watering as its author was at the Royal Wedding," he added.

But Ingrid Seward, editor of *Majesty* magazine, condemned the deal, accusing the arse of "cashing in" on its association with the royal family. "People will only buy this book because it's written by a pair of buttocks belonging to someone whose sister has married into the House of Windsor," she fumed.

"Whilst Pippa herself has always behaved with the utmost dignity, it must be said that her bottom is letting the side down by allowing itself to get involved in such a tawdry business," she added.

In 1998, the large breasts belonging to the Queen's niece Lady Helen Melons Windsor secured a £300,000 publishing advance for a lavishly-illustrated coffee table book charting the history of outsize door furniture. The finished volume, *Lady Helen Melons Windsor's Big Tits's Huge Knockers* sold 16 copies.

It Shouldn't Happen to a Plastic Surgeon!

Memoirs set to turn Hollywood facelift doc into James Herriot of cosmetic surgery

"Believe you me," says Prepuce, "Hollywood is the craziest place on earth. And when it comes to performing plastic surgery on the stars, nothing - and I mean NOTHING - ever goes according to plan!"

Rocky Around the Clock

"I remember once when I had *Rambo* star **SYLVESTER STALLONE** on my operating table. He was set to play a character much younger than himself in an up-coming movie, and was worried the lines round his eyes made him look too old. He had come to my clinic and asked if I could turn back the clock for him.

It was a routine procedure. I'd done similar facelifts hundreds

of times before on thousands of patients, and the operation went without a hitch. But imagine my surprise when I got home later that evening to discover that, whilst setting my video recorder to tape my favourite show that morning, I'd inadvertently turned the clock back on that too!

THE HILARIOUS reminiscences of a retired Beverly Hills cosmetic consultant are set to take the publishing world by storm. In his book *It Shouldn't Happen to a Plastic Surgeon*, **Dr Hymen Prepuce** recounts a series of madcap escapades, misadventures, gaffes and goofs from his long career as Tinseltown's go-to-guy for facelifts, nose-jobs and tummy-tucks.

Zoo Hit by Implant Scandal

AZOO in the Isle of Man is set to sue a French prosthetics company after many of its animals developed complications following breast enlargement surgery.

The Manx Wildlife and Conservation Sanctuary near Douglas claims that implants supplied by Grande Poivre Industries of Dijon were substandard, leading to an abnormally high failure rate. In addition, they claim that non-veterinary grade silicone was used in their manufacture.

penguins

Lions, penguins, elephants and antelopes are amongst the animals at the zoo whose implants have leaked or burst, leading to infections.

In one case, a giant tortoise suffered a double failure when both implants burst, leaking large quantities of industrial silicone underneath its

shell, leading to severe infections. The tortoise eventually became so ill that zoo vets had no option but to put it down.

"That was a particularly sad case," said zoo owner Preston Northend. "That tortoise was 230 years old. She would probably have lived another century if those implants had been made correctly."

"It's a tragedy," he added.

And, says Northend, the uncertainty of the situation is making matters worse for keepers at the 54 acre animal sanctuary.

puffins

He told us: "Because of the high failure rate, we're not sure what to do with apparently healthy animals.

For example, we have a White Siberian tiger with 38DD charms which isn't showing any symptoms at the moment. But its implants could burst any time, or they may already be leaking. We just don't know."

pelicans

"There are only 20 of those tigers left in the wild, and if this one were to die because of the unscrupulous behaviour of a French company, the whole species would be one step nearer to extinction," he added.

Time bomb: a woolly monkey worries about implants and (left) zoo owner Preston Northend

The zoo is also home to Ping-Pong the giant panda, who boasts an impressive pair of 48FF assets. But Northend was keen to emphasise that his star exhibit was in no danger.

"Ping-Pong underwent surgery two years ago, and we can assure visitors that her implants came from a different source than the rogue batch and are perfectly safe," he said.

Already one of the most popular exhibits at the zoo, Northend expects Ping-Pong to draw even bigger crowds next year.

"She's going in to get them made even bigger in the summer. We think around 48HH," he told a party of primary school children at the zoo yesterday. "And we might take the opportunity to have her vajazzled at the same time."

126

Instead of the episode of *Friends* I was expecting to watch, I'd managed to record *Spin City*!

It was certainly a "Rocky" moment, but in the end I had to laugh, and I'm sure the Italian Stallion would have laughed too ... if I hadn't given him strict instructions not to smile for at least a fortnight until his stitches got taken out."

Wham! Bam! Tank-you Pam!

"Another time I remember, I had glamourpuss **PAMELA ANDERSON** in for a breast enlargement operation, going from a double-D to a double-E fitting. It was a routine bread-and-butter procedure that I'd carried out countless times before, and it went without a hitch.

But later that evening when I was locking up my consulting rooms, I inadvertently switched off the fishtank heater along with all the lights. Needless to say, next morning my prize collection of tropical fish were floating belly-up in the water!

I had to laugh, and I'm sure that if I'd told her about my own "blonde moment", *Baywatch* star Pam would have split her sides too ... not to mention the freshly-stitched scars under her breasts where I'd inserted her new silicone implants!"

Scrotal Recall

"After thirty years at the top of the Hollywood cosmetic surgery tree, you get used to seeing famous faces across the consulting room table. So it was just another day at the office when *Conan the Barbarian* star **ARNOLD SCHWARZENEGGER** walked into my clinic and asked for a scrotal tuck.

It was a routine procedure I'd carried out a million times before and it went without a hitch. But when I got home that evening I had to laugh. Because the muscle-bound *Terminator* actor's penis had only been an inch-and-a-half long. And it would have seemed rude to laugh at it in front of him."

Dr Prepuce's book It Shouldn't Happen to a Plastic Surgeon (Almond Croissant Publishing) is available in all good poundshops priced £1.

★ ★ ★ ★ ★ ★ ★ ★ ★ ★ ★ ★

THE BITS THE MOVIE STARS DON'T WANT YOU TO SEE!

Fanny Batter's HOLLYWOOD cosmetic gossip

With their toned physiques and million dollar smiles, we look upon our favourite movie stars with envy. But lemmetellyou, the glamorous A-listers of Tinseltown are just as uncomfortable in their skins as the rest of us mortals. And it's time to present my very Academy Awards to the most embarrassing bodyparts that shame the heroes and heroines of the silver screen...

★ ★ ★ ★ ★ ★ ★ ★ ★ ★ ★ ★

The Oscar for the Worst Supporting Feet goes to ...
★ BO DEREK ★

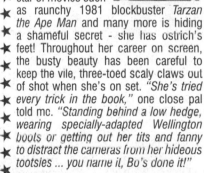

Watching her movies, you'd never guess that bodacious Bo's body was anything but a perfect 10. But you'd be wrong, for the sexy star of movies such as raunchy 1981 blockbuster *Tarzan the Ape Man* and many more is hiding a shameful secret - she has ostrich's feet! Throughout her career on screen, the busty beauty has been careful to keep the vile, three-toed scaly claws out of shot when she's on set. "She's tried every trick in the book," one close pal told me. "Standing behind a low hedge, wearing specially-adapted Wellington boots or getting out her tits and fanny to distract the cameras from her hideous tootsies ... you name it, Bo's done it!"

The Oscar for Worst Torso in a Leading Role goes to ...
★ BRUCE WILLIS ★

Hunky star Bruce sets the ladies' pulses racing in his action-packed thrillers such as *Die Hard, Die Hard 2, Die Hard With a Vengeance* and many more. But have you ever noticed that he never appears on screen without his vest on? Even viewers with a Sixth Sense would never guess why, but the truth is that Willis has spent his entire career hiding the fact he's got eight pig's teats arranged in two rows of four down his torso. "Bruce may have starred in 1989 smash *Look Who's Talking*," a close pal told me. "But one thing's for sure - he sure doesn't like talking about his disgusting, lactating sow's udders!"

The Oscar for the Worst Butt goes to ...
★ JENNIFER ANISTON ★

Aniston is one of Tinseltown's highest paid stars and repeatedly features in lists of the world's sexiest women, but even the former *Friends* star's best friends don't know why the 43-year-old Golden Globe-winning actress never does nude scenes. Aniston may pretend it's because her scripts simply never require her to strip off, but rumour has it the real reason is that she's been concealing a peculiar disfigurement since childhood - a vestigial, furry tail which sticks out from between her buttocks and whips from side to side when she's excited. "Jen's ass is a ticking time bomb," one Tinseltown wag told me: "If the public catch sight of her disgusting tail, it'll be box office poison!"

Gland Design!

WE'RE used to hearing about celebrities who undergo cosmetic surgery in order to preserve their youthful good looks, so it's no surprise when yet another personality decides to go under the knife. But one household name recently booked himself into a Harley Street clinic for a facelift that wasn't on his face. It was on his **MANHOOD!**

According to a close pal, nightclub owner **PETER STRINGFELLOW** had a small image of his own grinning face tattooed onto his bellend in the 1970s. Nearly four decades later, the image had become degraded and so the Sheffield-born entrepreneur took the decision to undergo the cosmetic op to give it a new lease of life.

professional

Stringfellow's doctor told us: "Due to reasons of professional medical confidentiality I am unable to confirm or deny any details regarding procedures that Mr Stringfellow may or may not have undergone."

"However, I can confirm that a patient matching Mr Stringfellow's description

By our Medical Correspondent
Dr. Rosemary Noappointments

EXCLUSIVE!

was admitted to my clinic last week in order to undergo a series of cosmetic operations on a face tattooed upon his bellend," he continued.

"The bags under the tattooed face's eyes were removed, wrinkles were erased from its forehead and the corners of its mouth, the jowls were reduced and the double chin was removed from Mr Stringfellow's ... I mean the patient's banjo," he added.

Meanwhile, a spokesman denied that Stringfellow had undergone a facelift on

Stringfellow ~ Face tattooed on his bobby's hat

his herman jelmet. "Peter is perfectly well and has not been in hospital," he told us.

downstair

But a photographer working for a downmarket tabloid newspaper yesterday used a long lens to photograph the 71-year-old pole-dancing magnate sitting wincing in his Soho apartment whilst wearing a pair of MC Hammer trousers with a big ice-pack on his crotch.

127

Bo-*DIY* Beautiful!

SELF ESTEEM in the UK is at an all-time low, with two-thirds of Britons dissatisfied by some aspect of their appearance. According to a report published last month, 25% of us are clinically depressed by our less-than-perfect bodies, whilst an astonishing 1 in 2 of us will commit suicide at some point in our lives as a result of our physical failings, flaws and foibles.

What's more, the pressure to attain the unrealistic standards of beauty which bombard us daily in books, magazines and the media is driving more and more of us to consider undergoing plastic surgery. An amazing 80% of us - that's nearly 9 out of 10 of the population - say they would be happy to go under the knife in pursuit of physical perfection.

However, the bad news is that film star good looks don't come cheap, with cosmetic clinics routinely charging five figure sums for facelifts, nose-jobs and tummy-tucks. But one man who has found a way to give himself the body beautiful without breaking the bank is Redditch bricklayer **NOBBY GOODYEAR.** 58-year-old Nobby has spent four decades rebuilding hundreds of houses across the West Midlands, transforming crumbling wrecks into desirable luxury properties. And now he has done the same for his own dilapidated structure - carrying out an amazing series of operations on himself using techniques he picked up during his 40-year career as a jobbing builder.

simple

He told us: "Believe me, if I can do it, anybody can. All that's needed is a few simple handtools, some materials you can get from your local DIY store for a few pounds, and somewhere reasonably clean such as your shed or garage, where you can carry out the work."

Goodyear began his quest for physical perfection in 2009 when his wife of 36 years left him for another man. He explained: "It was a real wake-up call when the missus upped sticks and went. I realised I'd let myself go."

"My lifestyle of pies, beer and ciggies had taken a toll on my appearance. I was a wreck. I knew if I was ever going to win back my wife, or hopefully someone a bit younger and better-looking, I was going to have to get myself back in shape, and fast."

"Obviously, I was too old to start exercising or change any of my bad habits, so the only option left was for me to go under the knife."

Builder Nobby's a self-made man!

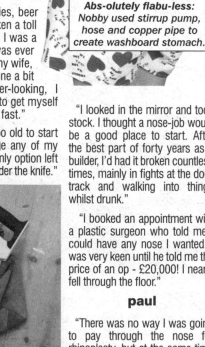

Abs-olutely flabu-less: Nobby used stirrup pump, hose and copper pipe to create washboard stomach.

Goodyear for the poses: Builder Nobby's lost his spare tyre and has transformed himself into a perfect physical specimen.

Tools of the Trade: Goodyear eschews traditional theatre equipment such as scapels, forceps and swabs in favour of the more traditional hammer, key-hole saw and rasp.

"I looked in the mirror and took stock. I thought a nose-job would be a good place to start. After the best part of forty years as a builder, I'd had it broken countless times, mainly in fights at the dog-track and walking into things whilst drunk."

"I booked an appointment with a plastic surgeon who told me I could have any nose I wanted. I was very keen until he told me the price of an op - £20,000! I nearly fell through the floor."

paul

"There was no way I was going to pay through the nose for rhinoplasty, but at the same time I've been in the building trade all my life and I knew an easy job when I saw one. I've ripped out and re-fitted hundreds of fireplaces in my time, and it occurred to me that a nose is nothing more than a facial fireplace. The nostrils are like the chimney flues and the bridge is nothing more than a skin mantlepiece. I decided to set to work and re-furbish my own nose in the shed. After all, how hard could it be?"

"Before I started, I had a few drinks to numb the pain. After downing a couple of large whiskies and a can of strong lager, I can honestly say I never felt a thing."

"As it turned out, it was an even easier job than I expected. I won't go into details because it's a trade secret, but suffice to say the whole procedure only took me about twenty minutes using nothing more complicated than a pair of pliers, half a hacksaw blade, a couple of feet of scrim and a small tube of decorator's caulk."

barry

"The next morning I couldn't wait to take the bandages off and have a look at my handiwork in the mirror, but even I was surprised by the result.

"I'd done a lovely job, even though I say so myself. I had the film star nose I'd always dreamed of. It was intoxicating. I felt a new confidence, a new vigour. I looked good and what's more I knew it. From that moment on I was hooked."

Nobby's next project was his abs. He told us: "When I left

school and started work on the sites I was built like a whippet. There wasn't an ounce of fat on me."

"But four decades of fried breakfasts, fish & chip lunches and builder's tea with six sugars had left me with a discernible paunch to say the least. I was tipping the scales at eighteen stone in my pants."

treasure

"Like most blokes, I yearned for a Peter Andre-style six-pack like I'd seen on the telly and in magazines. But this time the surgeon quoted me an eye-watering £15K for liposuction. Well, I didn't have the stomach to cough up that kind of cash. It seemed obvious to me that extracting subcutaneous cellulite was no different in principle from stripping out old cavity wall insulation, a job I've done countless times. The next day I was back in my shed preparing for another DIY operation."

"This time I used a stirrup pump, a few feet of garden hose and a length of micro-bore copper pipe sawn off at an angle. The procedure was fairly straightforward and took about an hour, including a few drink breaks to deaden the pain. I have to admit, this time it did hurt quite a bit, even after I'd downed six cans of Stella and the best part of a half-bottle of Scotch."

"But when I'd finished, the results were nothing short of fantastic. My spare tyre was gone and in its place was the chiselled washboard torso I'd always wanted but could never be bothered to do the sit-ups to get. Job done, and instead of fifteen grand, the whole job had left me with change out of twenty quid."

tool

The next item on Nobby's to-do list was his pecs. And this time he didn't even bother making an appointment to see the plastic surgeon. He told us: "Although there's not really an equivalent job in the building trade, I had a word with a pal who's a chef in a factory making chicken Kievs and who knows about this sort of thing. He told me that, just like when you stuff a turkey or make a beef Wellington, the implants have to go under the muscle, not over the top. So the next day I got a tube of silicone window sealant and prepared to give myself the he-man chest I'd always wanted."

"Now I know there's been a lot of talk in the press recently about so-called dangerous implants being made out of this type of silicone or that type of silicone. Well, I've been in the building trade all my life and I can tell you it's all the same stuff. Take it from me, there's no difference between ordinary frame sealant costing a fiver a pop and the stuff the doctors charge you hundreds of pounds for. They only call it medical grade so they can hike the price up."

"Anyway, I used up nearly a tube and a half, squeezing as much of it as I could under each pec and squashing it into shape before it went off. The finished result was nothing short of sensational. I looked like a Greek God. It seemed a shame to waste the half tube I had left over, so I did myself some calf implants too."

Over the course of the next 6 months, Goodyear performed a remarkable series of procedures

"There's been a lot of talk in the press recently about implants being made out of the wrong type of silicone. Well, I've been in the building trade all my life and I can tell you it's all the same stuff."

on himself using techniques he'd learned in the building trade. And his transformation was finally completed when he managed to carry out a hair transplant on his own balding pate.

"I'd seen how the proper trichologists did the job on a documentary," he told us. "They take small plugs of hair from somewhere else on your body and plant it into holes punched into the skin of your scalp."

"Well, I've always had an exceptionally hairy barse, so I simply lowered myself repeatedly onto a ½" holesaw bit mounted in an upturned router ... after a few stiff drinks for Dutch courage, of course! Before I knew it, I had two hundred plugs of lovely thick hair arranged in a biscuit tin lid, waiting to be planted into my thinning pate. Putting them in was a sight less painful than getting them out, I can tell you."

"But that's where my building experience really came to the fore. The mistake that hair transplant surgeons make is putting the plugs in using a square grid pattern, like a toothbrush. Now I've done more roofs than I care to remember, and it seemed obvious to me that the hair should be put in just like roof tiles, with each succeeding row pulled half along from the one above. That way, you get an overlap, better coverage and a much neater finish."

job

"It was a long afternoon, but by the end of it I had a barnet to be proud of - thick, black and lustrous like a teenager, and even better it hadn't cost me ten grand!"

After three years and countless home operations, Nobby had finally finished the process which he'd begun when his wife left him for another man. And when they accidentally met in the street outside her now home, she couldn't believe how good he looked.

He told us: "When the missus saw me at the peak of physical perfection, she immediately regretted leaving me and begged me to go out with her again. But I had to tell her I was already spoken for, because by that time I was going out with a supermodel."

monkeys

Goodyear has transformed himself, and he believes anyone who is reasonably good with their hands should be able to follow his example. Now he has decided to share his amazing home surgery secrets in a new book - *Nobby DIY's Perfect - The Book the Plastic Surgeons Tried to Ban* (Kedgeree Publishing £4.99). He told us: "Don't believe the hype. You don't have to pay thousands of pounds to get the body you've always wanted. Everything you need to know in order to do it yourself for pennies is in my book."

"Needless to say, the Royal College of Plastic Surgeons are none too pleased, but they can fuck off," he added.

The Price of Beauty

Builder Nobby Goodyear has given himself the body beautiful for a fraction of the price charged by cosmetic surgeons. Here's a breakdown of exactly what it cost him, and just how much he saved...

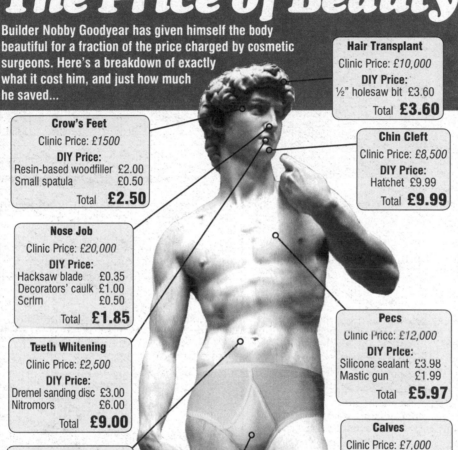

Hair Transplant
Clinic Price: £10,000
DIY Price:
½" holesaw bit £3.60
Total **£3.60**

Crow's Feet
Clinic Price: £1500
DIY Price:
Resin-based woodfiller £2.00
Small spatula £0.50
Total **£2.50**

Chin Cleft
Clinic Price: £8,500
DIY Price:
Hatchet £9.99
Total **£9.99**

Nose Job
Clinic Price: £20,000
DIY Price:
Hacksaw blade £0.35
Decorators' caulk £1.00
Scrim £0.50
Total **£1.85**

Teeth Whitening
Clinic Price: £2,500
DIY Price:
Dremel sanding disc £3.00
Nitromors £6.00
Total **£9.00**

Pecs
Clinic Price: £12,000
DIY Price:
Silicone sealant £3.98
Mastic gun £1.99
Total **£5.97**

Abdominal Liposuction
Clinic Price: £10,000
DIY Price:
Stirrup pump £8.50
Garden hose £5.00
Copper tubing (2m) £3.50
Total **£17.00**

Calves
Clinic Price: £7,000
DIY Price:
Leftover sealant
from other job Free
Total **£0.00**

Penis Enlargement
Clinic Price: £20,000
DIY Price:
Stanley knife + 6 blades £4.99
Pipe wrench £11.00
Stilsons £8.99
Angle grinder £39.99
Bradawl £1.50
No More Nails £5.50
Wire wool £2.00
Jubilee clips x 12 £3.00
Carpet tacks £1.99
Total **£78.96**

Total makover cost
Clinic Price: **£100,000** (+£20,000 VAT)
DIY price: **£128.87** (£100 for cash)

Cat Bin Woman Honoured

By Our Cat Abuse Correspondent Ada Chelstrom

Gong for controversial YouTube star

THAT woman who threw a cat in a wheelie bin is set to be awarded an OBE in the New Year's Honours list. Mary Bale, 47, has been granted the prestigious decoration in recognition of achieving more than 10 million Youtube "hits" for the 2010 video of her dumping Lola the cat into a dustbin.

Speaking from her home in Coventry, former bank worker Ms Bale said she was delighted and flattered to receive the honour. She told us: "I don't know why I did what I did. Putting that cat in a wheelie bin was a split-second lack of judgement that has cost me my job, my friends and my happiness. There have been numerous death threats made against me and people still spit at me on the rare occasions when I dare to leave the house."

confer

"But now her majesty has seen fit to confer this wonderful award upon me, it's all been worthwhile," she added.

The decision to honour Ms Bale was taken by Buckingham Palace after the Youtube video of her "moment of madness" became an internet sensation. Millions of viewers from more than a hundred countries tuned into the internet site to watch

That woman (top) putting that cat in a bin and (above) a cat similar to the one that that woman put into a bin (top)

the clip, which also featured on television news shows around the world.

decduous

Palace Honours Committee spokesman Peregrine Ptarmigan told us: "Mary Bale's video got ten million views on Youtube. That is a truly remarkable achievement by any standards. Her action of putting that cat in a wheelie bin has truly put this country on the map and well deserves official recognition."

Also receiving honours in this year's list are the Techno Viking, who gets a CBE, Fenton the dog who receives an MBE, and the Trolololololol man, who becomes a Knight Commander of the Order of the Garter.

TIME SHEDS

Store Tools and Travel in Time!

Size	Time Travel Capacity
6'x8'	200AD–2050AD
8'x10'	1000BC–3000AD
10'x12'	1,000,000BC–10,000AD

From just **£99.99**

*Price Includes
• Delivery
• Erection
• Map of Time

TIME SHEDS, PO Box 6, Winchester

The Imperial Mint is priapismically engorged with pride to introduce the

Tragic Event Teddy Bear Collection

Little Teddy Hinden-Bear™

THE FIRST in a unique heritage treasury of collector quality bears commemorating the greatest man-made disasters throughout history.

Little Teddy's so excited. Today he's going for a flight on an airship! And not just any old airship - it's LZ 129 The Hindenburg. Pride of the Luftschiffbau Zeppelin fleet, The Hindenburg is over 800 feet long and contains more than 7 million cubic feet of potentially explosive hydrogen gas.

But as the giant craft manoeuvres towards its mooring mast at Lakehurst Naval Air Station, New Jersey, Teddy's excitement turns to terror. There's a flash, the sound of a muffled explosion, and flames erupt through the skin of the airborne behemoth.

"Oh the Ursinity!"

Within moments, the Hindenburg is a giant, red ball of death, as it is consumed by fire. Passengers and crew leap to their doom, desperate to escape the inferno. Others are left trapped inside, screaming vainly for help as the conflagration consumes the gargantuan airship. Ground crew and spectators run for cover, powerless to comprehend the dreadful enormity of what they are witnessing.

Then, just 37 seconds later, it's all over. The once-proud craft has been reduced to a pile of charred, twisted, smoking metal. Thirty-two innocent people have been burned to death.

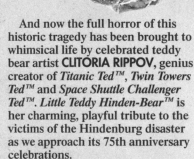

And now the full horror of this historic tragedy has been brought to whimsical life by celebrated teddy bear artist **CLITORIA RIPPOV**, genius creator of *Titanic Ted™*, *Twin Towers Ted™* and *Space Shuttle Challenger Ted™*. *Little Teddy Hinden-Bear™* is her charming, playful tribute to the victims of the Hindenburg disaster as we approach its 75th anniversary celebrations.

Limited Edition

Constructed using only the finest teddy material, with real kapok stuffing, hessian-backed dralon-pile fur and 24-carat glass-effect eyes, each limited edition *Little Teddy Hinden-Bear™* is hand-made by skilled craft-toddlers in China before being individually torched using genuine oxy-acetylene in our lock-up studios in Bermondsey.

A Keepsake and an Investment

In the tradition of the most sought after collectibles, this bear is guaranteed to be worth over One Million Pounds* within days** of purchase.

* Actual amount of pounds not guaranteed.
** Actual number of days not specified.

Only 16.66³
PRICE SHOWN UPSIDE DOWN
plus £2.99 postage and packing
Postage and packing shown slightly smaller than actual postage and packing of £129.99

Doubly Authentic

Each *Little Teddy Hinden-Bear™* comes with a Certificate of Authenticity. But that's not all. Each Certificate of Authenticity comes with its **OWN** Certificate of Authenticity, faux hand-numbered as a lasting testament to your bear's Certificate of Authenticity's veritability.

... SERIOUS COLLECTORS ONLY ... SERIOUS COLLECTORS ONLY ...

Heritage Reservation Application

Hurry! Don't miss your chance! Fill in the form immediately!
*No, don't make a cup of tea. Fill it in **NOW**!*

Yes, I've got £4000 hidden:
☐ under the bed ☐ in a biscuit tin
☐ in a teapot ☐ behind the clock

Name..
Address ....
....

Do you have a dog?
☐ Yes ☐ No

If Yes, what sort of dog is it?
☐ Small and easily frightened ☐ Big and bitey

If Big and bitey, would it eat meat pushed through the letterbox?
☐ Yes ☐ No

Signed ....

You will receive further Tragic Event Teddy Bears each week on Approval for the next 35 years. If you are not utterly delighted with them, simply send them back in their original packaging. They are yours to pay for whether or not you decide to keep them.

The Imperial Mint, PO Box 6, Bermondsey SE16. No callers.

OH, LORDY! IT'S THE FAT SLAGS

EEH! THAT'S A GOOD'UN...Y' LOOK LIKE A DUCK WI' PILES

NAA-AAA! THAT'S THE FACE BAZ PULLS WHEN HE'S DOIN' YOU UP THE SHITTER, IN'T IT?

THAT'S NOT A GOOD 'UN...YER ALL BOZ EYED

WELL, YOU'D **FARTED**

NAA-AA! I THINK I'LL SAVE THIS 'UN F' ME NEXT PASSPORT

NAA-AAA!

Y'CHEEKY SOD! THAT'S ME FACEBOOK POUT, THAT IS.

I DON'T KNOW...I'VE NEVER **SEEN** 'IS FACE WHEN HE'S DOIN' ME UP THE SHITTER, 'AVE I?

NAA-AAA! I KNOW...SOZ... EGGS ALWAYS DOES THAT T' ME)

Y'D 'AVE T' GET YER TITS OUT AT CUSTOMS

WELL IT WOULDN'T BE THE FIRST TIME

EEH, THEY'RE A RIGHT LAUGH THESE THINGS ARE, AREN'T THEY?

AYE...SHALL WE DO IT AGAIN SOMETIME?

AYE...WE'LL FIND A BIGGER ONE, THOUGH

NOT BE LONG NOW, LADIES...WE'RE GOING TO TAKE THE SIDE OFF

FOTO-U INSTANT PICTURES

PLATFORMS 1.2.3.4 ▶

WELL, 'URRY UP...

...WE'VE BIN IN 'ERE TWO HOURS AN' I'M BUSTIN FORRA PISS

BIG VERN

THIS IS A NICE PUB, VERN.

PROPER VILLAIN'S BOOZAH THIS ERNIE...THEY ALL BIN FROO THAT BOBBY MOORE... SCOTCH JACK...MAD FRANKIE ...THE KRAYS...

SEE THAT MARK ON THE BETTY? THAT'S WHERE RON STABBED JACK THE HAT FROO 'IS MINCE.

GOSH.

...TOOK FREE BIG GEEZAHS TO PULL THE DRUM AHT 'IS MUSH BEFORE THE UNDERTAKER COULD CARRY THE STIFF AHT THE GAFF.

WEREN'T A PRETTY SIGHT, ERNIE, BELIEVE ME.

...EXCUSE ME...WOULD EITHER OF YOU GENTLEMEN LIKE TO BUY A COPY OF THE WAR CRY..?

GET DAHN ERNIE!

IT'S THE FILF!

BLAM!

BLAM!

BLAM!

LETTERBOCKS

Viz Comic P.O. Box 841 Whitley Bay NE26 9EQ
letters@viz.co.uk

I HAVE been watching *Fake Britain* on BBC1 for a few weeks now and they have still not covered breasts or orgasms. Come on Dominic Littlewood, forget toxic lead-filled children's toys and cover the stuff we all care about.

Dan Dan the Musicman, e-mail

I RECENTLY attended a gig by Frank Turner and the Sleeping Souls. Unfortunately, I was so refreshed that I dozed off and kipped through the entire set. Have any other readers inadvertently joined a backing band in this way? Perhaps you broke up with someone at a Tom Petty concert, or spontaneously combusted whilst watching Georgie Fame.

Terry Bullweather, e-mail

STAR LETTER

IT has always been my ambition to dab my mouth with a table napkin and then fling it down angrily on the table, before storming out of the restaurant - just like they do in a Noel Coward play. So, can I appeal to KFC to replace their flimsy paper napkins with cloth ones? The paper ones just flutter around and invariably fall on the floor with absolutely no dramatic effect whatsoever.

T C, Frampton-on-Stour

I FOUND the face of renowned atheist Richard Dawkins burned into my slice of toast the other day. It reconfirmed my belief in the essentially random nature of the universe.

Chandler Raymond, e-mail

WHEN the Queen gets to a hundred, does she write a letter to herself, and if so, does she address it to Elizabeth or Your Majesty? If someone can answer this question it would really help my piles, as they've really come down with all the time I've spent sitting on the shitter thinking about it.

Professor Yaffle, e-mail

WHILE passing through London last Sunday I visited a pole-dancing bar at 11 in the morning despite having already just wanked off twice to a sex telephone line in my Ibis hotel room. Can any other *Viz* readers boast a less religious start to the Lord's day?

Sam White, e-mail

I WAS going to write in and say that I'd once gone out with a girl named Fanny Hare in a poor attempt to win five pounds. I didn't, and I'd like to take this opportunity to apologise to your readers.

Gordon Bennet, e-mail

WHY are Scandanavian detectives so popular on television all of a sudden? I have only met one Scandanavian detective, who interviewed me after I was arrested for fitting miniature cameras in a women's changing room in Narvik. He spoke reasonable English but shouted a lot and seemed to regard me with a great deal of contempt.

K Wittgenstein, Maltby

I'M sick of those adverts that tell us that we can't dodge paying our telly licence because they can track us down. I reckon it's all bollocks. I saw that picture of Osama Bin Laden watching his telly and it took the Navy Seals to find him. Where were the omniscient telly-licensing people when that was going down, dare I ask?

Terry Cardboard, e-mail

TOP TIPS

PUB landlords. Cheer up the mood in your pub by replacing the CO_2 beer gas with helium and laughing gas, for a fun-filled evening of high voices and hilarity.

S Mac Rat, e-mail

MAKE wasps less angry by putting a 50:50 mixture of prozac and jam in a jar outside the cunts' hives.

Tam Dale, e-mail

BURP the words 'Excuse me' to save valuable time.

Paul Townend, e-mail

RE-LIVE the excitement of the Sea Empress oil disaster by dunking your pets in treacle then scrubbing them with a toothbrush.

Nic Ledger, e-mail

CONVINCE your friends you're a television detective by picking everything up with a pencil.

Alex Zeal, e-mail

MEN. Don't spend half the time worrying about the length of your penis. Remember, women consider girth just as important, so spend half the time worrying about that instead.

Tuula Canavan, e-mail

ENVIRONMENTALISTS. A swan's neck and head with a scaffolding pipe up the middle makes an ideal organic golf club.

Tam Dale, e-mail

PRETEND to be in a lift by painting a vertical row of numbers on the inside of your wardrobe and standing inside humming Carpenters songs.

Spenner, e-mail

LADIES. Don't waste money on expensive high heels. Simply buy standard priced flats and walk around on tiptoe.

Tuula Canavan, e-mail

MAKE family photos more fun by getting one of your relatives to wear a red and white striped jumper and bobble hat and hide in amongst the crowd.

Carolyn Martin, e-mail

DRY stone wall enthusiasts. Try putting a bit of mortar between the stones in your wall. That way you won't have to rebuild the sodding thing every six months.

L Cemlyn, e-mail

toptips@viz.co.uk

Dear... Miriam
YOUR PROBLEMS SOLVED

Dear Miriam,

I THOUGHT I had a happy marriage to a hard-working plumber, but now I fear my husband has a secret life. I am 51, my husband is 53 and we recently celebrated our silver wedding anniversary. Like all plumbers, he has always rifled through the drawers of the houses where he's been working and brought back ladies' underwear in. But recently, I found some men's underpants and string vests that he had stolen from a house where he'd been fixing a leak. When I confronted him, he told me he must have accidentally rooted through the husband's drawer instead of the wife's. Like a fool, I believed him, but it's happened several times since then and now I'm worried that he might be gay.

GM, Surrey

MANY normal, heterosexual plumbers like to dress up in men's underwear from time to time. It's perfectly natural and nothing to worry about. Chances are your husband is merely exploring a different side of his personality. My guess is that this is merely a temporary phase that he is going through and he'll soon be back to stealing women's underwear to wank in again.

MIRIAM'S HELPLINES

Knocking noise when cold tap turned on	081 8177
Toilet flush needs three pushes	08 18177
Outside tap won't stop dripping	0818 177
Hubby doesn't want immersion heater	08181 77
Vaginal dryness	0 818177

Calls cost £45+VAT for the first 15 minutes plus £20+VAT per 10 minutes thereafter and include 6 cups of tea with milk and five sugars. Discount for cash. Calls terminate in your wife's knicker drawer.

EXCUSE ME, BUDDY...DO YOU KNOW THE WAY TO THE CITY MUSEUM?

hmmm...

YES.

MORE LOGICAL HILARITY NEXT TIME!

I BROKE down in my traction engine the other day and while I was waiting for the AA man to turn up, who should appear but the ghost of the late puppeteer and amateur TV aerial repair man Rod Hull, all dressed in white like he was, but still holding that damn emu.

Sidney Spanner, e-mail

I REALLY liked the recent teenage lesbian story line in *Coronation Street*, but I thought they could have included some very graphic lesbian love-making scenes just to make it more realistic for the viewers.

Stuart Achilles, e-mail

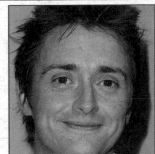

THE best day of my childhood was when I found a porno mag in the woods with my mates and we all took a page home. Now kids just put 'arse' into google and there it is. Kids have it so easy these days.

Ross Kennett, e-mail

EVERYTIME I see a TV programme that begins Richard Hammond's... I switch over. I really can't be bothered finding out what the irritating wanker is doing now.

R Dunlop, Goodplumber

Jimmy Nail's HAMMER

FACTS № 2031

THE APOLLO 14 astronauts took a hammer all the way to the moon. However, in the gravity-free vacuum of the lunar surface, it weighed less than a feather and was useless for knocking nails in!

I JUST found my rusty old Grifter pushbike in the garden shed and I managed to do a wheelie on it for almost 7 yards before I fell off and broke both my arms. Can any of your readers beat that?

Bobby Bowels, e-mail

WELL done to the kids on the bus that mooned that French coach. Those tourists will certainly think twice before coming back to our country and driving up and down our roads. Those children should all be recognised in the Queen's New Year's Honours List.

Hampton Fassbender, Hull

I HAVE wondered for a long time whether dogs and cats ever wonder why their two-legged owners don't fall over.

Michael Crowhurst, e-mail

Ming *for a* Day

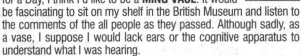

We've all dreamed about what it would be like to be *Ming for a Day*. But with so many different Mings to choose from, which one would you be, and how would you spend your 24 hours as Ming? We approached a selection of top celebrities and asked them: "What would **YOU** do if you got the chance to be *Ming for a Day?*"

Shaun Ryder, *Happy Mondays front man*

Throughout all my wild years of excess, I always wondered what it would be like to be an elderly politician. Whilst I enjoyed the drugs, sex and wild partying that went with the territory on the Madchester scene, at the back of my mind I always yearned to experience the lifestyle of an ineffectual, septuagenarian former leader of the Liberal Democrats. That's why, if I got the chance to be Ming for a Day, I'd choose to be mild-mannered Scottish MP **MING CAMPBELL**.

Clare Balding, *National Treasure*

Everyone agrees that I'm a national treasure, but I'd love to be a real piece of treasure, such as a priceless antique. That's why, if I got the opportunity to be Ming for a Day, I think I'd like to be a **MING VASE**. It would be fascinating to sit on my shelf in the British Museum and listen to the comments of the all people as they passed. Although sadly, as a vase, I suppose I would lack ears or the cognitive apparatus to understand what I was hearing.

Noel Edmonds, *Crinkley-Bottomed Swap Shop host*

Since I was a child, I've longed to launch an attack on all the people of the world, so if I was Ming for a Day, I think I'd like to be **MING THE MERCILESS**. From a futuristic fortress on my home planet of Mongo, I would use a giant death ray machine to target the Earth, until its inhabitants bowed to my evil will. Then I would fly down in War Rocket Ajax to personally deliver a "Gotcha" Oscar to the few puny humans who had somehow survived my wrath.

I DON'T know why Kate Middleton made such fuss about topless pictures of her appearing on the internet. A lot of the ladies I've seen in adult films have also had their breasts displayed across the internet, but they don't go making a song and dance about it. And most of theirs are covered in jizz, too. As is my computer screen. And my walls. Oh, and the cat.

Bobby Bowels, e-mail

IT was most unpatriotic of Kate Middleton to get them out for the French press rather than the British. After all, it's us who contribute towards the the Civil List. He who pays the piper should see the tits.

Tosh Belmarsh, Ely

IS it just me, or would Health and Safety go mental about the stairs in Hogwarts Castle?

Ross Kennett, e-mail

"I'm Having Two Weeks Off From Caring" ~Bono

Tireless environmental campaigner and human rights activist **BONO** last night announced that he was taking a two-week break from caring about issues such as global warming, destruction of the rainforests and African debt relief.

In a statement to the United Nations, the singer, 52, explained that following Live Aid he had been caring about global problems constantly for more than a quarter of a century, and that he now needed a bit of 'me time'.

holiday

He told delegates: "I've been concerned about all sorts of stuff 24/7 since 1985, and in all that time I haven't had a holiday from it."

"If I don't put my selfless compassion to one side for a couple of weeks, I'm going to burn out."

solstice

And the U2 front man was at pains to point out that the suspension of his

Pop Bellend's Social Conscience Takes a Break

concern would start at the end of November and would be temporary. He continued: "A fortnight of utter complete indifference to worthy causes should recharge my batteries. And I'll come back in mid-December, even more benevolent and humanitarian than before."

"But for those two weeks I couldn't give a shit how many animal species become extinct. And the starving millions can go fuck themselves," he added.

WE'VE GOT SOLICITORS

OH DARLING! ISN'T IT MARVELLOUS, MOVING INTO OUR FIRST HOME TOGETHER!

YES DARLING. I LOVE YOU SO MUCH.

SHORTLY

DARLING, I'VE JUST BEEN LOOKING UP IN THE LOFT.

COME AND SEE WHAT I'VE FOUND.

WHAT IS IT, DARLING?

OH, HOW ADORABLE! A PAIR OF SOLICITORS HAVE MADE THEIR NEST BEHIND THE WATER TANK!

HA HA! YES, I SUPPOSE WE'LL HAVE TO GET RID OF THEM.

OH NO, DO LET'S KEEP THEM, DARLING. THEY LOOK SO SWEET!

HA HA! WHATEVER YOU SAY, SUGARPLUM.

LATER

MMMM! THAT COOKING SMELLS ABSOLUTELY SCRUMPTIOUS!

I WONDER WHAT TIME TEA WILL BE READY?

DON'T WORRY, MR PERKINS. I'LL CONTACT YOUR WIFE'S SOLICITOR AND TRY TO GET AN ESTIMATED TIME FOR YOUR TEA

I HOPE IT WON'T BE TOO LONG — I AM RAVENOUS!

MY CLIENT INSISTS THAT HIS TEA MUST BE FORTHCOMING IMMEDIATELY. HE OBJECTS THAT MRS PERKINS'S PREPARATION OF IT IS *prima facie* UNREASONABLY PROTRACTED.

IS THAT SO?. I SHALL CONVEY THAT MESSAGE TO MY CLIENT.

MRS PERKINS, YOUR HUSBAND HAS LODGED A FORMAL COMPLAINT REGARDING THE DELAY TO YOUR COMPLETION OF HIS TEA.

WHAT?!

HE ALLEGES THAT YOU HAVE CAUSED HIM DISTRESS AND PERSONAL SUFFERING THROUGH NEGLECT AND MALNOURISHMENT.

I CAN'T BELIEVE CEDRIC WOULD SAY SUCH A THING! HE... HE ALWAYS USED TO BE SO LOVING AND CONSIDERATE...

"USED TO BE", EH?. I'LL MAKE A NOTE OF THAT AND GET BACK TO HIS SOLICITOR

MY CLIENT ASSERTS THAT MR PERKINS HAS BECOME COLD AND DISTANT TOWARDS HER, WITHHOLDING AFFECTION AND FAILING TO SATISFY HER SEXUAL NEEDS.

INDEED?

AS SUCH SHE MAINTAINS THAT SHE IS *quid pro quo* RELINQUISHED OF HER OBLIGATION TO PROVIDE HIS EVENING MEAL.

IT SEEMS THAT YOUR WIFE HAS ISSUED A COUNTER-CLAIM ACCUSING YOU OF EMOTIONAL ABUSE AND SEXUAL IMPOTENCE.

WHAT?!

BUT... BUT THAT'S SIMPLY NOT TRUE!

MY CLIENT REJECTS THE *ad hominem* ALLEGATIONS AS BEING *primus inter pares* A TISSUE OF LIES!

VERY WELL! MY CLIENT WILL FILE A PETITION FOR DIVORCE *sic transit gloria* ON THE GROUNDS OF IRRETRIEVABLE MARITAL BREAKDOWN!

THE COW! HOW COULD SHE DO THIS TO ME?!

DON'T WORRY, SHE DOESN'T HAVE A LEG TO STAND ON. WE'LL FIGHT HER EVERY INCH OF THE WAY!

THE INITIAL COURT HEARING IS SET FOR NEXT WEEK. I WOULD STRONGLY ADVISE THAT YOU HAVE NO PERSONAL CONTACT WITH YOUR HUSBAND IN THE MEANTIME.

SUITS ME! I NEVER WANT TO SEE HIM AGAIN!

GOOD. THE LAW IS A COMPLEX PROCESS AND BEST LEFT TO THE PROFESSIONALS.

BY THE WAY, HERE IS MY INVOICE FOR YOUR LEGAL COSTS INCURRED SO FAR...

GASP!

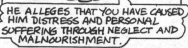

SHAFT, FLEECE, STERMROLLER & BLEED

INVOICE

YOU SHOULD FIND THAT YOUR HALF OF THE PROCEEDS FROM THE SALE OF THIS HOUSE WILL JUST ABOUT COVER THE FIRST INSTALLMENT.

A CHEQUE WILL DO NICELY, MR PERKINS.

WELL AT LEAST MY SHARE OF THE HOUSE WON'T BE GOING TO THAT SLAG!

FOR SALE

SEE YOU IN COURT, BITCH!

I'VE BEEN ADVISED NOT TO SPEAK TO YOU, YOU BASTARD!

DRINKIES BACK UP IN THE NEST, CLARENCE?

RATHER, OLD BOY. LET'S OPEN A BOTTLE OF BOLLY.

SPOILT

BASTARD

137

SNEAKY-PEEKY FUN WITH UPSKIRT COBAIN
PHWOOAAR! PIPPA MIDDLETON, EH..? I'D LOVE TO UPSKIRT HER!
DAILY NEWS
NEW BRANCH OF ALDI TO BE OPENED BY PIPPA MIDDLETON
SO...
I'VE MOUNTED A CAMERA AND FLASH ONTO THE ENDS OF THESE CLOWN SHOES! WHEN HER ROYAL HOTNESS COMES OVER TO ACCEPT THIS BUNCH OF FLOWERS, I'LL GET A TASTY SNAP OF TOMORROW'S WASHING!
PIPPA! PIPPA! OVER HERE, YOUR MAJESTY! I'VE GOT YOU SOME FLOWERS!
OH, HOW LOVELY. THANK-YOU.
AW, FUCK MY LUCK. SHE'S GOT A TROUSER-SUIT ON.
FLASH! FLASH! FLASH!
SHORTLY...
...RIGHT, IT'S FRIDAY NIGHT AND THE TOWN IS FULL OF LADIES IN SHORT SKIRTS..! I THINK I'LL GO AND TAKE FIDO FOR A WALK... HEH-HEH!
WA-HEY! HERE WE GO!
PUB
TIME TO LET THE DOG SEE THE RABBIT-TAIL!
FLASH! FLASH! FLASH!
BAH! IT'S JUST A RUGBY PLAYER ON A STAG NIGHT.
FANCY ANOTHER PINT, REG..?
CHEERS, STAN.
WHAT A SWIZZ!
SHORTLY...
BUS STOP
BIN
...YOU KNOW WHAT THEY SAY, READERS... IF AT FIRST YOU DON'T SUCCEED, FOLLOW A BIRD IN A SHORT SKIRT UP THE STAIRS ON A BUS! TEE HEE!
PHWOOAAR! I HOPE HER KNICKERS ARE ALL LACY AND SHE'S GOT STOCKINGS ON!
T6SS CH!
BUS STOP
AW BOLLOCKS.
LATER...
THERE'S A DEMONSTRATION TODAY, READERS... PRETTY LADIES AGAINST SEXISM!
...AND THEY'RE GOING TO MARCH RIGHT OVER THIS MANHOLE!
OOER! HERE THEY COME NOW!
FIT BIRDS AGAINST SEXISM
EQUAL RIGHTS FOR SEXY LADIES
RUB RUB
BEST MAKE SURE ME LEN IS CLEAN SO'S ALL ME GUSSET SHOTS COME OUT PIN SHARP!
I'M SORRY LADIES, BUT I'M GOING TO HAVE TO DIVERT YOU... THERE'S A HAIRY-ARSED SCOTTISH MALE PRIDE PARADE COMING THROUGH ON THIS STREET.
OKAY, OFFICER.
SO...
BRAW RICHTS FOR THE SCOTCH!
OCH THE NOO!
FLASH! FLASH!
...RATS' COCKS.
SHORTLY...
RIGHT! I'M BORING THROUGH TO AUSTRALIA, READERS!... SEE IF I CAN'T GET A BIT OF UPSKIRT ACTION "DOWN UNDER"!
DRILL! DRILL! DRILL!
8000 MILES
EXTENDING DRILL SET No10
6 MONTHS LATER...
A-HA! THAT'S THE LAST DRILL BIT. I MUST BE NEARLY THROUGH.
DRILL! DRILL!
POP!
WA-HEY! NOW TO FEED ME NEW ULTRA-LONG TELEPHOTO THROUGH THE HOLE TO THE "PANTIE-PODES"!
FINGERS CROSSED I'VE BROKEN THROUGH DIRECTLY UNDERNEATH ONE OF THE MINOGUE SISTERS...
DROOL!
FLASH! FLASH!
WELCOME TO ALICE SPRINGS PILES & FLATULENCE CLINIC

Led Zeppelin and the LAND THAT TIME FORGOT

SEMINAL BRITISH ROCK BAND LED ZEPPELIN WERE ON A TOUR OF THE COUNTRY'S CHARITY SHOPS, AUTOGRAPHING COPIES OF THEIR CLASSIC ALBUMS

WHERE TO NEXT, ROBERT?

THE AGE CONCERN SHOP ON BARNTON HIGH STREET, JIMMY! THEY'VE GOT A COPY OF OUR 1973 LP "HOUSES OF THE HOLY" THAT NEEDS AUTOGRAPHING.

SOON LED ZEP WERE SIGNING THE BATTERED SLEEVE OF THEIR TOP-SELLING FIFTH ALBUM—

HEY, CHECK OUT THESE GROOVY SHIRTS AND LOON PANTS, GUYS!

SUDDENLY JOHN PAUL JONES STUMBLED... AND DISAPPEARED BEHIND THE CLOTHING RACK!

WOW! WHERE'S JOHN PAUL GONE?

WE'D BETTER GO AFTER HIM!

AND WHEN THE OTHERS PUSHED THEIR WAY THROUGH THE MUSTY PAISLEY SHIRTS...

OH - WHERE HAS THE CHARITY SHOP GONE?

WHAT IS THIS PLACE?!

JIMMY PAGE LOOKED THOUGHTFUL

IF I AM NOT MISTAKEN, THIS IS SIXTEENTH CENTURY ENGLAND!

WE MUST'VE PASSED THROUGH SOME KIND OF TIME PORTAL... BACK INTO THE DAYS OF HENRY THE EIGHTH!

GADZOOKS! WHERE DID THESE STRANGELY-DRESSED FELLOWS APPEAR FROM?

MAYHAP THEY ARE SORCERERS!

KING HENRY HAS DECLARED THAT SORCERY IS PUNISHABLE BY DEATH!

WE'D BETTER MAKE OURSELVES SCARCE, GUYS!

OTHERWISE WE REALLY WILL BE CLIMBING THE "STAIRWAY TO HEAVEN!"

LOOK, A MONASTERY!

WE CAN SEEK SANCTUARY HERE AND LIE LOW FOR A WHILE!

LED ZEP WERE WELCOMED INTO THE MONASTERY BY A KINDLY FRIAR

MAKE YOURSELVES AT HOME, WEARY STRANGERS

PLEASE REFRESH YOURSELVES WITH A GOBLET OF MEAD.

ROBERT PLANT DRANK A MOUTHFUL OF MEAD, AND HIS EYES TWINKLED MISCHIEVOUSLY

THIS BOOZE IS PUTTING ME IN THE MOOD FOR SOME OF OUR LEGENDARY ROCK 'N' ROLL ANTICS!

WHOOPING AND SHOUTING, THE WILD MEN OF ROCK SET ABOUT TRASHING THE MONASTERY

OUTSIDE THE KING AND HIS GUARDS WERE PASSING BY

ZOUNDS! WHAT IS ALL THIS COMMOTION?

SOMEONE HAS HURLED AN ILLUMINATED MANUSCRIPT THROUGH THE MONASTERY WINDOW!

SUCH WANTON VANDALISM MUST BE PUNISHED!

GUARDS! TAKE THESE MEN TO THE TOWER!

WAIT! WE MEANT NO HARM, YOUR MAJESTY - WE WERE MERELY INDULGING IN SOME ROCK 'N' ROLL HI-JINKS.

YOU SEE, WE ARE A FAMOUS ROCK BAND FROM THE FUTURE, WHOSE ALBUM SALES TOTAL MORE THAN 200 MILLION WORLDWIDE

HENRY THE EIGHTH LOOKED STERN

IF WHAT YOU SAY IS TRUE, THEN THERE IS ONLY ONE THING THAT WE CAN DO....

THE KING PICKED UP A CHAIR AND SMASHED IT ON THE FLOOR

LET'S HAVE A PAR-R-TY!

WOO! LET'S HAVE A PARTY TONIGHT!

I NEVER REALISED THAT TRASHING A MONASTERY COULD BE SUCH FUN! NOW I'M GOING TO SMASH UP ALL THE MONASTERIES IN THE COUNTRY

AND THEN I'LL STICK A SHARK UP ANNE BOLEYN'S FANNY.

SOON IT WAS TIME FOR LED ZEP TO RETURN THROUGH THE MAGICAL CLOTHING RACK

THANKS FOR TEACHING ME HOW TO ROCK 'N' ROLL, LED ZEPPELIN!

HERE, TAKE THIS SIGNET RING, AS A TOKEN OF MY GRATITUDE.

WOW - WE'RE BACK IN THE CHARITY SHOP AGAIN!

MAYBE THE WHOLE ADVENTURE WAS JUST A DREAM!

IF IT WAS A DREAM, THEN HOW DO YOU EXPLAIN THIS?

HENRY THE EIGHTH'S SIGNET RING!

GASP! IT WASN'T A DREAM, AFTER ALL!

The End.

West Midlands auto trader tells of his crooked treatment at the hands of Tinseltown celebrities...

Used Cars of the Stars

Taken for a ride: Shorty bought lemons from movie stars in good faith.

A TIPTON MAN has been left out of pocket and out of business after a string of Hollywood movie stars conned him into buying second hand cars that were unroadworthy. *SHORTY MEDLOCK* is bitter that he has been forced to take the rap for the criminal acts of silver screen heroes like *BRAD PITT*, *JOHNNY DEPP* and *SCARLET JOHANSSON*.

"A-listers wrecked my business," says Tipton-based Wheeler Dealer

Magistrates last week fined Shorty £8,000 after finding him guilty of trading in stolen, written off and dangerous vehicles. But the 58-year-old garage owner says he sold the motors in good faith after purchasing them from a succession of Hollywood A-listers. Now he says he's determined to get even with the Tinseltown celebrities who ripped him and his customers off.

❝ When my previous business *AA1 Medlock Motors* closed down at the start of 2010 after a fire, I set up AAA1 Medlock Motors on the same site. In all the time the garage was open, I can honestly say I hardly ever had a single complaint.

budget

My customers were mainly people on a tight budget, looking for good quality, low-mileage motors at a fair price. Every car I sold came with a comprehensive 3-week warranty, covering all the major components, except engine, chassis, brakes, steering, exhaust and gearbox. And electrics and bodywork. My guarantee wasn't written down, but it didn't need to be. People knew me and trusted me. My reputation was my bond.

turnover

The trouble began one day in January. The business was quite successful, and there was a healthy turnover of stock. As a result, I was always on the lookout for quality used vehicles for my forecourt. So

Gears Johnny: Crafty Depp packed Nissan's transmission with sawdust.

I was pleased when someone pulled up in an E-reg *Nissan Bluebird*. It was a real head-turner, a credit to its owner. Nevertheless I couldn't have been more surprised when the driver's door opened and out stepped Jack Sparrow actor *JOHNNY DEPP.*

He explained he had bought the car as a runaround whilst he was filming the latest *Pirates of the Caribbean* movie at Pinewood Studios. Now he was back off to Hollywood and wanted to get rid of it quickly. He told me the motor had only ever had one previous owner - a vicar's wife who had only used it for short trips to church on a Sunday.

I took the Nissan for a spin round the block. It drove like a dream. Johnny told me it had a full service history, but he'd temporarily mislaid it whilst packing for his trip back to Tinseltown. It's a story I've heard more times than I care to mention, but I believed Depp. He was one of my favourite stars and I'd seen all his movies. He wanted £500 for the car, but after I pointed out that the spare tyre was bald we shook hands on £450.

crumble

It was a nice looking motor. The 1987 model Nissans are always popular with the punters and this one was no exception. I sold it to a woman that very afternoon. She was a midwife looking for reliable transport. I didn't take much of a profit on the deal. I may even have sold it at a loss, I can't remember. But as I waved another happy motorist away off my forecourt, I reflected that you simply can't put a price on customer satisfaction.

macintosh

So I couldn't have been more surprised when she turned up in my office two hours later, furiously demanding her money back. She told me the gearbox had seized up shortly after she set off and she'd had to drive 20 miles along the M9 in second gear. I took a look underneath and my worst fear was confirmed. *The gearbox*

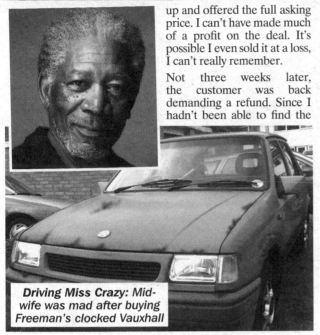

Driving Miss Crazy: Midwife was mad after buying Freeman's clocked Vauxhall

was shot and Depp had filled it with sawdust. I'd fallen for the oldest trick in the book. Johnny had had me for a mug.

anorak

If I had been responsible for filling the transmission with wood shavings, I would happily have given the customer a refund. But as I explained to her, I had bought the car off Depp in good faith, so her beef was actually with him. It wasn't my fault that by this time, the *Edward Scissorhands* star was sitting pretty in Beverly Hills with my 450 knicker in his back pocket. 99

After his experience with Depp, Shorty vowed never again to take the word of a Hollywood star at face value. But the next week, when MORGAN FREEMAN pulled up at the wheel of a shiny Vauxhall, the starstruck car dealer once again allowed his heart to overrule his better judgement.

66 It was a 4-door B-reg 1.6 Cavalier, a very sought-after set of wheels. It was 25-years old, and I couldn't believe it only had 2,000 miles on the clock. Freeman assured me he'd owned it from new, and had only used it for short trips to the shops on a Sunday morning. I know I should have smelled a rat, but this man played God in *Bruce Almighty*, and the word of God was good enough for me.

kagoul

We agreed on a price of £350 for the Vauxhall, and he handed over the keys. He told me all the dockets were in the glovebox, and I believed him. I parked it out on the forecourt and it wasn't long before a customer turned

up and offered the full asking price. I can't have made much of a profit on the deal. It's possible I even sold it at a loss, I can't really remember.

Not three weeks later, the customer was back demanding a refund. Since I hadn't been able to find the logbook in the glovebox, the chap who bought the car had written off to Swansea for a new one. When he showed me the replacement V5C, you could have knocked me down with a feather. For the Cavalier wasn't the low-mileage, one-owner example I'd bought in good faith. It had done 215,000 miles, had sixteen owners, and had been purchased just a month earlier from a car auction in Dudley. The star of *The Shawshank Redemption* had paid just £20 for it.

Sure enough, when I had a look at the back of the instrument binnacle, it was clear that Freeman had been up to no good. He'd taken a tin-opener to the rear of the speedo and wound the clock back. I would have loved to give the customer a full refund there and then, but unfortunately the situation was completely out of my hands. You see, due to the car's age I had only been able to offer a 20-day guarantee, and tragically it had elapsed just minutes earlier.

The customer was so cross with how he had

Freeman had been up to no good. He'd taken a tin-opener to the rear of the speedo and wound the clock back

been ripped off by Morgan Freeman that he actually threatened to punch me, and I had to set one of my big oily alsatians onto him. From the mood he was in as the dog chased him off my lot, I doubt he'd be watching any Morgan Freeman films any time soon. 99

Part-exchanges made up a sizeable proportion of Medlock's business, so he didn't give it a second thought when MERYL STREEP turned up at the garage, interested in trading in her Ford Escort cabriolet for a 1996 Citroen Saxo.

66 Streep's bodywork was in fine shape considering her age, and the Ford looked in pretty good nick too. Nevertheless I gave it the full Medlock Motors comprehensive 4-point check and it passed with flying colours. The car was worth about £500 trade, but she wanted £600 off the Saxo. We settled on £450 cash plus the car.

I decided to valet the convertible before putting it on sale, and wheeled it into my workshop and set about hoovering out the footwells, polishing the dash and painting the car a different colour. Suddenly, I felt a tap on my shoulder. It was a policeman, and he told me he had reason to believe the car I was working on was stolen. I assured him that it wasn't, as I had taken it that morning in part-ex from Meryl Streep.

He insisted on looking under the bonnet anyway, and as he had a search warrant as usual, there was nothing I could do to stop him.

escort

He pointed out that the Vehicle Identification Number had been filed off the engine block, and to my horror I realised I had been fucked over again by yet another star of the silver screen. Streep had probably hot-wired the Escort that very morning in a nearby railway station car park, but I knew my story wouldn't stand up in court. Even though I was completely innocent, I decided to accept a police caution for receiving stolen goods.

Out of Africa and *Kramer versus Kramer* used to be two of my favourite films, but to this day I can't watch anything with Streep in without my blood boiling. 99

The car business is notorious for sharp practices and dodgy dealings, and it's a sad fact that honest traders like Shorty often end up being tarred with the same brush as their more unscrupulous counterparts. There are a lot of sharks in the second hand motor trade, but from first hand experience, Shorty knows that much worse crooks are to be found on the silver screen.

66 In this game, your reputation is only as good as your last deal, so I'm always very careful when buying a car and selling it on. But I forgot my golden rule when ANGELINA JOLIE turned up at my lot wanting £150 for her FSO Polonez.

razzle

It was the 'Leisure' edition, a prestige vehicle, so I didn't quibble over the price. Jolie assured me there was a full service history and loads of bills, which her hubby Brad Pitt was sending over from California. At that point, alarm bells should have rung, and I should have walked away from the deal. But it's not every day that a Hollywood sex goddess turns up on my lot, and she was such a good actress I believed her when she said the paperwork was in the post. Like a starstruck idiot I handed over the £150.

It's the Pitts: Brad & Angelina's FSO was death-trap, says Shorty.

Meryl the Peril: Streep's Ford had been nicked.

The car sold the next day to a man with a young family who needed something safe and dependable for the school run. I assured him that the FSO Polonez was built like a tank. I didn't make much on the deal, I maybe even took a loss. That's the way this business goes. But I was gutted when he returned the next day with the police.

big churns

It turned out that the Polonez had conked out at the lights and a milk float had rear-ended it. Under the impact the car had split in two.

I couldn't believe it when the copper told me that the vehicle I had bought in good faith off Angelina Jolie was a cut and shut - welded together from the remains of two written-off vehicles. I had been conned by the actress, and that hurt, but my real concern then was for my customer and his young family. A minor shunt with a milk float had burst that death-trap like a wet paper bag. God knows what would have happened to him and his kiddies had the accident taken place at high speed.

I was speechless with shock, so much so that I couldn't answer the policeman's questions, which he said may count against me if the customer pressed charges.

Even though I had bought the car off the *Tomb Raider* star in good faith, I still felt an obligation to make things right with my customer. I told him to come back the next morning when I would give him his money back in full. Unfortunately there was a fire on my lot that evening and AAA1 Medlock Motors - along with all its past and future liabilities - went up in smoke. 99

Next week: Shorty bounces back with the opening of AAAA1 Medlock Motors, and buys a 1987 Volvo 340DL off Clint Eastwood, only to discover it has an outstanding loan from a credit company against it. And false number plates.

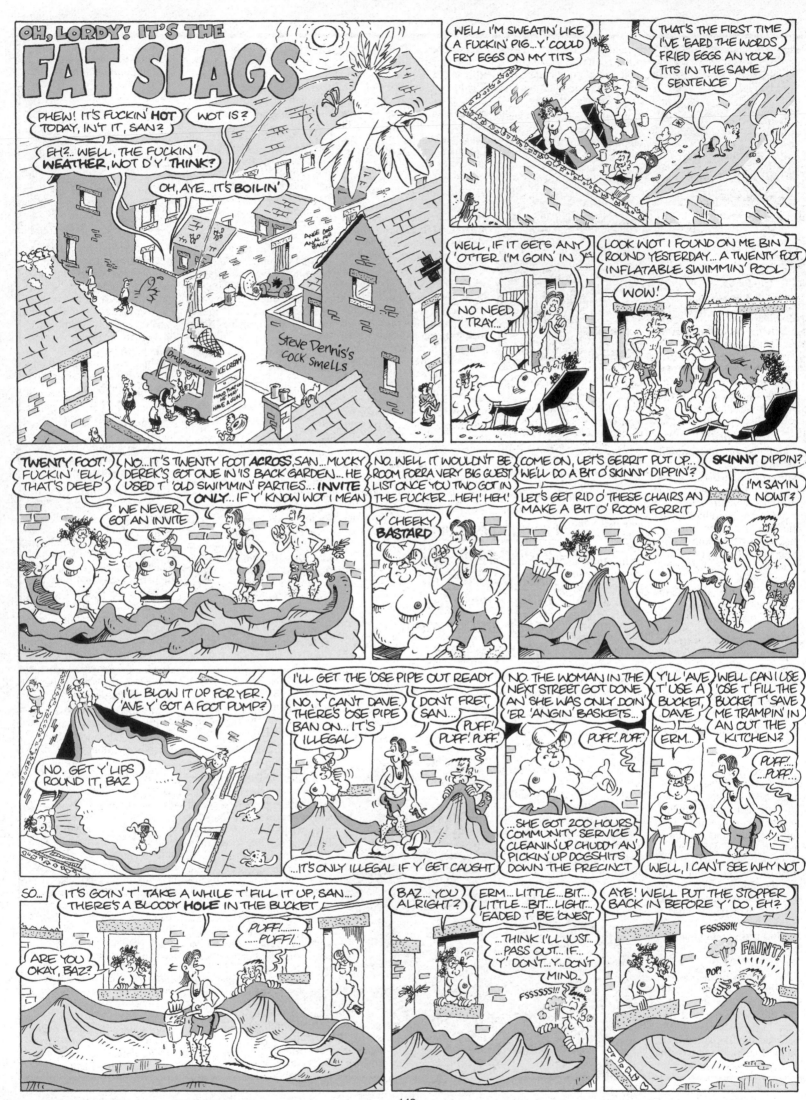

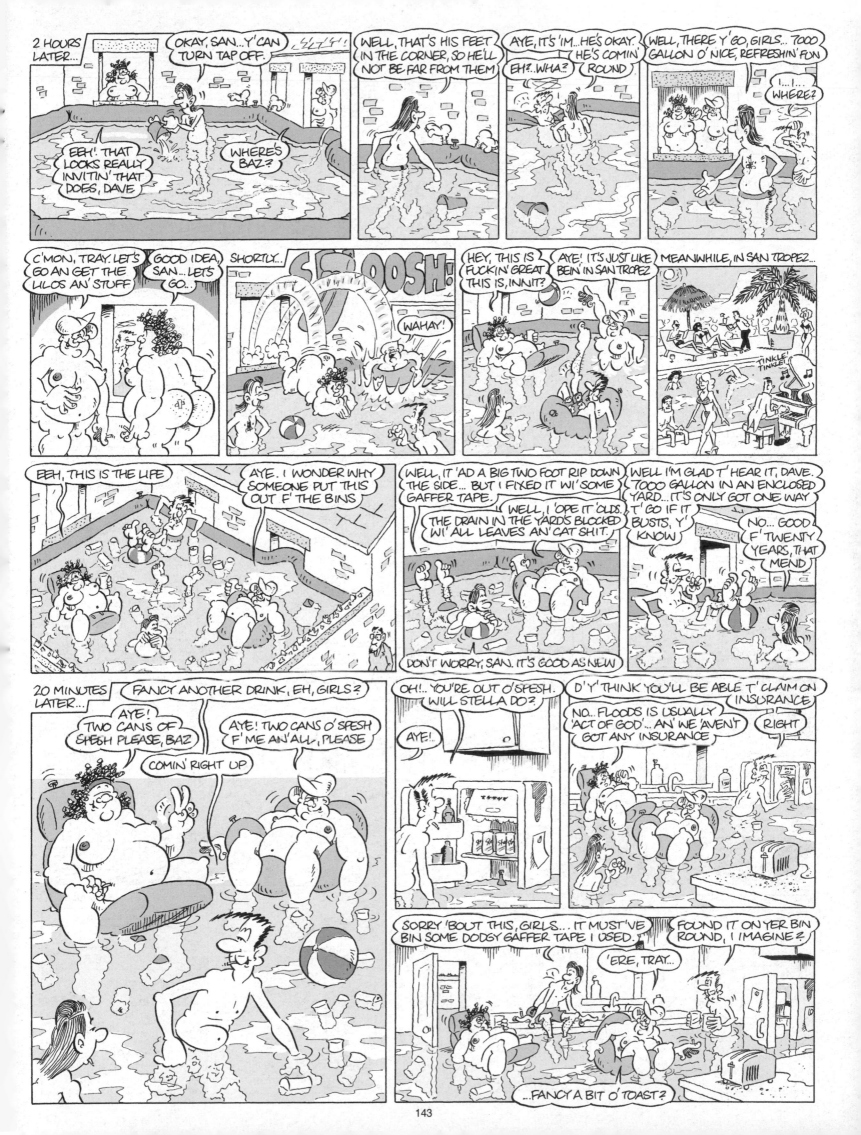

143

the REAL ALE TWATS

IN THE PUB ..AND SO THE GAME GOES INTO PENALTIES.. AND THE ATMOSPHERE HERE IN THE STADIUM IS ELECTRIC..

FOR UNITED, EVERYTHING DEPENDS ON WHAT HAPPENS IN THE NEXT FEW MINUTES.. ...AND IT WAS AT THE 1982 MORTON-ON-LUGG BEER FEST THAT I FIRST SAMPLED OWLD ALMOND'S FOAMING MOUTHFUL ....

...DAVITT SHOOTS... BUT I AM NEGLECTING MY DUTIES CASKETEERS! OUR GLASSES ARE EMPTY, AND I AM IN THE CHAIR FOR THIS NEXT ROUND!

..AND HE SCORES! I SHALL VENTURE FORTH TO THE BAR AND RETURN WITH A BRACE OF BRIMMING TANKARDS!

GET OUT THE FUCKING WAY! YELP! YOU'RE BLOCKING THE TELLY, YOU FAT TIT!

REALLY BARLORD! SOME OF US HAVE COME TO THIS PUB FOR A DRINK AND A CONVIVIAL CHAT BUT THE OVERBEARING PRESENCE OF TELEVISED SPORT IS MAKING THIS NIGH-ON IMPOSSIBLE!

WELL, THERE'S NO TELLY THROUGH IN THE LOUNGE. WE'RE STILL SERVING FOOD, BUT YOU SHOULD GET A SEAT

OH DEAR ME, THIS IS NO BETTER, I'M AFRAID. FAMILIES WITH SQUAWKING KIDS RUNNING AROUND EVERYWHERE.

FOR US MENFOLK, THE PUB IS A SANCTUARY AWAY FROM WIVES AND CHILDREN IF I WANTED TO BE SURROUNDED BY THE DOMESTIC HUBBUB OF FAMILY LIFE, I COULD HAVE STAYED AT HOME THIS EVENING.

EARLIER THAT EVENING, AT HOME TICK TOCK TICK TOCK TICK TOCK TICK TOCK

COME, CASKETEERS! WE SHALL FIND ANOTHER HOSTELRY MORE CONDUCIVE TO OUR EVENING'S DRINKING.

ALAS, THE UBIQUITY OF "SKY SPORTS" IS WRECKING THE GENIAL AMBIENCE OF OUR BELOVED PUBLIC HOUSES

LOOK AT ALL THOSE TENSE AND ANGRY FACES! ONE WOULD THINK THAT THEIR LIVES DEPENDED ON THE OUTCOME OF A "FOOTY" MATCH!

THE PUB SHOULD BE A PLACE TO RELAX — TO SIT AND SUP, AND FORGET THE CARES OF THE WORLD. OHO! THE BEARD AND SPIGOT! HERE AT LAST IS AN OASIS OF SANITY AND CALM.

EVENING, GENTS. ARE YOU TAKING PART IN THE QUIZ TONIGHT? A QUIZ, EH? WELL, WHY NOT?

SIT YE DOWN, CASKETEERS. LET US WHILE AWAY A MERRY HOUR OR SO, EXERCISING OUR INTELLECTS ON THE PUB QUIZ. IT'S ALL JUST A BIT OF FUN, OF COURSE.....

SHORTLY IMBECILE! I TOLD YOU THAT SPIELBERG'S FIRST OSCAR NOMINATION WAS FOR "CLOSE ENCOUNTERS" IN 1978! GACK! CHOKE! YOUR INSISTENCE THAT THE ANSWER WAS "E.T." HAS COST US A PRECIOUS POINT!!

WHAT do you look forward to most about Christmas? The big turkey dinner? The Bond film? The presents? Believe it or not, in a recent survey an amazing 100% of Brits nominated CHRISTMAS CRACKER JOKES as their highlight of the festive season.

But these comical gems of wit and humour don't write themselves. Each one is the end product of a complex process that involves the hard work of hundreds of talented and creative people. Few of us ever stop to think about all the time and effort that goes into the badly-printed wisecracks that crease us and our families up each December 25th. Let's follow the journey of a single Christmas cracker rib-tickler, from its earliest conception to its final realisation. It's time to read & learn & look & wonder & learn all about ...

XMAS CRACKER JOKES

THE STORY of a brand new CCJ (Christmas Cracker Joke) begins with a board meeting in January, where the directors of a large cracker corporation suggest, discuss and explore various themes they believe will provide a popular cracker quip for the upcoming festive season, still the best part of 12 months in the future. Amongst the topics under consideration this year are the unattractiveness of mothers-in-law and the inabilty of women to drive. Each area is discussed and its merits forcefully debated, but the directors finally decide that the laziness of husbands is a fruitful area that could yield a good joke for 2012.

ONCE the topic has been agreed and rubber-stamped by the board, it is submitted to the creative department of the company. Here, over endless cups of coffee, some of the sharpest minds in the business attempt to spin comedy gold about the laziness of husbands. At this stage in the process, no ideas are deemed off-limits or too outrageous for consideration; "blue-sky" and "outside the box" thinking are actively encouraged. Set-ups are suggested and rejected, punchlines are written and re-written, then discarded and re-written again. Eventually, after hours of discussion and countless drafts, a joke emerges: "Q: *What is a husband's idea of helping with the housework?* A: *Lifting his feet up so the missus can hoover underneath them.*"

THE JOKE is still a work in progress at this stage, and it is sent to be tested on a focus group selected at random from members of the general public who buy crackers. Each member of the group listens to the joke on headphones before filling in a detailed questionnaire; Which bits did they like? Which bits didn't they like? How do they think the joke could be improved?

THE RESPONSES from the focus group are sent to a scientist, who uses a powerful computer to crunch the numbers. The results are interesting: 84% of those polled think the gag is strong, 7% think is very strong and 2% think it is the funniest thing they've ever heard. Overall, it's a promising result, although several of the respondents feel that the word "missus" might be old-fashioned, outdated and sexist. The new CCJ is still a long way from being included in a cracker. There are several stages it must undergo before it is ready to be printed and inserted in a cracker.

TAKING into account the comments of the focus group, a professional gagsmith is charged with the tricky task of honing the joke to a fine edge. A cracker industry veteran with over 40 years of joke and motto writing under his belt, he is truly an expert in his demanding craft. He sets to work tweaking the wording of the one-liner; he knows that the insertion of a comma here or the removal of a semi-colon there can make all the difference between a Christmas dinner side-splitter and a tumbleweed moment over the turkey.

THE PROVISIONAL final draft of the joke is submitted to the company's legal department, where it is read by a highly-paid barrister. It is his responsibility to make sure that the new wording - "Q: What is a husband's idea of helping with the housework? A: Lifting up his feet so his wife can hoover underneath." - doesn't fall foul of the law. His trained lawyer's eye immediately spots a problem and he raises the alarm. The word "hoover" is a registered intellectual property owned by the Hoover Corporation of North Canton, Ohio USA. The legal eagle suggests that to avoid the risk of a successful court action, the offending trademark should be blacked out or removed completely.

THE JOKE, along with the legal advice, is returned to the editorial department. At a tense meeting attended by the cracker factory's key creative personnel, the problem appears unsurmountable: The word hoover is essential to the punchline and without it, the joke makes no sense. The meeting drags on until late at night with no apparent solution in sight. It looks like the CCJ has fallen at the final hurdle. More than two-thirds of cracker jokes suffer a similar fate, never seeing the light of day due to legal complications of one sort or another. Then, at the eleventh hour, a senior executive has a brainwave. Why not replace the word "hoover" with the word "vacuum"? Everyone holds their breath whilst the new version is re-submitted to the lawyer. Then, relief all round when he gives it the thmbs-up.

WITH the last legal barrier to publication finally eliminated, the joke is typeset and loaded onto a giant press, which roars into life. Running round the clock, it prints off countless millions of copies, which are folded up and placed inside Christmas crackers, along with a snap, a shit novelty and a paper hat that rips when you put it on. The finished Items are then loaded onto lorries and delivered to shops all over Britain in time for the Christmas shopping season.

IT IS Christmas Day, and at dinner tables from John's End to Land O'Groats Britons pull their crackers and eagerly read the joke contained on the slip of paper inside. The "lazy husband" wisecrack proves a great hit and the sound of helpless guffaws bursts from every dining room in the country. The whole team at the corporation can give themselves a pat on the back, congratulate themselves on a job well done, and take a few moments to sit back and relax. But not for very long. In the cracker gag world, you're only as good as your last joke, and there's a board meeting scheduled for 8.30 am sharp on January 2nd, when work begins in earnest on a new quip for Christmas 2013.

Showbiz Exclusive!

My Favourite Cracker Novelty

We asked some of Britain's top celebrities what their favourite thing that had ever fallen out of a cracker was...

George Osborne
Chancellor of the Exchequer

"About eight Christmases ago, I got a fortune-telling fish in my cracker. You put it on the palm of your hand and it tells you what is going to happen in the future. It's just a silly bit of fun, but I still find it useful even today. If it curls to the left, I raise petrol duty in line with inflation, if it curls to the right I lower the minimum lending rate, and if it stays flat I adjust the exchange rate mechanism by a quarter of one percent."

Tamara Para Tonkinson
It girl

"I regularly spent Christmas at Klosters with the Royal family back in the eighties, and once at dinner I pulled a cracker with Prince Charles. I won and the novelty was a small plastic magnifying glass, which I still have all these years later. I use it every morning in my dressing room when I'm looking for my bra."

Kylie Minogue
Popstress

"My most treasured cracker novelty is a small, yellow plastic comb that I won when I was round at my sister Dannii's house for Christmas. Few of my fans realise that I have got a very hairy arse, right down to my tinter, and I use the comb twice a day to keep it neat and tidy. I don't use my other comb in case I've got winnets and I end up getting them in my hair."

Tinie Tempah
Rap singer

"I've got one of those little packs of playing cards that are about half normal size. They're great for me, because as my name suggests, I'm extremely small. Last year I went on tour with Tinchy Strider, who's even smaller than I am, and we whiled away the hours on our Bedford Rascal tour bus playing snap with them."

Clint Eastwood
Cowboy actor

"I was pleased as punch when I pulled a cracker with Martin Scorsese and won a set of three miniature screwdrivers in a plastic wallet at Christopher Walken's Christmas party. Foolishly, I later swapped them with Jack Nicholson for a plastic compass and I haven't stopped kicking myself since. It never worked, pointing every which way but north, and I ended up throwing the goddamn thing in the trash can. Imagine how sick I felt when I saw Jack at last year's Oscars mending his glasses with the screwdrivers I swapped him."

Letterbocks

Viz Comic
P.O. Box 841
Whitley Bay
NE26 9EQ

letters@viz.co.uk

STAR LETTER

I'VE just been manically struggling to stay standing and slash into a filthy shitpot on a fast-moving coach. While staring at someone else's banger and mash with piss flying everywhere, my iPod played me Celine Dion's soulful ballad, *My Heart Will Go On*. Have any of your readers ever had a more inappropriately soundtracked event in their lives?

Lewis, e-mail

I GOT fetched from work yesterday because my son had been sick during a maths lesson at school, and it got me wondering; What would Ben Dover do if he was at work making a porn film and his son's teacher rang up to say young Tyger Drew had thrown up in a maths lesson? Would he drop everything and drive straight round to the school still with a big bone on? Or would he wait until he had blown his stack up some woman's back and then go in to fetch him?

Egbert Catattack, Finchley

YOU never see anything in the news about Finland, do you? It's too quiet over there, and I think those Finns are up to something. Have any of your readers been to Finland lately, and if so, did they see anything suspicious?

Hampton Crackpipe, Luton

I CAN'T see the point of ID cards. If I was sober I'd know who I am, and if I was drunk, I would probably lose it or forget where I put it. So what is the point?

Alan Heath, e-mail

SCIENTISTS say that a 10km wide crater is the site of a meteor strike that wiped out the dinosaurs. Well I simply don't believe that all the dinosaurs on earth were huddled together in this one crater when it struck. These so called scientists should really think through their theories before making such outlandish claims.

Charles Turner, e-mail

I CAN'T believe it when prostitutes complain about the way they are forced to make their money. Getting paid to have it off with members of the opposite sex would be my dream job.

George Panhandle, Birmingham

DO ANY readers know when the official cut-off point is for people talking about 'funny things that happened on *Friends*'? It's just that they stopped making it over 10 years ago and someone in my office still manages to discuss a quote, incident or episode on most days and it's starting to wear a bit thin.

D. Milner, Durham

I DON'T mind sending a few bob over to Africa now and again but as well as building schools and wells, why don't they use a bit of it to build a bridge for all those wildebeests who get eaten by crocodiles every year crossing the Serengeti River?

Terry Corrigan, e-mail

Christmas Winners
How our Olympic heroes will celebrate the festive season...

Mo Farah
Gold, 5,000 & 10,000 metres
"Every day is a training day to me, and Christmas Day is no exception. I'll get up at 5am like I always do and go for a 25-mile run, getting back home in time to see my family open their presents. After breakfast, I'll go for another 25-mile run, and do another 25-mile run before lunch. Then I'll tuck into a massive traditional Christmas dinner, consisting of turkey, roast spuds, sprouts, Yorkshire puddings and all the trimmings, followed by two big bowls full of Christmas pud with custard and brandy butter, plus a big plate of mince pies. Then it's straight back out on the road for a quick 25-mile run, before coming home and flopping on the sofa in front of the Bond film. Later in the day, I'll try to squeeze in another 25-mile run before bedtime, setting my alarm for 3am so I can have a quick 25-mile run before I get up on Boxing Day."

Jessica Ennis
Olympic Gold, Ladies' Heptathlon
"Every day of the year I practise each of the seven different events that comprise the heptathlon. Except on Christmas Day, when I take the opportunity to kick back and relax with my friends and family. However, I make up for it by training twice as hard on Boxing Day when I practise fourteen different events."

Bradley Wiggins
Olympic Gold, Tour de France
"December 25th is my favourite day of the year. I get so excited wondering what presents I'm going to get that I simply can't sleep the night before, and I'm always the first one down in the morning to see what Santa's left under the tree. Last year it was a brand new six-speed bike. Come to think of it, he's brought me a new bike every Christmas for the past twenty years."

Andy Murray
Olympic Gold, Men's Tennis
"Every day of the year I'm out on the courts, practising my game. Unfortunately, my training partner Ivan Lendl likes to take Christmas Day off, so on 25th December I train with 82-year-old Rabbi Lionel Blue who, as a Jew, doesn't believe in Christmas. However, one year in seven, when December 25th falls on a Saturday, even he won't train with me, and I have to go out in the garden and play swingball on my own."

WHY do people on the American continent give hurricanes names? Maybe you would get more sympathy from the rest of the world if you didn't get so emotionally attached to these violent gusts of wind.

Tulip Cock, e-mail

THEY say an apple a day keeps the doctor away. I wish I had listened to them as I have eaten a pear every day for 41 years, and am now suffering from chronic depression. What's more I've got a big boil on my arse which needs lancing.

Tam Dale, e-mail

Numbers don't exactly add up

Regarding *Register your quad bike before taking it off-road* (September 24), please note that "quad bike" is a misnomer. As "quad" equals four and "bi" equals two, it should be quad cycle.
W Vize, Ajman

I THINK this guy could be related to Mr Logic!

Andy Rignall, e-mail

I WAS watching a bongo flick on the internet today where a bird shoved an empty champagne bottle up her arse... *blunt end first!* I couldn't believe my eyes. Who can afford champagne these days?

Graham Flintoft, Gateshead

TOP TIPS

INSTEAD of looking left and right while crossing a road, why not save time by looking straight ahead, as the resulting tangent is the same.

Keith, e-mail

SAVE money on expensive summer and winter duvets by using a large sheet of raw puff pastry in summer and then cooking it in winter.

Tam Dale, e-mail

TOFFEE lovers. If you've mislaid your toffee hammer, simply post the intact slab to yourself using Parcelforce. It will eventually turn up on your doorstep broken into hundreds of bitesize pieces.

Stu Mandry, e-mail

SAVE money on eye-patches by poking out one lens of an old pair of sunglasses.

R Chudleigh, e-mail

GET THE feeling of spending a week in Guernsey by spending an afternoon in Guernsey.

Dr Grafenberg, Jersey

LEAVE reminder messages for flatmates by shouting your message into a sandwich bag, closing it very quickly, then leaving it on the bench for the recipient to open. You could perhaps leave a note telling them what it is.

Chops the Spacedog, e-mail

KEEP a Tim Curry 'Doctor Frank-n-Furter' outfit handy by the front door in case someone has a flat tyre and wants to use your house phone.

Luke Newland, e-mail

OLD fashioned undertakers. Mince pies on the eyes of the deceassed instead of coins make a nice festive touch at Christmas.

Chad Elliott, Bristol

MAKE neighbours think you have alcoholic mice by hiding miniature bottles of scotch behind a crack in the skirting board and using a teaspoon of porridge to simulate small pools of vermin vomit.

Collins Boostsy, e-mail

PREVENT your pet worm from getting lonely by cutting it in half.

Bill, e-mail

FOOL people into thinking you have a self-drive car by driving at top speed a few inches from the car in front whilst playing the bongos.

Paul Cartwright, e-mail

toptips@viz.co.uk

Rude Kid

ARE YOU LOOKING FORWARD TO SANTA COMING, YOUNG MAN?

FUCK SANTA. AND FUCK HIS FUCKING REINDEER!

❄ **CAN** someone tell me what the latest terror forecast is? Only I wanted to pop down the shops and don't want to get blown to bits by some fanatic in the name of some God or other, thank you very much.

Edna Ednathorpe, e-mail

✱ *Yes, Edna. A quick call to the Home Office reveals that the terror forecast is 'yellow to amber', which means that you can go to the shops for essential items, but be vigilant and report any people not dressed the same as you to the police.*

❄ **ON MY** way to work each day I pass a tree that is shaped like a man with a huge penis standing on a bridge. If your readers have any similar photos I really don't care.

Arthur Sixpence, e-mail

Just £10 a month can help a kitten get out of a boot.

This Christmas across the UK, over 10,000 kittens are stuck inside boots. We receive no government funding and we urgently need your money to help get them out. Donate online at www.kittensstuckinaboot.org

❄ **HAVING** fancied her for some time, I climbed into my wife's best friend's bed and gave her one during a holiday in Devon recently. Imagine my surprise when our grunting and bad language managed to wake up her husband, who was sleeping next to her at the time. Thankfully, being British, he had the good manners to let us finish, before ordering a cream tea for us all and deciding never to talk about it again in case it spoiled the holiday.

Edgar Lardgutsen, e-mail

❄ **WHEN** my daughter had the mumps, Shakin' Stevens lacked the decency to call to find out how she was faring. We are still waiting for him to show any degree of concern. If we are ever

introduced to him I shall give him a piece of my mind.

Sheila Trump, Taunton

❄ **WHY** don't they try Jimmy Savile by ouija board, similar to a court video link but with some gobshite claiming to be contacting the dead? I'd pick that Derek Acorah to carry out the nonsense, aided by Yvette Fielding who could scream hysterically now and then for fuck all. Then once Savile is 'in the room', Acorah's Indian spirit guide Sam could chop his balls off with his tomahawk.

Paranormal Investigator, e-mail

❄ **IN** *The Sound of Music*, why didn't Mary Poppins simply hide the Von Trapp family in her big handbag and then fly them off to Switzerland with her magic umbrella? A big hole in the plot there, I think.

Richard Warr, e-mail

❄ **WELL** if you ask me, kiwi fruits just look like shaved tarantula arses. No thanks, fruit 'n' veg police.

Howitt, e-mail

❄ **I FIND** it fascinating that the staple diet of Bedouins is lamb, which by coincidence, is also the name of their religion. Have any other readers know of any staple diets that correspond to the name of the religion of the people who actually eat the stuff ?

Terry Corrigan, e-mail

❄ **WE'RE** told in the Bible that Lazarus was raised from the dead after his sisters, Mary and Martha sent word of his death to Jesus. In a bizarre modern day parallel of this Biblical tale, a chap down my road called Leighton also recently died. This is where the similarities end however, as his two sisters failed to report his death to anyone and instead continued to cash in his giros for 3 months until neighbours complained about the smell.

Tarquin Cockfondle, e-mail

Non-cognate Interlexical Homographs Text Vote

'Away in'   'Pret'

or

...Which is YOUR favourite
'A Manger?'

Text AWAY IN or PRET to

018 11 8055

Martin Lewis's SOAPBOX

❝ *The Christmas TV ratings battle between Coronation Street and EastEnders is already underway. My sources tell me that viewers are in for some of the most spectacular finance related storylines in years...* ❞

In **Corrie**, *Sally* comes home early to find *Kevin* on the phone to his bank about interest charges. When Sally and Kevin secured the mortgage on their terraced property in the 1980s, Kevin was missold PPI and is now desperately trying to claim back the money before Sally finds out. With their relationship already on the rocks after Kev's disastrous decision to take out a 5 years mortgage at a fixed rate of 7%, could this be the final straw for long-suffering Sally? *Watch this space!*

££££££££££££££££££££££

In another controversial storyline, *Tyrone* opens a current account that requires a regular monthly credit of £1,000. When Kevin docks his wages for turning up drunk his balance dips under a grand and he loses 0.5% in interest bonus. When he finds out, there's the showdown of showdowns in the Rovers as Kevin openly brags about his online regular saver - a building society account that pays up to 1% more than Tyrone's equivalent product! *Sparks will fly!*

££££££££££££££££££££££

In a double ratings boost, a New Year's spectacular sees *Ken Barlow* accidently exceed his cash ISA limit by taking out a stocks and shares ISA with *2 providers!* Ken's life begins to unravel as he receives a letter from the tax office asking him to pay back the additional tax relief and explaining to him the current tax free savings threshold. With *Deirdre* threatening to leave him over the matter, Ken has nowhere left to turn and on New Year's Day viewers will see the street veteran slumped at his computer in tears as he desperately trawls through financial comparison websites! According to one insider, *"Ken manages to find a good rate of interest for an ISA saver product but accidentally presses 'Back' in his web browser and has to start the application process again."* **Could this be what finally pushes Ken over the edge?**

££££££££££££££££££££££

After being trounced in the ratings war by last year's festive Corrie overdraft charges plot, **EastEnders** will be looking to take back the Christmas ratings crown with the explosive culmination of a storyline involving *Pat Butcher*. Over the moon about her credit card balance transfer, the smile is wiped off Pat's face when she checks her statement and discovers that a 2% admin fee has been charged to her account - *£24 in total* - money she was hoping to use to buy a pay-as-you-go mobile!

Prosperous viewing folks! *Martin x*

HAMMER MANNERS
with the Duchess of Northumberland

MY NEIGHBOUR borrowed a hammer from me to put some picture hooks up. However, shortly afterwards his wife and children were killed after being dragged into the mechanism of an escalator. That was yesterday, and my neighbour is understandably still in a state of shock. I don't want to intrude on his grief, but the thing is, I'd really like my hammer back as I'm intending to build a rabbit hutch this weekend. Obviously, if it was a cheap hammer I'd probably just let him keep it what with all he's been through, but it's a 14oz stainless-steel-shafted Draper claw hammer with a vulcanised rubber grip, so I'm quite keen to get it back. How can I retrieve my hammer without coming over as too insensitive?

Barry Battleships, Bingley

I'M AFRAID that your hammer may be the last thing on your neighbour's mind. You should go round and offer your condolences, perhaps taking a bunch of flowers or a box of chocolates. Offer him a shoulder to cry on, and once he opens up, try to gently steer the subject away from the tragic accident that has befallen his family and onto your hammer. Perhaps you could start talking about coffins, expressing an interest in the way they are nailed together, and hope that it jogs his memory.

OUR BABY daughter was baptised last week, and as a christening gift from my husband's mother she received a 4lb lump hammer. The problem is, my sister also bought her an identical lump hammer. Do you think it would be unforgivably rude of me to ask my in-laws or sister for the receipt, or would it be better to simply say nothing?

Frances Tellme, Telford

YOUR mother-in-law and your sister have obviously put a lot of thought into their choice, and they undoubtedly both want their own gift to be unique and special - something that your daughter will treasure for the rest of her life. In this case, honesty may well be the best policy. Put the two relatives in touch with each other, explaining the situation. I'm sure that one of them will decide to return their lump hammer to the shop and exchange it for an alternative christening gift, such as a set of chisels or an electric router.

On das buses

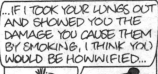

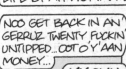

RAYWATCH

IF YOU saw Redcar lifeguard **RAY PILES** in the street, chances are you wouldn't give him a second glance. You'd never suspect for a moment that the portly, bespectacled, unemployed 58-year-old leads a remarkable double life.

Yet you would be wrong. For Ray is a real life superhero - Redcar's only full-time celebrity lifeguard - and when he's not shopping in the Spar or looking for a jobs in the local library reading room, he's patrolling the Teesside town's beaches 24 hours a day on the lookout for stars in distress.

Famous faces who get into difficulties in the sea have every reason to thank Ray, who selflessly plunges into the chilly waters several times every day to save them from drowning. In his 30 years as a frontline lifeguard Piles has also pulled hundreds of A-list celebrities from the treacherous surf of Redcar Bay.

"I've lost count of the number of stars I have literally plucked from the jaws of death," he told us. "And the roll-call of Holly-

EXCLUSIVE!

wood A-listers who owe me their lives reads like a soggy *Who's Who* of Tinseltown royalty."

Now, to mark the publication of a sensational authorised biography written by his best friend Keith Eggs, Ray is set to embark on a sell-out tour with a one man show about his adventures. Throughout January he will visit Women's Institute branches in Redcar, Coatham and Marske-by-the-Sea, showing slides and telling anecdotes featuring many of the showbiz celebrities he's met during his exciting career.

Speaking in his bachelor pad overlooking a disused BASF bromine smelter, Ray gave us a preview of some of the fascinating tales he'll be telling in his show.

"If I told you some of the household names I've rescued from the surf off Redcar beach, you'd think I was making it up. I remember this one time I spotted a woman waving for help from out beyond the groynes. She'd been bobbing about on an old tractor inner tube in the shallows, and had been pulled out into the deeper water by a current.

I've seen it happen a million times. People get out of their depth and they panic. I've got one of those floats like David Hasselhoff has got in Baywatch, which I made out of a big Lenor bottle. I immediately grabbed it and ran out into the water to rescue the woman. The water was rough, but I'm a strong swimmer, and I soon reached her.

When I saw who it was, I couldn't believe my eyes. For there, clinging desperately to the tractor tyre in the pounding waves was Lara Croft actress **ANGELINA JOLIE**!

Above the noise of the crashing surf, I shouted to her to hold onto me, and swam back to the shore. By the time I got her on the beach, Angelina had swallowed a load of sea water, so I had to do the kiss of life on her.

For most men, locking lips with the luscious *Tomb Raider* star would be a dream come true. For me, however, it was all in a day's work. After about ten minutes of kissing her, she came back to life, thanked me and went home to the boarding house where she was staying. I went straight back to patrolling the beach. As a lifeguard, I'm constantly on duty 24-7 in case someone else gets into difficulties and needs my services.

I didn't think any more about Angelina until the next day, when I got a phone call from her hubby **BRAD PITT**. *He was so grateful that I'd saved his wife's life that he wanted to give me a reward... of a million pounds! But I turned his offer down flat.*

As I told him, I'm not in this game to make money. I'm in it to save people from drowning... especially the stars.

It's not just unpredictable tides that can get people into trouble, says Ray. Lurking just below the surface of the sea off Redcar, there's also dangerous wildlife waiting to prey on unwary visitors who foolishly stray from the safety of the beach.

Anyone who's ever seen the film *Jaws* knows that the Great White Shark is the most dangerous fish in the ocean. With its razor-sharp teeth, voracious appetite for human flesh and lightning speed, it's the ultimate underwater killing machine.

So I was worried to say the least when one was spotted swimming around in the sea off West Scar. I tried to evacuate the beach, but there was a sandcastle competition on that day and the Lord Mayor of Redcar was insistent that it should go ahead as planned so as not to cause panic.

Suddenly, I heard a load of screams from the water. To my horror, I saw a pedallo full of girls out beyond the breakers, desperately trying to get back to the safety of dry land. I noticed straight away that they were **PAN'S PEOPLE**, the sexy dance troupe off *Top of the Pops*. Behind their boat, and bearing down on it at great speed, was the unmistakeable form of a shark's fin!

Without a thought for my own safety, I ran into the water and swam after the shark as fast as I could. I caught up with it just as it rose out of the water with its mouth open, ready to eat Pan's People.

Using all my strength, I grabbed it round the head and we rolled round and round in the water. Luckily, I had one of those daggers strapped to my leg like divers have in films, and I used it to stab the shark over and over.

Me and the shark sank beneath the waves, still locked in a deadly embrace. Up on the surface, it was all calm except for a big pool of bright red blood bubbling up to the surface. Pan's People were speechless with horror, looking at the deceptively calm water. They thought I was a goner.

There was a long silence during which nobody spoke. Then I popped out of the middle of the blood, clutching the dagger between my teeth and the girls all cheered.

The blonde with the legs and the short one with dark hair helped me into the boat and I pedalled them to the shore. Once they were safely back on the beach, the girls couldn't thank me enough for saving their lives by stabbing the shark. To show their gratitude, they offered to take me back to their B&B and do a special sexy dance routine in their bikinis just for me.

They made it clear there would be audience participation. Now I'm as red-blooded as the next man and I would be lying if I said I wasn't tempted to take them up on their offer, but in the end I had to turn them down. For I knew that the treacherous waters of Redcar had to be watched round the clock if they were not to claim any more innocent celebrity lives. And I would never have been able to forgive myself if another innocent star had perished in the sea while I was frolicking with Pan's People in skimpy bikinis.

have had hot dinners," says real life David Hasselhoff

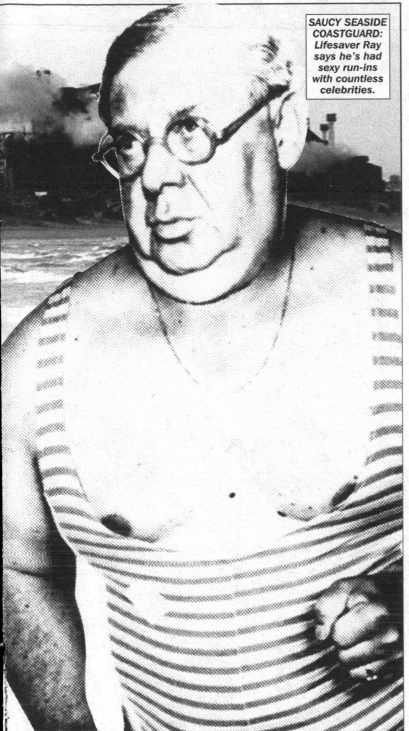

SAUCY SEASIDE COASTGUARD: Lifesaver Ray says he's had sexy run-ins with countless celebrities.

sea and onto the sand. But something was wrong, the *Crazy in Love* singer wasn't breathing and her heart had stopped.

The cause was obvious to me at once. Beyoncé had fallen in near Redcar's main sewage outlet and had swallowed a blob that had become lodged in her throat. I fished the blob out and cleared her airways, but I knew I had to start her heart again, and quick, or she would die.

I loosened her clothing and started doing that thing like on *Casualty*, pressing up and down on her tits to start her heart again. Anybody who walked past and saw me sitting astride one of the world's sexiest stars with my hands on her ample charms would have wondered what on earth was going on!

Eventually, after about ten minutes of me pushing her knockers up and down, Beyoncé came back to life. She opened her eyes and thanked me for getting the blob out her throat and starting her heart again. Then she said she'd like to show me her gratitude properly by going to bed with me behind the public bogs in the car park on East Parade. It was the opportunity of a lifetime. Most men would give their eye teeth for a chance to sleep with the sexy singer out of Destiny's Child.

But it was yet another offer I was going to have to turn down flat. I set my professional standards too high to allow me to take advantage of someone I'd rescued from Redcar's deadly depths. As far as I was concerned, simply knowing that I had saved the life of yet another well known personality from the world of showbusiness, was reward enough. **"**

Sometimes, the stars that Ray risked his own life to save were the last people on earth you might expect to get into difficulty in the sea.

" After starring in *Baywatch*, you'd think that busty blonde bombshell **PAMELA ANDERSON** would actually be at least be able to swim, but you'd be wrong. And to say I was surprised to see her in her familiar red swimsuit, floundering in the shallow waters off Redcar beach would be an understatement.

Apparently, Barb Wire star Pam had been metal-detecting on the wet sand and had found herself cut off on

a sandbar by the incoming tide. She had panicked as the waters rose, and by the time I spotted her, the water was up to her trademark chest. It was January, and the survival time in the icy waters off Tees Bay was less than ten minutes so I knew I had to act fast.

Like her real-life ex co-star, *Knight Rider*'s **DAVID HASSELHOFF**, I plunged into the freezing surf and pulled her to safety. As we lay side by side on the beach, I noticed that her nipples were sticking out like chapel hat pegs - a tell-tale sign of hypothermia. I knew that if I didn't raise her core body temperature immediately she would slip into unconsciousness and probably die.

I decided the best way to conserve her warmth was to cuddle right up to her with my hands on her breasts, which due to their large surface area were particularly prone to heat loss.

As a thank-you for saving her life, Pam asked me if I'd like to take part with her in one of her famous sex videos, like the one she did with her former husband, the drummer out of Mötley Crüe. I'd seen the video on one of the computers at the library before I got banned, so I was quite tempted to say the least. But I knew my duties as a lifeguard always have to come before my own personal pleasure.

For if a Hollywood star or famous pop singer had drowned off Redcar beach whilst I was doing sex on a boat with Pamela Anderson, then I would never have been able to forgive myself.

If you look through the archives of the local paper, you will see that not a single Tinseltown A-lister has perished off Redcar beach whilst I've been on patrol. That fact to me is worth more than all the sex I've had to turn down over the last three decades. **"**

Raywatch: The Life & Times of Celebrity Lifeguard Ray Piles by Keith Eggs is due to be published early in the new year as soon as the manuscript is completed. In the meantime, could anyone who has a ribbon suitable for a 1968 Boots portable typewriter please contact Mr Eggs c/o Flat 3a, above the Happy Haddock Fish & Chip shop, Gibbet Street, Redcar.

In his three decades of patrolling the town's seafront Ray has saved countless lives. But his position as Redcar beach's chief lifeguard is an unofficial one as he has never undergone any training.

" There was a slight problem a few years ago when I tried to save some youngsters who were drowning in a rock pool on the beach. It turned out they weren't drowning after all and my attempts to resuscitate them were misunderstood by some overzealous parents. To cut a long story short, I'm not allowed to be a proper lifeguard because I'm banned from coming into contact with children.

That doesn't bother me, as the legal restrictions on my movements have never stopped me from going out and doing what I do best ... and that's saving the stars.

I'll never forget this other time when I spotted bootylicious R'n'B star **BEYONCÉ** flailing about in the water. It turned out she'd been fishing for crabs off the potash dock and had slipped on some bait and fallen in. She'd been struggling against the undertow, got tired and now she was drowning.

It was the sort of bread and butter rescue I ate for breakfast. I dived into the surf to rescue her and within seconds I had dragged her out of the

Raffles The Gentleman Thug

AH! A SOJOURN TO CLACTON-ON-SEA, RAFFLES! I AM PARTICULARLY KEEN TO VISIT THE NEAPOLITAN PERGOLA ON THE PROMENADE, RIDE ON THE FAMOUS FUNICULAR RAILWAY AND SEE THE PANOPTICAL CAMERA OBSCURA...

FORAMINATE THAT, BUNNY...

...I'M HERE TO ABSTERSTICATE MY FUCKING NUTS...

...AND I HAVE IT ON MOST EXCELLENT AUTHORITY THAT ESSEX WOMEN SPREAD AS EASILY AS MESSRS FORTNUM & MASON'S QUINCE JELLY ON A FRESHLY-BUTTERED ENGLISH MUFFIN.

COME ON. LET'S GET PARKED.

...I AM AFRAID THAT YOU CANNOT LEAVE YOUR AUTOMOBILE THERE, SIR. THIS IS THE TOP OF THE LIFEBOAT SLIPWAY.

≥TSK≤

THAT'S A DISCOMFORT IN THE FUNDAMENT, FOR I HAVE SWITCHED OFF THE ENGINE, AND STARTING IT AGAIN IS A MOST WEARISOME PROCESS.

NOTWITHSTANDING, I UNDERSTAND THAT INGRESS AND EGRESS MUST NOT BE HINDERED AT ANY JUNCTURE.

≥SIGH≤ COULD YOU PASS ME THE STARTING HANDLE PLEASE, BUNNY...?

HERE YOU GO, RAFFLES...

CAPITAL.

WATCH HOW I TAKE A FIRM GRIP ON THE HANDLE... AND... ONE... TWO...THREE...

SPANK!

NOW, SHALL WE EMBARK TO THE BEACH, BUNNY? I UNDERSTAND THE LADIES HEREABOUTS ARE MOST IMMODESTLY DRESSED IN A MANNER THAT LEAVES LITTLE TO THE IMAGINATION.

I SAY!

OH YES. WHEN THEY EMERGE FROM THE WATER IN THEIR FLANELETTE SWIMSUITS, YOU CAN SEE EVERYTHING... DECOLLETAGE... CORYBUNGUS... CONTRAPUNCTUM... THE FUCKING ENTIRE ENSEMBLE.

SHORTLY...

COME ALONG, BUNNY...

LET'S GO AND PULL OURSELVES SOME HIRSUTE PATISSERIE.

EXCUSE ME MADAM, BUT MIGHT I POLITELY ENQUIRE IF YOU ARE AT ALL PARTIAL TO PHEASANT?

INDEED, SIR. I HAVE AN INCORRIGABLE FONDNESS FOR GAME MEAT OF ALL KINDS.

WELL IN THAT CASE, MY DEAR LADY, WOULD IT BE TOO FORWARD OF ME TO SUGGEST THAT YOU MIGHT CARE TO SUCK MY COCK, AS IT IS LIKEWISE BOTH "WELL HUNG" AND "FOUL"...?

EURGH! YOU BEASTLY GENTLEMAN!

SLAP!

OBVIOUSLY AN INVETERATE SAPPHIST, BUNNY.

I SHALL INFORM MY CHAPERONE - THE REVEREND COLEFAX - OF YOUR OBNOXIOUS ADVANCE, SIR.

WHAT...? THAT DOZY STREAK OF MICTURATE BURIED IN THE SAND...?

OOH! I'M DEFECATING MY BREECHES.

WAKE UP, REVEREND COLEFAX! THIS DISCOURTEOUS FELLOW HAS BUT LATELY FAVOURED ME WITH A MOST DEPLORABLE IMPLICATURE.

OH GOODNESS GRACIOUS. I AM GREATLY DISPLEASED TO HEAR THAT, MISS CARDEW...

...BECAUSE, IF THERE'S ONE THING THAT GETS MY DANDER UP, IT'S DEPLORABLE IMPLICATURES.

PHALLICIZE MY FORTUNE.

IN HOSPITAL...

NURSE... HERE'S A CONUNDRUM FOR YOU... WHAT'S GOT TWO BROKEN THUMBS, TOOK FIRST CLASS HONOURS IN FRENCH AT MAGDALEN COLLEGE OXFORD, AND LIKES BLOW-JOBS...?

"I'm in Two Minds about Bumming"

~ Archbishop

RETIRING Archbishop of Canterbury **DR ROWAN WILLIAMS** has finally come clean about his views on homosexuality. And his tendentious broadside on the emotive subject is set to shake the Church to its very foundations.

In a wide-ranging interview with *PC Pro* magazine, Dr Williams confronted the issue honestly. He said: "I'm very definitely in two minds about bumming."

Throughout his 10 years at the C of E's helm, Williams, 61, has felt constrained from speaking out candidly on the controversial subject. But since announcing his retirement, he says he is at last able to speak out publicly and plainly express his true opinions.

"I can now state categorically that I am 100% unsure about the matter," he continued. "In a sense, it seems to me that it I can neither condone nor condemn it."

In pinning his colours so firmly to the middle ground, the Archbishop is

sure to provoke a furious debate. But in the interview, he spoke of his relief at finally being able to be so openly noncommittal on the vexed topic.

"People have accused me of sitting on the fence about gayness, but now I'm very firmly off the fence and able to sidestep the issue square on," he said through his beard.

Heart scare for Kerry

Docs' warning for non-entity Katona

BRAVE *KERRY KATONA* has opened up her heart once again despite being warned by doctors that if she opens it up one more time, it may never close.

"It was a real wake-up call to be honest," the car-crash ex-reality star said to anyone who would listen. "My lifestyle of repeatedly opening up my h e a r t has left

Katona Hot Tin Roof: Atomic Kitten Kerry has opened heart once more.

me with very little of substance to open up my heart about."

heart

"That's why I'm opening up my heart about being told not to open up my heart."

Speaking candidly to passing pedestrians, the ex-Queen of the Jungle opened up her heart about her hectic lifestyle of failures, comebacks and failed comebacks.

"When I get up in the morning, sometimes it's hard to tell if I am making a comeback from failure that day or failing to come back from a previous failed comeback," she said.

clout

"The beauty of my career is that no day is ever the same.

"One day I might be teetering on the brink of financial and nervous collapse, and the very next day day I can be spiralling out of control in the morning, bouncing back in the afternoon and picking myself up off the floor in the evening," the former face of Iceland added.

Bishop! Bosh! Loadsa Dosh!

Bumper payday in store for new AB of C

WHOEVER is crowned the new Archbishop of Canterbury next year, one thing is certain... he's set for a bumper payday. For the lucky incumbent of the C of E's highest office gets a wages package that would make Fred Goodwin green with envy.

A basic salary of £70k tax free would be enough for most people in cash-strapped Britain, but it's pin money compared to the host of lucrative perks on offer, with the whole package adding up to a whopping £20 million a year! Here's where all the money comes from.

1 SALARY: Tax free, £70k basic plus a chauffeur-driven Bentley limousine and a free Central London palace.
£200,000

2 HOSPITALITY & GIFTS: Visiting dignitaries such as Popes and Dalai Llamas etc. hand over expensive gifts as tokens of their esteem plus free 5-star hotel accommodation when travelling overseas.
£600,000

3 WINE & BISCUITS: A perk of the job, as much as he can eat or drink, thrown in gratis.
£5,000

4 COLLECTION PLATE, TIPS ETC.: Parishioners are encouraged to give generously at the end of services, and with 52 services a year in a 1,000-seater Cathedral, the cash soon adds up.
£100,000

5 VESTMENTS: The Archbishop of Canterbury gets a bumper clothing allowance, but if he makes do and mends his threadbare old robes, he can simply pocket the lot.
£60,000

6 JOURNALISM, WRITING ETC.: Tabloid newspapers pay good money for a religious leader's considered views on the big moral issues of the day, such as *Britain's Got Talent*, the Go Compare meerkats and Paris Hilton's latest sex video.
£150,000

7 BIBLE ROYALTIES: The Archbishop of Canterbury receives 3% of the cover price of every Bible sold in the UK.
£300,000

8 PERSONAL APPEARANCES: He can charge up to £10,000 to open a fete, visit a hospice or offer solace at the site of a natural disaster.
£1,500,000

9 PRODUCT ENDORSEMENTS: Mitre and crook manufacturers, incense producers and holy water bottlers fork out hefty fees for high-profile clergymen to be seen using their products.
£5,000,000

10 PERFORMANCE-RELATED BONUS: Paid in Church of England shares to avoid attracting the attention of the taxman.
£2,000,000+

TOTAL: £20 MILLION